The Inclusive Teacher

This quick-reference, highly practical guide is designed to help teachers successfully include students with a disability in the classroom, as well as being a research text.

Armstrong and Roy focus on key 'sticky' issues often referenced by teachers, schools, and government as preventing inclusion, filling in the gaps in current teacher capabilities in responding to these issues. They cover, for example, how to record educational progress for a student with a disability on an Individual Education Plan (IEP), how teachers should respond to occupational violence in a classroom by a student with a disability, and the need to teach routines. The authors provide learning activities and use vignettes throughout the book to offer a story format and help the reader understand how to overcome persistent challenges to educational inclusion for those with a disability. The guidance provided is mapped to relevant Australian teacher standards and government recommendations, and has been successfully road-tested with Australian state governments, schools, and thousands of pre-service teachers.

An essential read for pre-service teachers, this book will also be of interest to new and in-service teachers in the mainstream sector as well as in the special education and alternative school sectors.

David Armstrong (Dave) is a specialist teacher, researcher, teacher educator, and adviser to government. Dave has led courses/pathways in Teacher Education Programs on disability and inclusion in Australia and the UK. Dave has successfully published two books with Routledge: *Educational Trends Exposed* (2022) and *Key Perspectives on Dyslexia* (2014).

David Roy is a passionate, ethical, and inclusive lecturer and researcher with over 31 years' experience in schools and tertiary education. He has a deep passion for developing and implementing a wide range of educational practices, policy changes, and research for learning and teaching, and works closely with politicians, governments, and education bodies regarding implementing change. David has had 11 books published.

The Inclusive Teacher
A Practical Guide to Inclusion
in Australian Classrooms

David Armstrong and David Roy

LONDON AND NEW YORK

Designed cover image: Cover image by Ian Roy

First published 2026
by Routledge
4 Park Square, Milton Park, Abingdon, Oxon OX14 4RN

and by Routledge
605 Third Avenue, New York, NY 10158

Routledge is an imprint of the Taylor & Francis Group, an informa business

© 2026 David Armstrong and David Roy

The right of David Armstrong and David Roy to be identified as authors of this work has been asserted in accordance with sections 77 and 78 of the Copyright, Designs and Patents Act 1988.

All rights reserved. No part of this book may be reprinted or reproduced or utilised in any form or by any electronic, mechanical, or other means, now known or hereafter invented, including photocopying and recording, or in any information storage or retrieval system, without permission in writing from the publishers.

For Product Safety Concerns and Information please contact our EU representative GPSR@taylorandfrancis.com. Taylor & Francis Verlag GmbH, Kaufingerstraße 24, 80331 München, Germany.

Trademark notice: Product or corporate names may be trademarks or registered trademarks, and are used only for identification and explanation without intent to infringe.

British Library Cataloguing-in-Publication Data
A catalogue record for this book is available from the British Library

Library of Congress Cataloging-in-Publication Data
Names: Armstrong, David (Lecturer in teacher education) author | Roy, David M. S. author
Title: The inclusive teacher : a practical guide to inclusion in Australian classrooms / David Armstrong and David Roy.
Description: Abingdon, Oxon ; New York, NY : Routledge, 2026. | Includes bibliographical references and index.
Identifiers: LCCN 2025031707 (print) | LCCN 2025031708 (ebook) | ISBN 9781041134053 hardback | ISBN 9781041134015 paperback | ISBN 9781003669630 ebook
Subjects: LCSH: Inclusive education--Australia | Children with disabilities--Education--Australia | Students with disabilities--Australia
Classification: LCC LC1203.A8 A76 2026 (print) | LCC LC1203.A8 (ebook)
LC record available at https://lccn.loc.gov/2025031707
LC ebook record available at https://lccn.loc.gov/2025031708

ISBN: 978-1-041-13405-3 (hbk)
ISBN: 978-1-041-13401-5 (pbk)
ISBN: 978-1-003-66963-0 (ebk)

DOI: 10.4324/9781003669630

Typeset in Galliard
by KnowledgeWorks Global Ltd.

For Fraser and David

Contents

List of tables ix
Foreword x
Acknowledgements xii
Introduction xiii

PART I
Educational inclusion: The why 1

1 Attendance and the unfolding crisis in education 3
2 Objections to this book and myths about inclusion 6
3 Understanding inclusion 10

PART II
Educational inclusion: What and how 25

4 Disability: Becoming a developmentally informed teacher 27
5 Differentiation and Universal Design for Learning (UDL) 57
6 Feedback and effective praise 67
7 Establishing routines in the classroom 74
8 Building strong parent-school partnerships 82
9 Behaviour: Building and maintaining calm and productive classrooms 88
10 Mental health and well-being in schools 115
11 Inclusive assessment 144
12 Safety in school and bullying prevention 163

PART III
Final words
181

13 Key learnings
183

References
191
Index
211

Tables

0.1	Book structure	xv
3.1	Implications	12
3.2	How this book maps to recommendations by the Disability Royal Commission Final Report (DRC, 2023)	23
4.1	Categories of disability	38
5.1	Connections	58
5.2	Differentiation is and is not	62
6.1	Feedback Levels	73
7.1	Routine myths	75
7.2	Start of the day routines	78
7.3	End of the day routines	78
9.1	The evidence base for effective behaviour interventions, programs and supports	101
9.2	Practical strategies to motivate students to replace negative behaviours with positives	111
10.1	Public mental health services in Australia	126
11.1	Arrangements and supports	159
12.1	Practical strategies to motivate students to replace negative behaviours with positives	170
12.2	Critical incident response plan	175

Foreword

Foreword by Senator David Shoebridge for 'The Inclusive Teacher: A Practical Guide to Inclusion in Australian Classrooms'.

The Inclusive Australian Teacher Handbook arrives at a pivotal moment in Australia's educational development.

Every class, in every school, contains a wonderful spectrum of children with skills, passions, challenges, talents and experiences unique to them. Every one of them deserves to be taught and respected as their own unique bundle of hope and opportunity. Unfortunately, due to a lack of essential resources and misplaced practices, too often this opportunity is lost.

The result is we are witnessing a crisis in Australian education, with declining attendance rates that disproportionately affect our most vulnerable students, including those with disabilities.

This crisis is particularly acute in our public schools, which serve the highest proportions of students with disabilities and complex needs, yet often operate with inadequate funding and resources compared to their private counterparts.

Behind these statistics are real children, whose stories you'll encounter in these pages. Each represents not just a statistic, but a young person whose educational experience will shape their entire future.

When I was the Greens Education spokesperson in the NSW Parliament, I had the privilege of working closely with advocates, educators and families fighting for truly inclusive education. It was in this context that I first met David Roy whose tireless efforts to advance inclusive education have helped shape policy and practice across our state. I had the benefit of hearing directly from David in both private briefings and in his powerful advocacy in his evidence to Parliamentary committees.

It was through David and other brave advocates that I heard about, and campaigned against, practices that were occurring at schools that were so appallingly harmful to children with disability. David's truth telling about physical discipline, punishment and exclusion lead to genuine changes in how schools recorded and responded to reportable conduct instances and made children safer. I thank him for that.

I have been particularly concerned about the use of suspension and expulsions against children with a disability in schools. Excluding children from school often starts a downward spiral of less engagement, less learning and more disruption. This book refuses to accept that challenging behaviour should be grounds for exclusion. The escalation cycle model and de-escalation strategies outlined here offer clear alternatives to the punitive approaches that have failed too many of our students with disabilities.

The recommendations of the Disability Royal Commission Final Report provide a roadmap for transforming Australian education. This handbook serves as a practical companion to that transformation, equipping teachers with the knowledge and confidence to implement real change in their classrooms and schools.

The core message of this book resonates deeply with my own values: we must find ways to support all learners to succeed and achieve all they are capable of.

It's a simple fact that inclusion creates a learning environment that benefits all children and those who teach them. The authors have given us more than a handbook—they've provided a roadmap toward the kind of education system we need for the world our children will be living in. One that serves all students, supports all teachers, and strengthens our entire community.

Now, as they say, it's over to you.

Senator David Shoebridge
Australian Greens

Acknowledgements

The authors would like to thank the following:

All our families and friends for their support and advice. Vilija Stephens, Felicia Chan, Claire Midgley, Khadijah Ebrahim, and the editorial staff at Routledge. The staff of both La Trobe University and the University of Newcastle. Caroline Dock and Gill Armstrong for their support. Dr Anne Southall of La Trobe University for advice on trauma in school settings, Professor Paul Harper of the University of Queensland on expert advice on laws related to disability, Prof Susan Ledger of the University of Newcastle, and Murat Dizdar of the NSW Department of Education, who all offered particular assistance with the writing. Thank you to many students, colleagues, politicians, advocates, and organisations and over the years with whom we have worked, learnt from and shared experiences in inclusion. This text is based on empirical research but also the lived experiences of a multitude. Finally, may we thank the reviewers and colleagues from many universities who have offered valuable, constructive criticism.

Introduction

This book responds to the huge benefits but also real or perceived challenges of including students with a disability in Australian classrooms. Collectively, the authors have enormous teaching experience of successful inclusion in practice and are researchers on this topic. Authors also have lived experience of what we write about, either as a person with a disability or as a parent of a child with a disability or both. Lived experience of disability plus professional classroom experience does not make us the only voice worth hearing about successful educational inclusion in schools, but this combination does provide an authentic, real-life edge to what we recommend.

We offer evidence-based, up-to-date, very practical advice on the inclusion of students with a disability, including key teacher responsibilities in the classroom. Pragmatic guidance is also given on how to challenge or work around common negative attitudes, system failures, or shortcomings which currently compromise educational inclusion in Australian schools. The book content reflects this focus, addressing 'sticky' but vital classroom-based issues which teachers and research report in the inclusion of students with a disability and which include:

- Ensuring that students have positive mental health.
- Supporting positive behaviours by students in the classroom.
- Ensuring a safe and productive classroom, preventing dangerous, aggressive or violent behaviour.
- Delivering a student-centred curriculum using differentiation, effective praise and Universal Design for Learning (UDL).
- Establishing effective routines in the classroom.
- Engaging with the parents of a student with a disability.
- Understanding the learning process and how to use this knowledge to help overcome personal barriers to learning and achievement.

In writing this book, we have consciously addressed the alleged gaps in teacher education/teacher preparation, which are often (often unfairly) highlighted by the media or reports. Establishing routines, supporting positive behaviour, school safety, and understanding how typical students learn (the learning process).

Why this book focuses on students with a disability

Educational inclusion is far greater than the inclusion of students with a disability (Boyle and Anderson, 2020; UNICEF, 2017). Acknowledging this fact, we borrow the approach adopted by Slee (2018) and we position this book as focussing on one specific group (students with a disability) who face substantial disadvantage in many current Australian schools. This position does not in any way exclude students belonging to other highly disadvantaged groups in Australia, such as, for example, students who are First Nations people or who hail from refugee or asylum-seeker backgrounds. The urgency of enabling effective inclusion for students with a disability is sharply underlined by the fact that across Australia, increasing numbers of students with a disability face educational *exclusion,* with all the flow-on harms that this brings for them and their families (Armstrong and Armstrong, 2021; DRC, 2023). The book you are reading is our modest effort to provide greater equity and fairness for children and young people with a disability in the face of the worsening disadvantage they face in school.

Who will benefit from reading this book?

We have written this book for teachers in public primary *and* secondary schools in Australia, including those who are studying to enter the profession and who are called pre-service teachers or students of initial teacher education (ITE) across Australia. This book provides:

- Professional learning and updates for **existing/qualified teachers**.
- Essential learning for **pre-service teachers/students of initial teacher education** (ITE).
- Essential learning and updates for **school leaders** (principals, deputy principals).

While the focus of this text is on public schools, we suggest that teachers, school leaders, and other education professionals employed in other sectors of the Australian education system will realise the same benefits from reading this book and applying this knowledge.

Successful educational inclusion is also the responsibility of all adults involved in the education of a student with a disability – including students who have not yet received the formal label but are suspected of having a disability or undergoing assessment. Therefore, this book will benefit:

- **School support staff:** well-being leaders, school counsellors and behaviour support staff, for example.
- **Allied professionals:** psychologists, speech, and language pathologists; mental health professionals, for example.
- **Parents** of a child with or at-risk of a disability.

- **Public service professionals** responsible for developing or implementing educational inclusion in public school systems across Australia, for instance: the Victorian Department of Education, ACT Education Directorate, New South Wales (NSW) Department of Education, South Australian Department of Education, Department of Education Western Australia (WA), The Tasmanian Department of Education, Children and Young People, Northern Territories (NT) Department of Education, Queensland Department of Education, and Federal Department of Education.

Book structure

Rather than adopting a traditional chapter structure, the authors have chosen to provide sections devoted to core topics on the inclusion of students with a disability.

Many sections are concise and ideally suited for delivery as part of a professional learning update for existing teachers or as a short-focussed workshop or seminar with pre-service teachers/students in ITE. Each section in this book begins with explicit mention of the relevant **Australian Institute for Teaching and School Leadership** (AITSL) teacher professional standards it addresses. This mapping has been done to help give you confidence in how your learning meets AITSL professional standards relevant to the inclusion of students with a disability.

The book is also split into two parts, and as part of the hands-on but evidence-based approach used. **Table 0.1 Book Structure** below explains:

Table 0.1 Book structure

Part	Focus
Educational inclusion: *the why*	This short part of the book details *why* the educational inclusion of students with a disability is required from all Australian teachers. Your responsibilities towards students with a disability in terms of existing laws, professional standards, and educational policies are highlighted.
	Common everyday objections to inclusion are also outlined in this part of the book. This content helps the reader identify unhelpful, unprofessional, and misinformed comments about educational inclusion, which (unfortunately) still circulate in schools, communities, and/or society.
Educational inclusion: *what and how*	This longer part of the book details key practical knowledge relevant to the successful inclusion of students with a disability (the 'what'). Your successful application of this knowledge ('the how') in the classroom is enabled via vignettes, activities, recommendations, and resources.

Wider benefits of this book for you

The content in this book provides readers with skills, knowledge, and confidence which, if carefully applied, will improve teaching and the quality of all student learning in a classroom.

One misunderstanding about inclusion is that it solely or primarily benefits disadvantaged students, such as those with a disability (Armstrong and Squires, 2014; Boyle and Anderson, 2020; Slee, 2011). Early pioneering literature about inclusion emphasised that educational inclusion is a force for raising the quality of education for all students in a school (Booth & Ainscow, 2002). This observation remains true and applies here. Students with a disability will particularly benefit from the application of the knowledge provided in this book, but many other individuals in a class will gain if you read and then apply what we recommend in terms of, for example, using praise effectively or establishing strong routines in your classroom.

In this sense, *The Inclusive Teacher* is designed to elevate teaching and learning for *all* students in *all* Australian schools. We hope you enjoy reading it.

Part I
Educational inclusion
The why

1 Attendance and the unfolding crisis in education

> This short section will help you to:
>
> - Recognise the current stresses in the Australian education system and make sense of them.
> - Understand how educational inclusion is likely to be impacted by a system under structural pressures.
> - Realise that all teachers have a role in advocating for a more inclusive and equitable school system.
>
> The Australian Institute for Teaching and School Leadership (AITSL) Graduate Teacher Standards covered by this learning include:
>
> 7.1 Understand and apply the key principles described in codes of ethics and conduct for the teaching profession.
> 7.4 Engage with professional teaching networks and broader communities.

This book is premised on the idea that educational inclusion is a good thing and that teachers should be equipped and empowered to deliver inclusion using the best available evidence of what works. Unfortunately, this premise is under threat from events which we must now discuss.

A well-functioning and sufficiently resourced public school system is essential for delivering inclusion, as the United Nations (UN) states (UNICEF, 2017). Chapter 7 discusses this point in further detail in the context of students with a disability.

A crisis has engulfed the Australian education system while writing this book. It indicates that the education system in Australia is neither well-functioning nor sufficiently resourced and is in serious trouble. There are numerous manifestations of this crisis in education, suggesting that it has deep and extensive roots. Teacher education, which supplies new teachers for the profession, has seen declining numbers. Greater numbers of existing teachers are, it seems,

DOI: 10.4324/9781003669630-2

leaving the profession, a phenomenon known as teacher attrition (Heffernan et al., 2022). If we apply the core laws of 'supply' and 'demand' from economics, we can understand that the school workforce is being impacted from both directions: supply is reduced exactly at the same time as demand is rising. The result is a stressed school system with fewer teachers. An insufficient number of teachers to deliver the core curriculum leads to greater stress on the remaining school workforce, further professionals therefore leave or retire early if they can. Other teachers turn to professional bodies or teaching unions in response to this crisis. Industrial action, including strikes, has occurred in New South Wales (NSW), for example. A self-sustaining negative process known as a vicious circle could appear in school systems as an outcome of the current crisis.

Implications for quality teaching and inclusion

In this chaotic and concerning situation, the quality of the learning experience in classrooms across Australia for all students declines. Part of this outcome is due to a reduction in the quality of teaching, typically as temporary, or 'cover', teaching staff are employed to address gaps in staffing or regular teachers at that school are redeployed as short notice, often covering areas outside of their specialism. If schools cannot deliver the core curriculum, then logic suggests that inclusion might also suffer. This logic is supported by research, which highlights how inclusion is deprioritised by many working in the Australian school system (Slee, 2011). What is known about how disadvantage operates educationally would suggest that disadvantaged students will be hardest hit by disruption to learning, specifically the lack of a consistent teacher (Humphrey et al., 2020). Recent trends in publicly available educational data confirm these predictions. The issue of school attendance is especially important to discuss here when thinking about inclusion in the classroom.

Declining attendance and inclusion

Registering student attendance is a mundane daily administrative role for most teachers at some point. If you are a teacher, a decline in attendance can have several immediate impacts which vary. One immediate negative flow on impact of declining attendance in a class is that planning learning can be more difficult for a teacher, due to the difficulty predicting how many students will be present. Classrooms can also feel 'hollowed out' and emotionally muted due to depopulation. It could be, in the short term, that fewer students positively represent a chance to better support remaining students – this is an optimistic framing of falling attendance, which is now being tested in Australian schools.

In May 2023, the Australian Federal Education Minister, Jason Clare, called an urgent meeting of all states and territories due to data showing a decline in attendance at public schools across Australia (Clare, 2023). Clare also highlighted that this decline pre-dates, although it could have been accelerated by, impacts from the COVID-19 global pandemic.

Bills and Howard, important Australian researchers in this area, offered the following analysis:

> In 2014 eight out of every ten students were attending school for more than 90% of the time. In 2022 only five in ten students were attending at that rate. This suggests there has been a marked increase in the number of students who are missing at least a week of school a year.
>
> (2023)

As Bills and Howard (2023) also highlight, falling attendance is a longer-term process, pre-dating the appearance of COVID-19 in 2019.

Emerging data from families with a child who has a disability adds further information. According to this data, increasing numbers of concerned parents are withdrawing their child or children from schools and electing to home-school them. Furthermore, we know from public inquiries that the exclusion, abuse, neglect, bullying, or indifference experienced in the Australian school system by many students is what prompts this decision (DRC, 2023). These children are, most probably, included in the wider group of students referred to by Clare (2023), and Bills and Howard (2023). Right now, researchers are not clear how many of these families are included, but data from other studies offer strong clues. Furthermore, overall school attendance appears to be in accelerating decline at the time of writing. The latest national update on school attendance reveals a further decrease in the overall rate of school attendance with a corresponding increase in unauthorised absence (ACARA, 2024).

Over the last decade, suspensions and exclusions from school have risen for students with a disability (ABC, 2020). For instance, one of the authors has established that students with disability are greatly over-represented in data of school suspensions, making up over 60% of school suspensions by settings in NSW (Roy, 2020).

Bringing it together

Of itself, rising school suspensions amongst students with a disability are concerning and a clear setback for an inclusive school system. When considering dropping overall school attendance since 2014 (Bills and Howard, 2023) and most especially declining attendance by students with a disability (DRC, 2023), this trend can be seen as part of a pattern of indicators revealing that the education system in Australia is in long-term decline.

There is growing agreement in Australian society that actions must be taken to stem this decline and restore progress toward a sustainable and progressive future for our children and young people. Educational inclusion is a key part of this outcome and is a distinctive feature of a well-functioning and sufficiently resourced public school system. By reading this book and, if you can, applying the learning we offer, you are lending your strength to this brighter future.

2 Objections to this book and myths about inclusion

A list of likely objections to this book is given below.

Some objections arise from a negative lived experience, based often on anxiety by teachers about inclusion or unwillingness to change customs or practices. Other objections are simply 'thought termination' – phrases intended to stop any further curiosity and discussion – also called 'thought termination cliché' (Lifton, 1989 [1961]).

Other responses are simply part of teacher folklore ('myths') and are often spoken without further reflection. When these phrases given below are used (or similar), we recommend the reader consider who is making this point and for what purpose/motivation. Understanding the professional role of the person expressing this view within the education system often explains why they are trying to sway your view on the topic or have wider motivations (Armstrong and Armstrong, 2021). Poor coping or even the state of psychological exhaustion known as burn out can also be a driver for negative comments about inclusion (Armstrong, 2018).

Behaviour

Students need to just behave. Teachers need to manage student behaviour. Discipline and punishment are best at changing behaviour. Some children are simply bad. Some children are naughty. Teachers don't need to be curious about why children are bad or naughty. Disabled students can be dangerous for a teacher due to problem behaviours and can distract other students. Praise is bad. The teacher can fix problem children. Parents are to blame for their child's behaviour. Good discipline is more important than learning – discipline first.

Differentiation

Differentiation doesn't work and can't work. Students should be given the same resources and treatment, and it's up to them to work it out. If you don't know what differentiation is, you should say 'no' to learning about differentiation. Differentiation is just required for kids with a disability. Differentiation is hard. Differentiation is a fancy technical skill.

DOI: 10.4324/9781003669630-3

UDL

Students with a disability simply need to learn to adapt to how things are in schools. Few schools in Australia have applied Universal Design for Learning (UDL) because it doesn't work. Changing seating plans is enough for UDL. The ability to physically access school buildings is enough to say that the school has a UDL approach. If you don't know what UDL is, you should say 'no' to learning about UDL.

Inclusion

Teachers aren't social workers. Inclusion doesn't work and can't work. The fact that so many schools can't be inclusive proves that inclusion doesn't work and can't work. Inclusion is something that teaching/classroom assistants deal with. Sitting students near the front of the classroom is inclusion. If I am teaching, then students must be learning. Helping children learn through scaffolding and other supports is cheating and unfair to other students. Teaching must be the same for all students. If you don't know what inclusion is, then just say 'no' to inclusion.

Parent-school partnerships

Parents need to listen to teachers, not the other way around. Some parents withdraw their child from school because they are neglectful. Parents are supporting snowflake children to withdraw from school and opt out of lessons if they are in school. Parents never need support and should 'toughen up' when facing difficulties so they can be a parent to their child. If parents don't engage with schools or reply to emails, calls, and so forth, then it's their problem.

Teaching and learning

Learning is just a change in long-term memory. Learning just happens. There is just teaching. It's all about academic results; nothing else really matters. There are shortcuts to better learning, which can help students with a disability. Special education has special pedagogy. Teaching students with a disability is best left to the specialists. Children have learning styles which teachers should cater for. Cognitive science, neuroscience, _____ (fill in the blank and add 'science') can transform student progress/attainment/behaviour/academic performance _____ (fill in the blank with whatever term is used).

Settings

If a child has a disability, then a special school is the best place for them. Disabled students can't perform at the same level as other students and need a special curriculum. Disabled students in a class automatically generate extra work for the teacher. Special schools will always exist in school systems;

it's inevitable. Special schools are part of an inclusive school system. Public schools are funded at the same level as non-public schools in Australia.

School safety and bullying

Schools should not concern themselves with safety – a safe workplace is for the union, principal to address or police. School safety is solely about kids with guns, knives or who are being aggressive or destructive. Preventing bullying is not the teacher's or the school's responsibility. Bullying never happens in my class/school! Bullying is best dealt with just by the teacher – it's their responsibility. Whole school bullying prevention programs are too expensive and time-consuming to even consider.

Funding

Integrated funding support in schools is both very specific in its requirement for medical diagnoses and standard score cut-offs, often leaving the determination of other difficulties to the discretion of school staff. Segregated schooling continues to increase as systems direct more funding into schools for specific purposes (SSPs)and considers separate schools to be congruent with inclusion. The emphasis placed by the United Nations Convention on the Rights of Persons with Disabilities (UNCRPD) on inclusive education for students with disabilities carries significant implications for policy, practice, and societal perspectives. Shifting the focus to inclusive education, the legislative and policy obligations for supporting students with disabilities in schools encompass international, national, and state-level frameworks, but does have funding issues. These obligations aim to ensure equitable access to education, foster inclusive environments, and offer tailored support. Nonetheless, the intricacies of implementing these mandates become apparent when considering challenges related to funding, resource allocation, professional development, and shifts in attitudes.

All the political parties are correct in their respective policies of a need for increased funding and/or accountability, both for education in general and specifically for children with a disability. It is clear that pre-service training needs to be re-examined. A specialist course in 'Special Needs' Education just reinforces the concepts of 'other' for children with a disability. All children are diverse and should be supported based on learning needs rather than the 'label' of 'special needs'. Thus, all the pre-service training courses (on average four a semester/eight a year/32 over a 4-year degree – including discipline knowledge) should have diverse learner pedagogies embedded throughout. The funding issue is maybe a slight misdirection. Schools need more funding, of that there is no question. However, there is multiple evidence that suggests that 'diverted' funding by principals to support students with recognised needs is not actually directed in a method that supports the student's need but rather removes the student's need from distracting the other 'normal' learners. Funding teacher aides to support students is not the answer. One might consider that the children with the greatest pedagogical needs would be better supported by the staff with the deepest pedagogical training, rather than the all-too-common practice of the least trained staff being left to support those with the most complex needs. Increased funding will provide materials and staffing to allow adjustments to allow children to access the curriculum and schools. Funding will support staff training in the means and methods to implement tailored support for all students, but schools and education authorities need to be held accountable for their funding to ensure it does support the students it is aimed at.

Funding is an issue, but it is not the only issue. We need to offer all students access to an education that supports their learning, rather than highlighting their deficits. Deliberate choice by all of us as a community is what will make the difference.

Note your own myths about inclusion and the topics covered in this book

Research into educational trends indicates that education is a fertile place for myths and poor understanding, or even self-interested distortion about many topics like educational inclusion (Adey and Dillon, 2012; Armstrong and Armstrong, 2021). Therefore, we invite you to note any potential (or definite) myths or objections about topics covered in this book which you encounter, using what we have given above as a reference. Our recommendation: if you note an objection, following advice by Armstrong and Armstrong (2021, p. 123), we recommend that you also consider: 1. *who* is voicing the objection; and 2. For *what purpose*? How they frame the 'problem' they object to is likely to give you a clue about this purpose if it is not clear, and help you decide about whether it is a result of anxiety, a lack of knowledge, or self-interest.

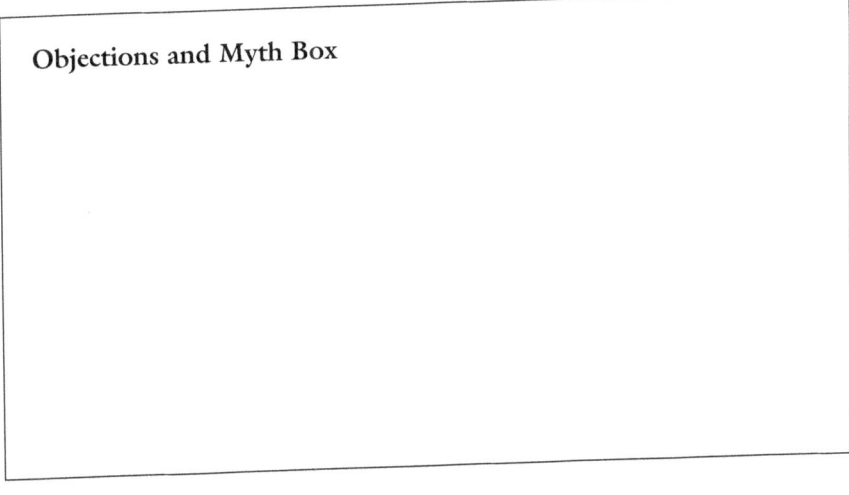

Objections and Myth Box

3 Understanding inclusion

> This section will help you learn how to:
>
> - Identify what inclusion is in practice.
> - Identify laws and polices relevant to inclusion (and differences).
> - Understand your legal and professional duty as a teacher in relation to inclusion.
> - Learn about inclusion in practice for an individual with a disability.
> - Learn about inclusion in practice across a whole school setting.
>
> Australian Institute for Teaching and School Leadership (AITSL) Graduate Teacher Standards covered by this learning include:
>
> 7.1 Meet professional ethics and responsibilities.
> 7.2 Comply with legislative, administrative and organisational requirements.
> 1.6 Strategies to support full participation of students with disability.

Educational inclusion in Australia laws and regulations

Internationally, declarations made by the United Nations (UN) are a legal basis for inclusion. Specifically, Article 24 The Right to an Inclusive Education, which is part of the Convention on the Rights of Persons with a Disability (United Nations, 2008) and the Convention on the Rights of the Child (United Nations, 1990) ratified by Australia, Canada, and the UK – along with 196 countries. These international, legal commitments are represented in the National Disability Strategy (NDS) 2021–2031 with 'education and learning' given as one of the seven important outcome areas for focus (Australian Government, 2024). The new national strategy (2021–2030) is awaiting finalisation but is likely to restate this legal commitment to inclusive education.

DOI: 10.4324/9781003669630-4

In response to this legal commitment, Australia has one law plus two important types of policy tools designed to regulate practice in schools, all of which come under the umbrella of inclusion.

- **Law**: The Disability Discrimination Act (Australian Government, 1992). This is a federal law which makes it illegal to discriminate against individuals with a disability. Each state in Australia has created a version of this law because delivering public education is a primary financial responsibility of states as per the Australian Constitution (Slee, 2018).
- **Standards for interpreting the Law (DDA, 1992) for education.**
  Disability Standards for Education (Australian Government, 2005). These Standards provide teachers and schools with an interpretation of how the DDA (Australian Government, 1992) applies in classrooms and the wider school. At the time of writing, the DSE is being updated.

  Website: https://www.education.gov.au/disability-standards-education-2005

- **Teacher Professional Standards. Australian Institute for Teaching and School Leadership (AITSL)**

  Professional Standards. AITSL standards unpack how key parts of the DSE (2005) and DDA (1992) apply in teacher knowledge, skills, and professional practice. In this book, we refer to specific AISL standards at the graduate level, which are relevant to inclusion, for example, 'Standard 1.5 Differentiate teaching to meet the specific learning needs of students across the full range of abilities'. AITSL standards (currently) focus on teacher professional practice and do not consider the wider systems which enable inclusion, such as schools' admissions policy or school systems providing personalised additional support for students who require it. When thinking about inclusion in the classroom, this absence is a limitation because teachers do not practice professional skills in a vacuum.

  Website: https://www.aitsl.edu.au/standards

The difference between laws and regulations

When considering laws and professional regulatory 'standards', it is important to realise that subtle but important differences exist between law and regulation. The DDA (1992) is the legal act that makes it illegal to discriminate against persons of any age with a disability and applies to all sectors of society, including health settings and workplaces, for example.

When applied to education, the DDA (1992) has, we and others think, two major implications required to prevent discrimination in education as shown in Table 3.1.

Reasonable adjustments

Changes made by the classroom teacher to enable students with a disability to participate in learning on the same basis as their peers (DSE, 2005) are

Table 3.1 Implications

Implications?	Who is responsible?
Setting and classroom environment. Students with a disability are educated with their typically developing peers, sharing the same space in their local school.	Schools and school leaders with oversight by the state or territory education department or equivalent.
Reasonable adjustment. Changes are made to the school environment to enable students to achieve educational success. These adjustments comprise more than sitting near the teacher or being able to physically access classrooms; they involve, but are not restricted to, the curriculum, classroom delivery by teachers, classroom assessment practice, and, also, wider school systems, such as enrolment and additional support arrangements for students.	The class teacher – with advice and support from colleagues, school leaders, advice from parents on a child's needs and specialist advice from any allied professionals (e.g. occupational therapist, psychologist).

central to preventing discrimination. For this reason, reasonable adjustment has been the focus of policy by the government designed to ensure that all schools meet this minimum standard (DSE, 2005). These efforts, in part, also stem from limited application of reasonable adjustment in practice, often accompanied by the incorrect perception, by some teachers, that they require elaborate, time-consuming and expensive changes to teaching, school buildings, and assessment (Page *et al.*, 2024). The adjustments to enrolment, teaching, assessment, and other aspects of school required by students with a disability are often modest (Armstrong and Armstrong, 2021). Legislation (Australian Government, 2005) is also clear that an element of reasonableness is important when considering the implications of adjustments required for a student in terms of a teacher's time or financial resources (Page *et al.*, 2024).

Many sections in this book, including this one, are designed to help the reader think about what reasonable adjustments look like in the classroom. To complement your knowledge of making reasonable adjustments in practice, excellent existing resources are also available. The federally funded organisation, Nationally Consistent Collection of Data on School Students with a Disability (NCCD), has high-quality resources, including case studies and tools illustrating practical application of reasonable adjustments (Australian Government Department of Education, 2024):

Website: https://www.nccd.edu.au/resources-and-tools

Defining what inclusion *is*

Since 2008, the UN has specified that schools and the whole education system should be fully inclusive, enabling the full participation and engagement of students affected by disability and/or disadvantage (UNICEF, 2017). This effort at clarification was made because some countries, including Australia, had effectively ignored their commitment to apply Article 24 in schools. UNICEF (2017) document *Inclusive Education: Understanding Article 24 of the Convention on the Rights of Persons with Disabilities* is crystal clear on how inclusion should be present in classrooms and wider education systems.

> **Education system**
>
> An inclusive education system is one that accommodates all students, whatever their abilities or requirements, and at all levels – pre-school, primary, secondary, tertiary, vocational, and life-long learning (UNICEF, 2017, p. 3).
>
> **Schools and classrooms**
>
> Inclusive education environments adapt the design and physical structures, teaching methods, and curriculum, as well as the culture, policy, and practice of education environments, so that they are accessible to all students without discrimination. Placing students with disabilities within mainstream classes without these adaptations does not constitute inclusion (p. 3).

The Australian school system(s)

There is general agreement that Australia has a complex education system, which differs considerably across states and territories. A major review of the Australian schools by Gonski *et al.* (2018) referred to the system as unnecessarily complex in its structure and funding. When educational inclusion is discussed, the following types of schools ('settings') are often referenced (Anderson and Boyle, 2019):

- *Mainstream schools.* Regular, 'ordinary' primary or secondary schools.
- *Special schools.* Schools which cater for students with a disability and/or complex health needs.
- *Alternative settings.* An eclectic category of settings which offer an alternative to mainstream- hospital schools, behaviour units, community schools.
- *Flexible Learning Options (FLO).* Educational provision for children who have dropped out of mainstream or who have been expelled/excluded from mainstream, special, or alternative settings.

Mainstream, special, alternative, and FLO are *relational* terms which arise from Australia's segregated and fragmented education system. Mainstream schools are 'regular' (primary or secondary) public schools which, in public at least, do not select enrolment based on a child's abilities but accept *all children* from their local area (DRC, 2023). Slee (2018) suggests that many Australian schools, of whatever description, present themselves as inclusive but are not, in fact, inclusive. Australian-based educational research has supported this point (Anderson and Boyle, 2019, p. 206).

School sector, involving governance and funding, is also very relevant when considering educational inclusion in Australia and overlays school type. There are three school sectors in Australia, namely government (or 'public'), Catholic, and Independent (ACARA, 2024). In 2024, 4,132,006 students were enrolled in 9,653 schools nationally. The government sector is the largest educational provider. In 2024, 63.4% of school-age students were enrolled in a government school (ACARA, 2024).

Nationally, schools in the government sector educate the vast majority of students who have a disability; 89% of a total population of 338,000 children and young people who comprise this population nationally. Since educating students with a disability can require additional funding for equipment or support staff, costs which disproportionally fall on the government sector, an important review by Gonski *et al.* (2018) recommended that every student with a disability have additional funding attached to meet their specific needs. Gonski *et al.* (2018) argued that this individualisation of funding was necessary to reduce inequity across the school system, and where the additional costs of supporting students with a disability act as a financial disincentive to some settings at enrolment.

According to the most recent data gathered in 2018, just 12% of students with a disability attended a special school setting (ACARA, 2024). At face value, this would suggest progress in Australia toward a more inclusive school system and away from the segregated schooling system characterised by some critics (de Bruin, 2019). Other research suggests a less positive picture for the inclusion of students with a disability in mainstream schools located in any sector (Slee, 2018).

What does *not* count as educational inclusion

UNICEF (2017), together with a range of research studies and public enquires in Australia, paints a vivid picture of what does *not* count as inclusion. For instance, researchers Chambers and Forlin (2021), in their review of the progress of inclusion in Western Australia, conclude:

> In reality, the range of educational placement options available continue to be the same as in the 1970s, although placement selection is now reversed. While initially movement was from segregated facilities into integrated ones, it is now from inclusive settings into more segregated ones.

They add:

> The names of the schools are less stigmatising and school sites expect to cater for considerably more diverse student populations, but it remains that for children with the most challenging needs, education for them is with a specialist teacher in a separate classroom. (p. 12)

Understanding inclusion through examining its very opposite, exclusion, segregation, and discrimination, is powerful. Slee (2018) adopts this approach in his passionate and personal account of 'the smelly side of schooling' (p. 11). Following this analogy, an inspired graphic used by Hehir et al. (2016) visually represents these odours in comparison to inclusion.

In considering special schools and other specialist settings (e.g. behaviour units), Lassig et al. (2024) offers a powerful summary of research evidence about the impact of segregated settings, which 'demonstrates that placement in segregated settings for students with disability has resulted in a marginalised population that has been institutionalised, undereducated, abused, neglected, socially rejected and excluded from society' (p. 14). In relation to education settings, literature has, correctly, pointed out that the normalisation of discrimination represented by segregated settings would not be acceptable in the workplace or other sectors such as health (Slee, 2011; United Nations, 2008).

Australian school systems and the lack of inclusion

In 2019, monitoring by the United Nations Human Rights Commission (UNHRC) raised the alarm that Australia was not following its legal obligations under the Convention on the Rights of Persons with a Disability (2008) and the Convention on the Rights of the Child (United Nations, 1990). This response by the UNHRC was a culmination of years of campaigning about the negative impacts of educational exclusion and segregation by disability advocacy groups. This news reached the Australian media and prompted political action in the Senate led by Greens Senator Jordon Steele-John passed with Labour's support, triggering the establishment of the Disability Royal Commission inquiry (see below).

Short answer questions

Q1. Would it be seen as acceptable if workplaces had a separate lunchroom or workspace for people with a disability?

A1. Separate lunchrooms or workspaces for those with a disability would not be regarded as acceptable by workplaces and would break the law. The majority of medium to large size employers in Australia have detailed organisational policies promoting inclusion and anti-discrimination.

Educational recommendations of the disability royal commission (DRC)

The Disability Royal Commission (DRC, 2023) delivered its Final Report in October 2023. Recommendations for education stretched over seven broad areas, and in the report are unpacked into detailed sub-recommendations. Elaboration of many points in the report is beyond the scope of this book, but here are some key points directly relevant to Australian teachers right now and going into the future.

Key recommendation

Removing barriers to inclusion in public mainstream schools

The DRC (2023) report states:

> 'All Australian governments and educational authorities should address and progressively overcome the barriers to inclusive education in mainstream schools'. (p. 338)

The report, specifically, highlights several concerning trends in the public mainstream education system, including a rise in number of special schools, rising levels of exclusion (including suspension) of students with a disability as a disciplinary measure (p.161), and, also, gross failure to meet children's personal and academic needs, including safety from bullying, violence and harassment (p. 51). The negative experiences of First Nations people with a disability attracted note (p. 141 Exec Summary). The introduction of the report summarises the current state of public education in Australia:

> Today, Australian schools do not consistently deliver an inclusive education that protects students with disability from violence, abuse, and neglect. Students with disability face multiple barriers to inclusive education, underpinned by negative attitudes and low expectations. Schools systematically exclude students with disability. They do this by not providing appropriate adjustments and supports to enable their participation in classrooms and in the broader school community. In many cases, through gatekeeping, students with disability are channelled into special/segregated schools and classes. Schools fail to engage students with disability and their parents in decision making. They use and misuse exclusionary discipline on students and fail to plan and support students' transition to further learning and work. (p. 10)

In response, the DRC (2023) states that 'A safe, quality and inclusive education can only be delivered through significant transformation of the school system' (p. 10).

The implementation ('making it happen in the classroom') and logistics of this major transformation of the school system are detailed by the DRC (2023).

This document makes recommendations that involve change at the federal, state, school, and classroom levels. If translated into action, with government investment in the resources and changes recommended, here is what we predict *should* happen.

- **Illegal enrolment practices end.** 'Gatekeeping' practices are currently used by some schools where students and their parents are dissuaded from enrolment and directed to special schools or similar. **Impact:** Gatekeeping will end after strengthening the law and measures to monitor enrolment in schools. Greater numbers of students with disabilities in regular, mainstream classrooms in public schools.
- **Attitudes changed and awareness raised amongst teachers and school leaders.** Teachers, school leaders and education professionals in state or territory government often are not aware of their legal and professional-ethical responsibility to students with a disability or key concepts such as 'reasonable adjustment'. Some professionals have a 'culture of low expectations' about students with a disability. **Impact:** raised awareness of legal and professional-ethical responsibility and acceptance that inclusion is necessary, normalisation of inclusion and widespread 'reasonable adjustment'.
- **Professional learning advanced and teacher capability strengthened.** Many teachers currently feel inadequately prepared to enable meaningful inclusion of students with a disability, using essential inclusive practices such as differentiation. **Impact:** teachers in schools receive ongoing high-quality professional learning, coaching and support to equip them to make inclusion happen. Providers of teacher education (universities) invest in expertise and resources due to strengthened AITSL standards and the elevation of inclusion so that it becomes a part of the core curriculum for teacher education.
- **Ongoing organisational/system support given to schools.** State and territories' governments do not, routinely, have distinct organisational units with the resources to support schools and teachers in implementing educational inclusion. **Impact:** public mainstream schools have ongoing specialist advice, support, and resources for making effective inclusion in their setting.
- **Parents of students with a disability are engaged with schools.** Many parents are alienated by illegal gatekeeping, integration without inclusion, and a culture of low expectations. Parents feel disempowered to ask questions, raise concerns or complain. **Impact:** parents are seen by professionals as key, equal partners with transparent processes introduced by schools to aid mutual trust and connection.

Response to the DRC Final Report

Government response to the educational DRC (2023) Final Report acknowledged their scale and necessity of educational and other reforms recommended. The establishment of a Federal Task Force was announced (Young, Edmonds and Campagnella, 2023), and the Federal Social Services Minister, Amanda

Rishworth, was reported as saying, 'The message of this report is clear — we do need to do better,' ABC, Young, Edmonds and Campagnella (2023).

Debate: the end of special schools or a fudge?

The publication of the DRC (2023) Final Report generated an intense public debate because it explicitly discussed the phasing out of special schools. Three commissioners called for the phasing out of special schools as soon as possible:

> Commissioners Bennett, Galbally and McEwin take the view the deliberate and systemic separation of people based on disability constitutes segregation. From their perspective, segregation describes situations where people with disability live, learn, work or socialise in environments designed specifically for people with disability, separate from people without disability. They consider segregating people based on disability to be incompatible with inclusion and believe it is unconscionable that segregation on the basis of disability remains a policy default in Australia in the 21st century. (p. 93)

It should be noted by the reader that Commissioners Bennett, Galbally, and McEwin had lived experience of disability, directly, or cared for a close family member with a disability.

The Chair and Commissioners Mason and Ryan, differed and claimed a more 'nuanced' view than their colleagues on the Commission (p. 93 Vol 7) advocating for a longer term, gradual, reduction in special schools and with an emphasis on inclusive mainstream schooling wherever possible, rather than as an absolute principle for all children with a disability, regardless of need.

Predictably, at the time of the Final Report's publication, many media headlines and content discussing education focussed on this split in the commissioners' views about the future of special schools. *The Sydney Morning Herald*, for instance, headlined: 'Royal commission split on future of special schools, group homes and workshops for the disabled' (Chrysanthos, 2023). In further response, *The Sydney Morning Herald* also presented the story of a student, called Lilli, who 'thrives' at a special school (Groch, 2023). Many charities and advocacy groups expressed deep disappointment at this aspect of the DRC (2023). Greens Party Senator, Jordan Steele-John, commented, 'They've suggested that we wait until 2050. In segregated education, for instance, that would mean that a disabled child born today would be likely to see their child educated in a segregated setting', and added, 'That's not acceptable.' (Grattan, 2023).

Armstrong (2023) argues that the timetable for phasing our special schools, or even whether they are closed at all is a distraction from the key finding of the DRC Final Report which is the dire need for major reform of mainstream, regular public schooling so that can deliver educational inclusion, a point emphasised in the Final Report where it says 'All Commissioners agree that mainstream schools need major reforms to overcome the barriers to safe, equal and inclusive education (p. 90, Vol 7). You can read more about Armstrong's views below.

Reading

Voice box 2.2: School A – One school's response to promoting inclusion and reducing exclusion

School A is a large, public secondary school which serves a socio-economically deprived area of an Australian state, 40 km from the state capital. In 2020, the school had 1,100 students enrolled, with 50 formally identified as having a disability according to data collected by the South Australian Department for Education. Just over 100 hailed as from an Aboriginal background. School A also respond to an area where disengagement, truancy, early school leaving (drop out), and academic under-achievement are recognised problems affecting children and young people. In the state, School A is recognised as an inclusive school and has operated a range of programs and school systems designed for children with disabilities since 2005. Wherever possible, students with disabilities enrolled in School A attend mainstream curriculum (English, Mathematics, Science, Humanities) classes for 100% of the school week and are enrolled in a form class with a dedicated form teacher. In mainstream classes, each curriculum area has a designated learning support assistant whose primary role is to ensure, in concert with their form teacher, that any children in receipt of funding from the state government are making good academic progress in that area. Each student's learning goals are recorded and monitored using an Individual Education Plan (IEP). This sets the focus for work across subject areas.

School A has a tiered system of support, which is designed to practically match resources with different levels of student needs present in a class and has some in-school provision designed for students requiring higher (Tier 2 and Tier 3) educational support temporarily or on an ongoing basis. To deliver Tier 2 provision, School A has an 'Inclusion Centre', a large, open-plan classroom with an adjoining sensory room, study room, and storeroom for resources. This space offers an Additional Support Class (ASC). Two full-time teachers who lead teaching (Ali and Mai), one part-time teacher (Jo), and two support assistants staff this class. The ASC has a higher staff-to-student ratio than regular classes offered by the school and a fluctuating cohort of 10–15 students, all of whom have a disability. Wherever possible, this class is a temporary, part-time home for students with the higher or highest level of needs and offers temporary intensive support rather than replacing their regular form class. The vast majority (85%) of students attending this class fully return to regular classes after 6–12 weeks attending the ASC, and much of the support provided is geared towards making up gaps in learning so that students can re-join their regular mainstream class for 100% of the school week.

The Inclusion Centre is centrally located on the ground floor of the school campus and in one of the main campus buildings. This prime geographical location sends the message that The Inclusion Centre is a key part of the school and practically helps students travel between this centre and their regular classes. Staff members Ali, Mai, and Jo lead professional learning activities for School A on inclusive learning and support staff on best practice in making curriculum adjustments and adaptations in regular classrooms in School A. Mai has an advanced and up-to-date understanding of a range of assistive technologies (hardware and software) that can be used to aid learning for children with disabilities and advises teachers at School A daily. Ali, Mai, and Jo also have input into the goal setting as part of producing IEPs at School A (see IEPs in this book), which are used to plan what curriculum adjustments and adaptations are required for individual students.

Drop-in sessions on literacy and numeracy are provided twice weekly in The Inclusion Centre and are open to all students. Students work in small groups of three to four members on common areas of need, as well as receiving 1:1 support with highly individualised instruction as necessary.

School A has an Inclusive Learning Leader, Ana Brown, who is a member of the school senior leadership team. Ana works with staff across the school, students' families, and many external agencies, providing specialist support around behaviour, speech and language, mental health, and health. Ana liaises with a multidisciplinary team consisting of social workers, an assigned mental health nurse provided by Child and Adolescent Mental Health Services (CAMHS), two visiting speech and language therapists, and two student behaviour specialists provided by the state education department. They have online case meetings each Monday morning in term-time to identify any issues affecting the health, welfare or safety of individual students with a disability and to coordinate actions or support necessary. Ana, Ali, Mai, and Jo liaise with families and external allied professionals (psychologists, social workers, speech and language pathologists) regarding any issues affecting a student's social, emotional, or psychological welfare.

School A has a strong anti-bullying program ('Bullying no-way') and an anti-exclusion school policy, accompanied by an initiative called 'Keep in'. The Principal, Jane Chloros, is passionate about reducing the risk of suspensions and exclusions/expulsion, and School A is known for its collaborative work with the local community and families to tackle educational disengagement and under-achievement, including strong links with community leaders and youth groups. Jane has a good reputation amongst the vast majority staff team and has their support for efforts to implement inclusion.

Jane is passionate that School A should meet the academic, developmental and social needs of all children in the local community. She promotes the idea that motivational teaching and a highly supportive but also highly structured classroom behavioural climate can reduce disengagement. Jane also promotes early intervention, and School A plans to adopt the Positive Behaviour Support and Interventions program in the next two years, aiming to further reduce problem behaviours before they start.

School A has a longstanding reputation in connection with vocational educational, offering work placements and vocational pathways for students into agriculture, the wine industry, hospitality industry, and furniture making – all employment sectors present in the state. Students at School A who are at risk of disengagement and exclusion are encouraged to access 'voc ed' streams, which are hosted in the dedicated VEd Centre on campus. Rhys Jones, the VEd Centre manager, describes these streams as a 'safety net for disadvantaged kids who would otherwise be out of school' and as a way of 'keeping in the system'. In keeping with state policy, the VEd Centre of School A delivers Flexible Learning Options (FLO), which is a program designed for secondary-age students who no longer attend school. This element of provision is particularly important in School A, given its location in a community with elevated levels of social and economic advantage and disengaged young people. FLO students physically attend the VEd Centre for two days per week, accessing an educational core curriculum consisting of literacy and numeracy, with a variety of heavily individualised other services delivered off-site for the remainder. Over 13 other providers deliver services via the FLO umbrella, ranging from careers advice to industry vocational tasters to the Positive Psychology and Wellbeing Toolkit.

Due to School A's growing reputation in the state for inclusion, a new 'special class' was introduced recently and which consists exclusively of students with a disability formally recognised under the Disability Discrimination Act (Australian Government, 1992). Enrolment in this class did not draw from School A's geographical zoning and was organised centrally by the state education department rather than by the school. This class was designed as a permanent rather than a temporary entity – unlike the ASC already offered. Some staff at School A expressed misgivings about this development as they believed that a permanent special class attended purely by students with a disability undermined inclusion and the RtI system used in School A.

Results in reading and mathematics, as well as in the state secondary exam (SSE) at School A, have been below the state average for most years since its founding in 1973. In response, the school has set goals for the next two years that seek to improve student attainment in reading, numeracy, and SSE, with a public-school improvement plan centred on these targets. Furthermore, the Deputy Director of State Education has privately suggested to School A Principal, Jane Chloros, that the school should drop plans to advance school inclusive policies and practices and should, instead, focus on raising academic attainment in English and mathematics. This recommendation is in line with an election commitment to 'raise standards' in literacy by the political party which won the election last year in the state where School A is located and is increasingly reflected in state educational policy. The Principal, Jane, is aware that she could be assigned to another school by the department at the end of her tenure next year and that a new principal might not advocate for inclusion to the same extent. This creates the ethical-professional dilemma of whether to resist the erosion of inclusive practice in School A and potentially be replaced by a principal who supports inclusion less anyway, or accept the changes desired but remain an advocate of inclusion for School A, hopefully limiting any erosion of inclusive practices.

Pause and think

Q1. Has School A made a credible effort to be inclusive?

A1. Yes – within the constraints it faces, School A has made credible and substantial efforts with the (important) leadership of the Principal, Jane Chloros.

Q2. Does the new 'special class' introduced in 2019 undermine inclusion in School A?

A2. Yes. The new 'special class' created undermines School A's efforts to implement inclusion and could be seen as an attempt to reassert control by the state's Department of Education, moving the school away from inclusion.

Q3. **Open Question.** *Are there any features of School A which deserve comment or which you find interesting or surprising? Why?*

Response to intervention (RtI) and multi-tiered systems supports (MTSS)

Designing flexible support systems that efficiently meet the diverse needs of students with a disability has been an enduring challenge in schools. In Australia, as in other countries such as the United States (US) and England, efficiency in allocating limited financial resources available has been a driver for these efforts (Armstrong and Armstrong, 2021). In the US, in the 1990s, educational researchers, working with schools, created a graduated (or tiered) support system called Response to Intervention (RtI) (Mellard *et al.*, 2010) The driving concept behind RtI was that how a student with a disability responded to intervention (i.e. educational progress visibly made) should guide the intensity of support subsequently received, with supports available divided into three tiers of increasing intensity (and therefore cost).

In a drive to improve the quality of standard, teaching in classrooms, effective, explicit and responsive teaching in the base tier (Tier 1) was emphasised as essential by advocates of RtI and as necessary before a student was escalated 'up' into Tier 2 (Buckman *et al.*, 2021; Fuchs, Fuchs & Compton, 2012).

Multi-Tiered Systems Supports (MTSS) is the latest name for RtI (Zhang *et al.*, 2023), and this rebranded term for RtI has been increasingly used in Australia, promoted by the Australian Educational Research Organisation (AERO, 2024).

Bringing it together

In the existing law of Australia, sector regulation and professional standards provide clarity about what is expected by teachers and by schools in terms of educational inclusion. Meeting the human rights of students with a disability underpins this expectation of the behaviours and actions expected of all those employed in education. The story here is that this clarity has, too often, failed to translate into action at the classroom, school, and system levels. The DRC Final Report (2023) can be seen as a crisis response to these failures to implement inclusion and, to our mind, offers a roadmap for the changes necessary – including major investment in teacher knowledge and capability to deliver inclusion. To advance the implementation of inclusion, this book provides guidance for teachers and for schools on how to be 'ahead of the curve' and meet the expectations set out in the key reforms recommended by the DRC Final Report (2023). How our book maps to recommendations relevant to teacher professional practice is set out in Table 3.2.

Public response to educational recommendations in the DRC Final Report (2023) was telling, indicating a reluctance by some in the education system and, in wider society, to accept educational inclusion on principle. In their review of inclusion as a powerful, global, educational trend, Armstrong and Armstrong (2022) go so far as to suggest that 'push back' against inclusion is a hopeful sign that it is a genuinely radical and socially progressive force for change.

Table 3.2 How this book maps to recommendations by the Disability Royal Commission Final Report (DRC, 2023)

Recommendation	Relevant book content
Awareness by teachers and schools of legal responsibility to include students with a disability.	• Understanding inclusion (this section). • Disability.
Teachers understand how to apply reasonable adjustment.	• Understanding inclusion (this section). • Differentiation and Universal Design for Learning.
Parents of students with disability are engaged with schools and make decisions together.	• Creating strong parent-school partnerships.
End negative attitudes and culture of low expectations towards students with a disability.	• Disability. • This book, as a whole, addresses this recommendation.
Educators should avoid the use of exclusionary discipline on students with a disability unless necessary as a last resort to avert the risk of serious harm.	• Behaviour in schools • Mental health in schools • Safety in schools and bullying prevention.
Professional learning advanced, and teacher capability strengthened.	• Teaching Routines. • Differentiation and UDL. • Effective feedback and effective praise.

Part II
Educational inclusion
What and how

4 Disability

Becoming a developmentally informed teacher

> This chapter will help you:
>
> - Understand key concepts in the field, including: 'disability', 'learning disability', 'intellectual disability', 'complex needs', and 'typically developing'.
> - Appreciate that disabilities can co-occur and conspire with other barriers to learning, which can generate complex support needs.
> - Understand that some developmental or specific disabilities are not always clearly evident but can present in subtle ways in students.
> - Identify important frameworks for understanding disability and difference: neurodiversity, medical and social models of disability.
>
> AITSL Graduate Teacher Standards covered by this learning include:
>
> 1.1 Physical, social and intellectual development and characteristics of students.
> 1.2 Understand how students learn.
> 1.6 Strategies to support full participation of students with disability.

Introduction

This chapter offers readers the confidence to apply inclusion in practice and a foundation to develop expertise in meeting the educational needs of students with a disability.

We set out in what follows how understanding how typically developing students learn (the process) is the foundation for understanding learning for a student with a disability and who may differ in their development from what is expected by a teacher due to the impacts of disability. Information is therefore given in this chapter on the typical learning process, and the reader is invited to consider how this applies to students experiencing disability.

DOI: 10.4324/9781003669630-6

We highlight how, when applied, this knowledge is *developmental* and is indispensable when making 'reasonable adjustment' in the classroom with associated classroom accommodations as are set out by the law (Australian Government, 1992) – as discussed in **Understanding educational inclusion, law, policy, and teacher responsibilities**. Practically, this developmental knowledge about the learning process benefits professional teacher practice when helping students with (or without) a disability when they encounter problems at a stage in the learning process.

Practical examples of students affected by disability (Ely, Jackie, and Zac) are provided to help convey the logic set out.

The knowledge gained in this chapter about the learning process and development is key to becoming a developmentally informed teacher and which will enhance teaching and learning for all students.

The World Health Organisation (WHO) state that an 'estimated 1.3 billion people experience significant disability', adding, 'This represents 16% of the world's population, or 1 in 6 of us.' (WHO, 2023). A core definition of disability must start with that used in the United Nations (2008), which is 'long-term physical, mental, intellectual, or sensory impairments which in interaction with various barriers may hinder their full and effective participation in society on an equal basis with others' (United Nations, 2008).

For teachers, every class/cohort will, most probably, have two or more students directly affected by a disability. Meeting the needs of these individuals is, therefore, a practical necessity for every teacher. Given the enormous importance of educational inclusion for students with disabilities and the many issues involved in this complex area, this chapter is intended as a starting point to prompt the reader to consider their own professional needs and interests in this area.

Vignettes

Here are three case studies ('vignettes') to help you consider the issues involved in supporting students with disabilities. These are an amalgam of real cases experienced by the author and are used in this chapter to illustrate the principles and theories discussed.

Ely

Ely is an affectionate child who likes stuffed toys and shows from children's television (TV). Ely attends Cherry Blossoms pre-school setting, but is leaving next month to move up to a local primary school. Ely can become very frustrated in social situations when he doesn't understand what to do and can become angry. Ely's development has previously attracted the attention of the local early intervention team. Ely does not live with his biological parents; he has been previously in the care system and recently placed with a foster family. Due to moving area, Ely is a year older than any of the other children at Cherry Blossoms and has just celebrated his sixth birthday. There are concerns that Ely might have an intellectual disability (ID); once he has transitioned to primary school, there are plans to have Ely assessed.

After an incident of rough-and-tumble play in the garden at the rear of Cherry Blossoms, Ely breaks a finger and is collected by his foster parents. It seems that several other children were making fun of Ely because he was pretending to be Iggle Piggle from the TV show '*In the Night Garden*'. Days later, Ely is showing signs of distress after the incident and appears withdrawn. The Manager of Cherry Blossoms, Ayisha, calls Ely's foster parents and social worker to discuss whether he can continue to safely attend school or should be withdrawn.

Jackie

Jackie, aged 11, has 'severe' difficulties with reading, writing, and study skills and is near the end of primary school. Jackie is, however, a diligent student and has a strong network of supportive friends in school. Outside of literacy, Jackie shows strong age-appropriate understanding and excels artistically, with digital art and pastel paintings showcased at several local art galleries. Jackie has a strong interest in art. Jackie's mother is supportive of her daughter but is 'wary of school' and recalls having had a 'crap time and being bullied by one teacher everyday'. Jackie has received some literacy support for two years after much campaigning by her mother, but does not have a formal disability. Jackie is becoming increasingly frustrated by her difficulties with reading, writing, and study, although making slow but appreciable progress. Last Tuesday, Jackie had a 'meltdown' according to her class teacher and had to be collected from school by her mum.

Zac

After a lengthy pre entry process, Zac enters a local high school. Zac, age 13, has a formal diagnosis of high-functioning autism and attention-deficit/hyperactivity disorder (ADHD). Zac's parents, both of whom are lawyers, have withdrawn Zac from a primary school and a high school previously due to dissatisfaction with his progress and the support provided. Zac's mother also runs an autism-friendly support group for parents (A for Autism). Zac likes history, which is his hobby. Initial assessment by the school specialist teacher/inclusion coordinator, Mr Armstrong, has identified that Zac will require small-group support with literacy (Tier 2) to help him keep up with the level of coursework required. Given Zac's educational background, it seems that Zac will also potentially require Tier 2 (small-group) or even Tier 3 (one-to-one, high-intensity) support with his behaviour, particularly as Zac can engage in physically dangerous conduct if overstimulated (see Chapter 2 for discussion of Tiers of support). Although the school is strongly committed to inclusion, the principal has expressed concern, privately, that 'we can't meet Zac's needs' to the school specialist teacher/inclusion coordinator.

Short Answer Questions

First, please answer the following questions:

Q1. Should Ayisha be concerned about this situation, and if so, why? What are the key issues facing Ely? What should Ayisha do next?

A1. Yes, Ayisha should be very concerned. Ely is facing exclusion from his peer group/collective bullying and is also at risk of suspension or exclusion from Cherry Blossoms. Ely's social understanding and interests appear less developed than might be expected at his age, and a developmental assessment by a pediatrician and/or developmental psychologist should be urgently arranged with the support of the early intervention team or equivalent.

Q2. What are the issues affecting Jackie's learning and welfare? What are the possible outcomes of Jackie becoming increasingly frustrated by her difficulties with reading, writing, and studying? How might this frustration present in Jackie's behaviour and actions?

A2. Jackie presents with a pattern of difficulties indicative of dyslexia – a disability described as a 'specific learning difficulty' and discussed later in this chapter. Jackie urgently needs a diagnostic assessment to determine whether she has dyslexia. Still, regardless, the school should assume that this is the case and urgently review Jackie's learning needs with follow-up actions for intensive literacy, wellbeing, and study supports. Due to a lack of action by the school, Jackie is at risk of disengagement and requires timely intervention to re-engage with focused support from the school counsellor and/or wellbeing team, plus Jackie's class teacher. Jackie's mum needs to be included in these efforts at re-engagement.

Q3. What are the key issues facing Zac? What should Mr Armstrong say to the school principal in response to her concerns about Zac? What issues might prevent Zac from succeeding in his new school?

A3. Zac requires multiple supports if he is to remain included in this mainstream school. Most important, the principal and senior leadership team must have confidence that Zac and other students like Zac can be successfully included. Mr Armstrong needs to remind colleagues that the school has a legal and ethical duty to ensure appropriate supports are in place and persuade colleagues that Zac can flourish in school, without adverse impact on other students' learning, if the right supports are in place. Negative attitudes by professionals and Zac's behavioural needs are the greatest barriers to his success. Mr Armstrong faces some challenges here!

Disability 31

Q4. *Are there any common issues for educational practice, or affecting how school systems enact inclusion, which can be identified from looking across the cases of Zac, Ely, or Jackie?*

A4. Common issues in the vignettes presented include: the need for pre-emptive behavioural and academic support systems to be in place to avoid damaging incidents ('Ely' and suspension/exclusion); doubts that inclusion can work undermine its implementation (Zac); and the risk of self-exclusion by students with disabilities due to schools not meeting their educational needs (Jackie and 'drop out'). Looking across these cases, we can see some of the threats to effective inclusion are systemic and often due to wholly preventable problems. Changes in attitudes by professionals, timely diagnostic assessment and unqualified use of classroom supports would have made a positive difference in all three vignettes.

Connection 8.1: who are learners affected by disability?

The UN Convention of the Rights of Persons with Disabilities states: 'Persons with disabilities include those who have long-term physical, mental, intellectual or sensory impairments which in interaction with various barriers may hinder their full and effective participation in society on an equal basis with others' (United Nation, 2008). The definition organises disabilities into physical, mental, intellectual and sensory categories – a structure which is widely accepted in Australia and beyond. Note also that Jackie and Ely do not yet have a formal diagnosis of disability but that across Australia students who are waiting for this assessment are afforded full legal protection from discrimination due to their disability as set out in the Disability Discrimination Act (DDA, 1992) and which should trigger all of the funded (and no-cost) supports necessary to meet each child's personal needs.

When thinking about a child/young person's growth in an education context, the term developmental disability, and also, the term learning disability are often used, emphasising the impact, respectively, of that disability on a child's development and on their learning. These terms are discussed in more detail shortly.

Definitions of disability are often used in legalistic contexts and for funding purposes, but are arguably of limited practical use in supporting affected individuals on an everyday level in school. Furthermore, definitions of disability are abstract and do not reveal how their impacts present in real children and young people. In a thought-provoking editorial published in *The Lancet* medical journal, The Lancet (2009) comments: 'There are 650 million people with disabilities in the world who all have their unique story to share. People with disabilities are individuals who do not all think or act according to the "disabled" label that society has assigned them.' (p. 1793).

The cases of Ely, Jackie and Zac suggest the complexities involved in ensuring that students with disabilities thrive in contemporary schools. Zac, in particular, often did not think or act according to the 'disabled' label that society has assigned him. With a 'hidden disability', Jackie did not fit the stereotype of disability at all, hence the lack of a formal label. This section uses Ely, Jackie, and Zac as references to discuss research, practice, and policy relevant to each student and help the reader appreciate some of the deeper issues affecting this population and move beyond categorical definitions. To enrich this consideration by the reader, important wider models of disability are explained below.

Pause and think

Zac has the label high-functioning autism (HFA). The American Psychological Association, who are recognised as a global authority on diagnostic labelling, describe HFA as 'a controversial, nonstandardised classification describing individuals who meet the DSM-IV-TR diagnostic criteria for autism but who have higher IQs and less severe impairment than seen in others with the disorder.' (APA, Dictionary of Psychology). HFA, which officially replaced the term 'Asperger Syndrome' in 2013, is a distinctive form of autism where individuals have 'normal cognitive functioning' but often require lifelong supports with gaining and maintaining friendships and with navigating complex social situations (de Giambattista *et al.*, 2019, p. 138).

In Australia, levels of autism have been increasingly adopted when discussing the support needs of affected individuals like Zac. Levels of autism are categorised by Health Direct, a government-funded agency, as:

1 Level 1: people requiring support.
2 Level 2: people requiring substantial support.
3 Level 3: people more severely affected and requiring very substantial support.

(Healthdirect Australia, n.d.; https://www.healthdirect.gov.au/autism).

Here are some questions to advance consideration of Zac's vignette.

Q1. Does Zac's high-functioning autism label signal what Mr Armstrong should do when supporting Zac to form healthy peer friendships or when supporting Zac to improve his reading comprehension? Does the label HFA (Level 1 autism) signal how Zac's teachers should support his learning and personal goals and suggest what strategies they should use?

A1. No – Zac's label does not directly help Mr Armstrong select and apply strategies which will help Zac form healthy peer friendships and improve his reading comprehension, or address any other areas for personal or academic development. Labels typically focus on what a child cannot do and their impairment, rather than indicating what will help address these identified deficits.

The medical model of disability, social model of disability, and neurodiversity

Several major models of disability exist and are important to understand because they help make sense of the topic, including the language often used to describe disability in education and how support for affected students like Ely, Jackie, and Zac is funded in Australia. Disability models are also important to know because they help make sense of the systems, practices, and customs used in the education system in Australia, England, and the US in connection with students identified as having special educational needs (Armstrong, 2017; Slee, 2018). The reader should also be very aware, when considering this discussion, that the special educational needs sector has faced persistent criticism for reproducing negative aspects of the medical model.

The medical model of disability was, until the 1980s, the prevalent frame for thinking about all students with a disability. The medical model has roots stretching back to the 19th century or even earlier, when many children with disabilities resided in hospitals or in asylums with a focus on treatment and care outside of mainstream society (Slee, 2011). Davidson (2006) emphasises the deficit framing of disability inherent in the medical model, suggesting that, 'The medical definition of disability locates impairment in the individual as someone who lacks the full complement of physical and cognitive elements of true personhood and who must be cured or rehabilitated.' (Davidson, 2006, p. 117).

Terms connected to a medical model of disability: identification, assessment, diagnosis, remediation, instruction, therapy, and intervention.

An example of a statement using a medical model of disability: 'Students must receive a diagnosis for disability which impacts literacy to fund their place on a reading program and to receive support from a teacher aide in class'.

During the 1970s and early 1980s, dissatisfaction with the medical model peaked in the US, UK (Brisenden, 1986). Parents of children with a disability, adults with disabilities, advocates and professionals increasingly demanded that the medical model be dropped and replaced by the social model in guiding how civil society – health, education, and the law – responded to individuals with disabilities. This collective was described as the disability movement and understood as a 'social movement for change' (Barton, 1996, p. 7). Disability was increasingly positioned as a human rights issue in public life in the US, UK, and Australia, including the right to be free from discrimination, and the right to access education and health services on the same basis as those without disability – a right enshrined in national legislation such as the Disability Discrimination Act (Australian Government, 1992). The medical model was framed as outdated and incompatible with societal efforts to enshrine these human rights. Davidson (2006), for example, contrasts the medical model with the social model, commenting, 'The social model locates disability not in the individual's impairment but in the environment—in social attitudes, institutional structures, and physical or communicational barriers that prevent full participation as citizen subject.' (Davidson, 2006, p. 117).

Terms connected to a social model of disability: discrimination, exclusion, learning environment, attitudes, stigma, systemic barriers, and supports.

Example of a statement using a social model of disability: 'Students face systemic barriers to participation and learning: the curriculum must therefore be modified, environmental barriers removed, discrimination tackled, and support needs met as presented rather than waiting for a categorical diagnosis'.

Many in the educational community (teachers, educational leaders, researchers, disability advocates, parents and affected students) have argued for decades that the education system in Australia should move to a social model of disability (All Means All, 2021; Slee, 2011). Students with dyslexia, like Jackie, have been singled out as particularly benefiting from education adopting a social model of disability with the argument that their difficulties with reading, writing and academic study are socially-constructed (Macdonald, 2009).

Children and young people with disability often receive health services and many disabilities, for instance, Down Syndrome typically confers wider health implications for those affected (Landes *et al.*, 2020). Clinicians, researchers and nurses working in public health or medicine have collectively called for the adoption of a social model of disability. In response some researchers in education have criticised the social model because it downplays 'the role of biological and mental conditions in the lives of disabled people' (Anastasiou and Kauffman, 2011, p. 367) and have argued that special education should be retained and modernised despite facing criticism from many who advocate for the social model of disability (Kauffman *et al.*, 2017).

Pause and think 4.1

What are your personal experiences of individuals with a disability? Do you have a family member, friend, peer, or work colleague with a disability? Do you have a disability? Using this experience, can you predict/reflect upon what personal strengths this person can bring to study? What are these strengths – can you describe them, e.g. 'perseverance'? How might a teacher harness these personal strengths?

Inclusion, the medical model, and the social model

During the early 1990s, the educational inclusion movement drew on the human rights perspective and energy of the disability movement, expanding its remit to argue that schools should meet the needs of all students who attended, including but not restricted to: students with disabilities; those from indigenous families; and those affected by poverty or disadvantage, including, for example, children who were asylum-seekers or whose families were migrants (Ainscow and Booth, 2006).

This comprehensive feature of inclusion was designed to avoid a 'narrow focus' on disability and children defined as having 'special educational needs' (Ainscow and Booth, 2006, p. 5) and is, arguably, more compatible in perspective with national (DDA, 1992) and international law (UNICEF, 2017) where a social model of disability does not fit with separate special schools and special labels for students with disabilities. Advocates of inclusion have argued that the special education system stigmatises students with disabilities by emphasising difference and deficit, segregating students outside of mainstream education (All Means All, 2021; Slee, 2011). Researchers have proposed a 'dilemma of difference' which explains this analysis where the provision of special educational services may, positively, enable personalised, developmentally appropriate, educational provision but may also, negatively, signal difference and entrench stigma and disablement by mainstream society in attitudes towards students with disabilities (Norwich, 2005).

https://www.unicef.org/eca/sites/unicef.org.eca/files/IE_summary_accessible_220917_brief.pdf

Stigma and attitudes toward disability in education

Despite perennial initiatives to change public attitudes for the better, students with disabilities often face negative attitudes from typically developing professionals and/or peers in education (DRC 2023). Quantifying the amount of discrimination occurring in schools is difficult (which teacher would wish to admit discriminatory behaviour?). A major study by Temple et al. (2018), using data from the 2015 Australian Bureau of Statistics (ABS) Survey of Disability, Ageing and Carers, found that 'Approximately 9% ... of people with a disability experienced disability discrimination in 2015 and 31% (of typically developing people) ... engaged in avoidance behaviours' (p. 1). 'Avoidance' behaviours, Temple et al. (2018) explain, are where a typically developing person avoids interacting with a person with a disability (p. 1). Worryingly, the number of special schools has risen across Australia over the last decade (AFDO, 2019), with many teachers and bureaucrats working in the Australian education system appearing to support a segregated education system (Slee, 2011).

Social beliefs underpinning these attitudes are often complex in form and range from overt hostility to more subtle forms of discrimination and bias. Low educational expectations (Slee, 2011) and well-meant stereotyping, e.g. all individuals with autism are like the film character Rainman (Siberman, 2015), are socially common manifestations of negative attitudes toward disabilities. Zac, who has HFA and ADHD, is at risk of experiencing stereotypes of this kind.

The sociologist Erwin Goffman is credited with establishing the modern concept of stigma and as it applies to individuals who, for instance, have a disability, mental health condition, or other difference which might be used to 'taint them' and mark them out as individuals to avoid (Goffman, 1963). Temple *et al.* (2018) in their study concluded that almost a third of non-disabled individuals (31%) admitted to this behaviour towards others with a disability; with the data used being drawn from the 2015 Australian Bureau of Statistics (ABS) Survey of Disability, Ageing and Carers. Coleman (2013) further explains that with stigma, 'People are treated categorically rather than individually, and in the process are devalued.' (p. 145). Stigma, therefore, refers to the experience of this devaluation and is highly contextual, operating via social interactions (Bos *et al.*, 2013). Indeed, this high level of variability means that 'What is stigmatizing in one social context may not be stigmatizing in another situation' (Bos *et al.*, 2013, p. 1). Developmental psychologists have explored how children learn to recognise and respond to difference, exploring its complex emergence in childhood and adolescence (Bos *et al.*, 2013).

As was explained in Chapter 2, **Myths about inclusion and objections to this book**, negative, sceptical, or ambivalent attitudes towards inclusion in Australia ('inclusion doesn't work' and 'I don't know if inclusion can work'), identified by research (Tan *et al.*, 2019), are a major factor in whether and to what extent inclusion is implemented in the classroom: attitudes matter because they underpin actions and behaviours in practice. The principal described in Zac's case epitomises this sceptical attitude to inclusion.

A research study about attitudes toward inclusion held by teachers by Boyle *et al.* (2013) pragmatically suggests that 'The variability of teacher attitudes is affected by the quality of the planning, and the support to teachers may not have been properly controlled for during the implementation of inclusion policies.' (p. 529), and points to a gap between policy goals and their enactment in school systems, customs and capabilities of teachers. Boyle *et al.* (2013) add that 'high exposure to inclusive teaching in the original university course modules' studied at teacher education/preservice level has been identified as an important factor in enabling positive attitudes towards inclusion in practice' (p. 529) – an observation which is hopeful because it suggests inclusion can prevail, if teachers enter practice feeling empowered and capable of success (Armstrong, 2018).

Neurodiversity

The Australian Sociologist Judy Stringer is attributed with coining the term neurodiversity in the 1980s (Doyle, 2020) and since then, some adults affected by ASD, dyslexia, or ADHD have argued that their disability is in fact simply a difference in how they think and process experience – a part of our diversity as a species (Armstrong, 2021). Researchers and philosophers have proposed that cognitive and perceptual differences experienced by individuals with ASD, dyslexia, or ADHD are an essential part of human evolution and connected to diversity in our species, exploring the many philosophical, social, and practical implications of this profound idea (Bertilsdotter Rosqvist *et al.*, 2020). Since the 1980s, neurodiversity has grown into a wide-ranging social movement for change in attitudes toward individuals with disabilities, including, but not restricted to, autism, ADHD, and dyslexia (Leadbitter *et al.*, 2021).

In a thought-provoking counter-response, some individuals with disability have said that this view of difference is simplistic and does not fit with their valid experience. Proponents of this view suggest that framing their disability as a mere difference devalues the very real difficulties they face with self-care, cooking, cleaning, working out their finances, and other everyday aspects of everyday life due to the effects of disability (Kenny *et al.*, 2016). This rejection of neurodiversity overlaps with criticism of the social model of disability highlighted earlier, especially that the role of biological and psychological impacts of disability is downplayed in the social model (Anastasiou and Kauffman, 2011). Like the disability movement, neurodiversity is an active, growing international movement for social change encompassing education, employment, and health (den Houting 2019). Students with ASD, dyslexia, and ADHD have been identified as neurodivergent populations (Kenny *et al.*, 2016). Armstrong and Armstrong (2022) make the point that if schools and wider society embrace the idea of neurodiversity, then classroom support (and funding) must be automatically provided to a student who is neurodiverse because, by definition, there is no disability present to test for in the first place.

Pause and think 4.2

Q1. This chapter does not attempt to list and outline the multiple disabilities listed under the major categories in Table 4.1 – *why is this?*

A1. Disabilities are numerous – it is unhelpful to offer lists of disabilities without any context, particularly when many disabilities are idiosyncratic in how they affect individuals and present to teachers. Autism is one such disability (Baron-Cohen, 2008).

Table 4.1 Categories of disability

Physical disabilities with a physical origin/impact	Mental disabilities with a psychological origin/impact	Intellectual disabilities with a neurological origin/impact	Sensory disabilities with a sensory origin/impact
Paraplegia, Cerebral palsy, for example.	Depression, anxiety, psychosis, for example.	Intellectual disability, Fragile X Syndrome, for example.	Visual impairment, hearing impairment, for example.

Recommendation for practice: to understand how a student is impacted by a disability, ask them (and/or their family)

To avoid assumptions, generalisations, or personal bias, the reader is strongly encouraged to speak to the student or any family/carers, as well as other professionals involved, to ask how this student's learning, socialisation, health, and/or psychological wellbeing is exactly impacted (Armstrong *et al.*, 2015).

Asking students or family/carers of students what helped the student learn best and what has worked in the past to enable their learning is also ethically superior, engaging students in the learning process and any modification or educational adjustments necessary. This emphasis on a student's capabilities or strengths is in line with the social model of disability highlighted above and is associated with a strength-based approach (Jones-Smith, 2011). As Elder *et al.* (2018) point out, a strength-based approach has already emerged in the discipline of counselling but has been strangely overlooked in education, despite its promise for improving professional practice with students who have disabilities.

Elder *et al.* (2018) detail how a strength-based approach can be used to enhance Individual Education Plans (IEPs). **Weblink:** Elder et al. (2018) https://files.eric.ed.gov/fulltext/EJ1182587.pdf

Defining developmental delay

Early identification by educators of any delay or difference in a child's development is vital for prevention of later problem and for making inclusion happen in practice – it is only by noticing any delay or difference in a child's development that appropriate support or interventions can be selected. Research has underlined how important this connection is and the costs of teachers failing to notice and act accordingly.

A high-quality international study by Squires (2020) highlights how students with disabilities are disproportionately affected by early school leaving (also called 'dropout') and that the damaging event where this happens is rooted in many missed opportunities to prevent it. Squires (2020) adds:

> dropout has often been portrayed as an outcome and therefore something that only secondary school teachers need to think about.

However, much of the literature suggests that this view is unhelpful and that Early School Leaving is the result of processes that run throughout childhood. This means that everybody involved in education and childhood development needs to consider how these processes operate. (p. 332)

'Everybody involved in education and childhood development' needs to therefore have knowledge of how to confidently notice any delay or difference in a child's development – providing this knowledge is the purpose of what immediately follows.

Ely is described by the Early Childhood Intervention Team as having developmental delay because developmentally his expressive language and social skills are below what might be expected for a child his age. A developmental delay means that Ely is not following expected norms in the pace of his development (Sheridan et al., 2008). For instance, Ely's play, language, social skills and understanding are similar to the youngest children in Cherry Blossoms (aged 3) but he is the oldest child who attends by over a year. Sheridan et al. (2008) details how developmental delay is graded: 'As a general rule, developmental delay is described as moderate where the development age is between two-thirds and a half. As severe where when it (it = progress against expected norms) is less than half of the chronological age.' Sheridan adds that 'It may be more informative to describe a child's strengths and difficulties to highlight needs' (p. 55). Under this criteria Ely's developmental delay might be classified 'moderate' with some uncertainty given his age and because children vary, often considerably, in their individual pace of development making it unwise to rush to comparison.

One major criticism of school systems in English-speaking countries is that teaching is aimed to meet the needs of children who are typical in their pace and level of academic and intellectual development but not for children who are either ahead developmentally, i.e. 'gifted', or behind expectations, i.e. 'require additional support'. This conclusion has been described as bell-curve schooling, referring to the Gaussian (bell) curve used to categorise and compare individuals statistically (Florian, 2019).

Weblink

Expressive language disorder

This is a useful link in explaining expressive language disorder:

https://www.betterhealth.vic.gov.au/health/HealthyLiving/expressive-language-disorder

Case study: what is intellectual disability?

The early intervention team and social worker who have been assisting Ely's foster family suspect that Ely's developmental delay is a sign that he has an ID but Ely has not had an assessment because this type of assessment is typically done at the start of formal schooling (APA, 2013). To be diagnosed as having ID Ely must score less than 70 on a standardised Intelligence Quotient (IQ) Test (APA, 2013). The APA explain that ID affects a person's everyday life including their reasoning, knowledge, and memory; empathy, social judgement, and social understanding; ability to manage money, care for themselves (self-care, e.g. learn oral hygiene), and self-organisation (APA, 2013). Many adults with ID live in supported housing and may need assistance in coping with everyday life. Children and young people with ID often overcome great challenges in learning to read, write, become numerate, self-manage study, and gain and maintain friendships. Helping students affected by ID learn to confidently self-advocate can bring lifelong, flow-on benefits (Anderson and Bigby, 2017).

Connection: IQ tests

The combination 'disability and intelligence' in education has a controversial and disturbing history. It is no coincidence that the early development of the IQ test in France in 1905 was triggered by the need to identify and cater for children who, it was thought, would not benefit from classroom instruction due to intellectual deficiency. The development of IQ test at that time by the French Government was bound up with the development of schooling and segregation of students into different groups based on academic ability (Harris and Greenspan, 2016). Some critics of special education argue that this ethically unsound historical practice is alive and well in segregated school systems (Slee, 2018) (see Chapter 2 for further discussion).

In modern practice, developmental psychologists use IQ tests as part of a range of assessments to determine how students function in terms of verbal reasoning, non-verbal reasoning and adaptive behaviours and to inform a support plan which fits the student's needs in education and at home (Armstrong and Squires, 2014). In practice, intelligence as measured by IQ tests is often an imprecise measure of what a child can or can't do and their understanding of concepts e.g. numbers (Alvares et al., 2020). Asking a child or young person carefully directed questions ('Show me how to add 10 and 2... What's the symbol I should use') and observing the response is therefore an important tool for teachers to use if this information is not already provided in reports about a child or young person. If a child has spoken language, then their response to questions, e.g. vocabulary, eye contact, ability to listen, can reveal much about their overall level of development and suggest areas for support.

Developmental disabilities, co-occurrence, and complex support needs

ID is considered under the greater umbrella term of developmental disabilities (Schalock *et al.*, 2019). Referring to guidance by the World Health Organization (2013) developmental disabilities 'are a heterogeneous group of psychiatric conditions that begin in childhood and interfere with typical development, causing functional impairment in one or multiple domains of life (i.e., cognition, learning, language, communication, and social interaction)' (Chan *et al.*, 2020, p. 103579). Some genetic conditions, e.g. Down Syndrome (Trisomy 21) can lead to developmental disability, including intellectual impairment and complex support needs, but have a genetic cause (Chan *et al.*, 2020).

> **Weblink**
>
> **Developmental disabilities – free resources**
>
> Here is a website by Developmental Disability WA (Western Australia) containing high-quality resources 'Our Key Focus Areas' outlines developmental disabilities and their impact on student's learning and development.
>
> https://ddwa.org.au/

Many students with disabilities, including those with complex support needs, attend schools without incident and can be amazingly resourceful and self-sufficient in making progress despite the everyday challenges they face. Jackie is one of these students.

Research indicates, however, that school environments can be particularly problematic for students with certain disabilities such as for example, ASD (Symes and Humphrey, 2012).

In mainstream school students with ASD are at elevated risk of bullied, impacting negatively on their mental health (Humphrey and Lewis, 2008). Noisy, socially complex school environments can provoke anxious, agitated or even aggressive behaviour by overwhelmed students who struggle to self-regulate (Larcombe *et al.*, 2019). Withdrawal from mainstream school by parents, suspension or even expulsion can occur as flow-on events of bullying or overloading. Students with disabilities, more generally, are over-represented amongst those who are suspended or excluded/expelled from school on account of behaviour (Armstrong *et al.*, 2019; DRC, 2020).

Zac was diagnosed with HFA and ADHD. The presence of one type of disability makes it more likely than another will also be present – a phenomena known as co-occurrence (Joyner and Wagner, 2020). Many types of disability co-occur, with students who have ASD, for instance, often also having ADHD (Panagiotidi *et al.*, 2019). When several disabilities act together their combined effect can be substantial on a child's development producing complex needs in the classroom. The term 'complex support needs' according to Collings *et al.* (2018):

> refers to the interplay of cognitive, developmental, psychosocial, physical impairment and/or health conditions combined with adverse environmental factors, for example, behavioural risks, substance misuse, criminal justice contact, insecure housing, cultural or intergenerational disadvantage or a history of violence, trauma and abuse. (p 142)

Individuals with complex needs are particularly vulnerable to mental health issues and older students have particular risk of incarceration (e.g. youth detention) or becoming homeless in Australia (Bigby and O'Connor, 2019).

Ely has complex support needs. Zac is on the autistic spectrum, affecting his social understanding plus ADHD impacting his self-regulation, which together generate some challenges for Zac in coping with social situations.

The following example is based on a real incident experienced by the writer while practicing as a specialist/senior teacher and designed to illustrate suggested best practice in responding to Zac when he becomes dysregulated.

Case study: Tuesday morning music performance practice

Case study: Tuesday am, 7C music practice

One Tuesday morning, Mr Armstrong is called urgently to the school music room no1. The music practice class is in chaos, staffed by a cover teacher who is struggling to cope with the boisterous behaviour of several male students. One of the youths is playing loud electric guitar while the teacher remonstrates with another student who refuses to cease playing a drum kit. Zac is struggling to cope emotionally in this chaotic, disordered and noisy environment, covering his ears with his hands and appearing agitated. One the female students laughs at Zac's reaction. Zac suddenly picks up a heavy electric guitar and begins to swing it dangerously above his head.

Questions

Q1. Does Mr Armstrong need to take action?

A1. Yes Mr Armstrong needs to act with urgency.

Q2. What should be the priority for Mr Armstrong in this situation?

Disability 43

A2. In order of priority:

1 Ensuring the safety of Zac, all students present and staff.
2 Deescalating the situation to enable learning to resume in a calm and orderly way
3 Supporting the cover teacher – who may be feeling professionally vulnerable.

Q3. What actions should Mr Armstrong take?

A3. Attract the attention of the cover teacher so they know support has arrived. If safe to do so, gently grab the guitar without touching Zac and lower it to the floor. Reassure Zac. If unsafe to do this, evacuate staff and students from the music room and seek support from other staff to contain the situation. Speak calmly but with authority to the boy on the drum kit asking him to desist. Give the boy playing electric guitar an opportunity to turn down the volume. If he ignores turn the amplifier off at the socket and say he is free to play quietly/unamplified. Avoid any secondary arguments and outright confrontation with students but act with authority to de-escalate the situation.

Q4. What should happen after the incident?

A4. In order of priority:

- Debrief the cover teacher who may need a break from teaching and some reassurance.
- Immediately inform senior staff in the school about the incident.
- Assess Zac's needs. Zac may need to have a break in a calm, quiet space in the setting before he can return to classes or his parents may need to collect him.
- Review goals, interventions, and/or strategies around behaviour set out in Zac's Behaviour Support Plan (BSP) in light of the incident. Amend the BSP if necessary.
- Complete any necessary documents, e.g. Critical Incident Documents.
- Learning point: identify what might have been done to prevent this situation in first place; does this incident have any learning points for school policy, procedures, or processes?

Jackie: hidden disabilities and learning disabilities

Many conditions, difficulties, or learning differences do not present obviously and are hard to formally classify but can nonetheless have major impacts on the long-term psychological welfare and academic progress of students. Children or young people affected can face multiple disadvantages because of the adverse academic, social or psychological impact of conditions or differences plus challenges inherent in identifying them, receiving the label and consequent classroom support they need. Conditions or differences present in this category are a varied group, often with poorly defined boundaries and confusing terminology. Following the UN definition, learning difficulties can become lifelong learning disabilities when and if they have a sustained disabling impact on a child's everyday life and wellbeing. The federal organisation *Learning Difficulties Australia* helpfully clarifies:

> 'Internal factors are intrinsic to the individual, can cause a person to learn differently, are usually life-long, and are usually considered a learning disability – also referred to as a specific or significant learning difficulty (in Australia and the UK), or learning disability (in the US and Canada)' and add 'Dyslexia is generally considered to be a learning disability, or specific learning difficulty.'
>
> (Learning Difficulties Australia Inc., n.d.)

These interconnected obstacles the process of identifying a learning disability, labelling a child, acquiring funding and accessing effective support can amount to substantial barriers to success for a child in school (Armstrong and Squires, 2014). Jackie illustrates how this can manifest in a real child who likely has dyslexia, to be discussed next. To reinforce the value of this focus on dyslexia the reader should note that dyslexia in a relatively common disability affecting 3–10% of the population (Peterson and Pennington, 2015). This means that most classrooms will have one or more students with dyslexia (Rose, 2009).

Case study 8.3: difficulties or disability?

When thinking about 'Jackie', the phrase 'difficulties' in relation to the phrase 'disability' requires discussion involving the added complication of how to interpret this relationship and apply it to the classroom. In the context of learning *difficulties* refers to the persistent challenges and obstacles to learning faced by a student and which may impede their progress when compared with their peers. For instance, a child may learn to read but do so slowly and with great difficulty, despite excellent classroom instruction and supports (Rose, 2009). As a term *disability* has a wider remit and is used to denote an impairment which impacts a child's daily life and functioning: 'long-term physical, mental, intellectual or sensory impairments which in interaction with various barriers may hinder their full and effective participation in society on an equal basis with others' (United Nation, 2008) and this expansive definition may or may not be relevant to teaching and learning or may do so in a complex way.

As the reader might gather, 'disability' and 'difficulty' are fuzzy, relational terms, open to interpretation depending on the criteria selected. Indeed, this lack of clarity has caused numerous problems for affected students, their families, and teachers, with many students receiving no support because they do not meet the criteria for being formally labelled with a recognised disability (Disability Royal Commission, 2020b). Critics of this negative educational outcome have described Australia as having a categorical system of support whereby funding for classroom support is reliant on a student clearly meeting the diagnostic criteria for a disability (Sharma *et al.*, 2019) and urged timely reform 'allocating individual funding to students based on the severity of a student's needs' (p. 4) as opposed to whether they fit a category. Sharma et al. (2019) add 'Such definitions remain highly deficit based and therefore contentious; offensive to people with disability and antithetical to the vision of inclusive education.' (p. 4).

Teaching approaches and strategies

What excellent quality classroom practice looks like for students with disability is impossible to meaningfully generalise. Disabilities impact students learning in very different and often unique ways. This reality means that a personalised educational response by a teacher to individual needs is best for students with a disability (Armstrong and Squires, 2014).

Professional frameworks often use vague statements such as 'know your learners and how they learn' (Australian Institute for Teaching and School Leadership, 2011) because further detail is impossible and would have to be specific to a child's specific educational needs. In thinking about professional practice Elliott *et al.* (2011) suggests that much of what teachers do in the classroom is based on tacit knowledge – that is knowledge which is not formally codified and explicit and therefore notoriously difficult to pin down and explain to another person. One myth in this area is the belief that there are teaching approaches and strategies which are uniquely suitable for use with students with a disability: a special pedagogy. Several studies about this issue suggest this is not the case (Norwich, 2013) and indicate that highly effective practitioners simply apply flexibility and imagination in classroom planning and delivery together with sound, but standard, teaching approaches and strategies (Armstrong *et al.*, 2015). This conclusion about what works and what doesn't work is also reached by listening to the educational experiences of students with dyslexia and is examined in Case study 8.4 below.

Case study 8.4: Charlie and Nic

Please watch the video 'Charlie and Nic', considering the questions below and which are designed to aid your focus. This video has been produced by SPELD (Specific Educational Learning Disorders) Victoria who are a charity aiming to 'assist those with Specific Learning Difficulties within our community' (SPELD Victoria, 2021).

Weblink https://youtu.be/xKLi19wl_R4

Q1. What difficulties do you think/guess Charlie faced in primary school:
- In reading?
- Writing?
- In efforts and performance?
- Motivation and persistence?
- Learning?

Q2. How has be overcome these challenges? What works for him?
Q4. What did Charlie's teachers do to help him? What didn't help?
Q3. From watching the above video what did you learn about how a teacher can help students like Charlie?

New South Wales (NSW), Western Australia (WA), South Australia (SA), and Queensland (QLD) also have their own SPELD Associations which the reader might search for depending on their location.

Weblink: https://auspeld.org.au/state-associations/

Stages and behaviours in the learning process

Although what excellent teaching approaches and strategies looks like for students with disability might be hard to represent without context, research does suggest a core set of common skills/behaviours which are vital for learning. Understanding these stages and where problems occur is essential for targeted teaching approaches and strategies which benefit all *students* but most particularly those with disabilities.

Looking across cognitive psychology, applied psychology and instructional design (Kubina *et al.*, 2009; Smith and Ragan, 2005) core stages and associated behaviours in the learning process can be identified. The result of a student successfully entering each stage in the process (what a teacher might note) is given at the end of each heading.

- **Attention/Acquisition.** As highlighted in the above discussion, attention is an essential foundation for learning any new skill or acquiring new knowledge. 'Switching on' an attentional spotlight (focusing on the teacher) and selecting what is relevant to attend to (what our teacher is exactly saying we should do next) are part of this stage. Attention is known to be part of a wider suite of capabilities collectively called executive-function and which help humans organise priorities and decide goals (called goal-orientated behaviour) (Zwosta *et al.*, 2015). Result: the student is ready to learn.

- **Application.** The result of this stage is a behavioural, where a student, often hesitantly at first, applies new knowledge learned (e.g. writes 10 + 1 = 11). Before a student can perform this behaviour they must first encode new information. The term 'encoding' is used to describe the initial process of committing new learning to memory, involving the contextualisation (maths, numbers, addition) prioritisation ('I need to learn this sum') and cognitive processing of incoming information, all of which are required for effective encoding in our memory (Knowlton and Castel, 2022). Information given by a teacher is never context free but involves 'rules' (sums must use signs such as + or =) around its application, purpose and value. As Knowlton and Castel (2022) point out, motivation is crucial when we encode new learning and is under-studied (p. 26). Result: a student can start to practise applying their new learning.
- **Fluency.** This refers to our capability to automatically, correctly apply new learning and without having to self-monitor or self-check. Like attention, fluency is itself a complex sub-process in learning, often, for example, involving the use of fine motor skills (when a teacher handwriting notes for instance in a staff meeting) as well as intellectual knowledge (Reber and Greifeneder, 2017) and attention to correctly application of 'the rules' governing new learning. Result: a student can automatically, correctly/accurately apply new learning and perform the expected behaviours.
- **Maintenance**. We must regularly practise and frequently apply our new knowledge to maintain it for future use (reducing the chance of it 'fading' in memory). Technically, practise is known as 'rehearsal' and involves regularly retrieving recent learning (and associated behaviours) from memory to ensure that we can perform the same task or behaviour in future (Williams and Lombrozo, 2010). Motivation to maintain knowledge, through regular practice and for future retrieval is vital for maintenance (Stefanidi et al., 2018). Result a student can accurately recall learning and perform the expected behaviour.
- **Generalisation.** Once we can confidently, accurately retrieve new learning (concisely explaining new learning to a friend or peer with accuracy, is a simple but effective test), we can generalise learning. Generalisation refers to the ability to apply new learning beyond the original context we learned and in a different situation or different context. (Ghirlanda and Enquist, 2003) and is regarded as an important ability when considering the overall development of children and young people (Carruthers et al., 2020). Result a student can apply learning beyond the original context in which it was learned.
- **Mastery.** Mastery refers to the social and/or professional recognition of competence in an area of knowledge and application in practice (Bloom 1968; Lengetti et al., 2020). In this definition mastery is a social evaluation involving judgements about the depth of understanding (including any gaps in personal knowledge) shown by a learner as evidenced by the depth of learning they demonstrate in formal or informal assessments (McGaghie

et al., 2014). Researchers have argued that a learner can deliberately aim for mastery by adopting a set of cognitive-behavioural strategies (Lengetti *et al.*, 2014; Zimmerman, 2008). This approach to learning is known as 'mastery learning' and has some empirical support in research studies (Winget and Persky 2022). Result: the student is recognised for their academic performance and knowledge.

Motivation and the emotional elements of learning are vital for progress and cut across stages in learning. Learning is not just about applying skills and knowledge but also about a learner acting on their motivation by applying the appropriate behaviours, including effective self-regulation of the emotions that arise along the way.

Impressive research over the last 40 years into self-regulated learning has suggested how important student behaviours such as goal-setting, self-monitoring and self-evaluation run in parallel with stages with the learning process (Shunk and Zimmerman, 2012; Zimmerman 2008) and offer teachable opportunities to raise the level of learning by students (Shunk and Zimmerman, 2012).

Scenario 8.3 in Chapter 8 helps the reader better understand how these abstract, conceptual stages apply in real learning.

Case study: new learning

Recall the last time you learned something new, for instance you might learn a new musical instrument like the guitar, a new language or how to make the perfect stir fry.

For focus let's discuss learning the electric bass guitar. Let's say for example that you want to learn how to play a simple bassline and have located an instructional video on YouTube to help. Here is how this learning applies to stages and behaviours in the learning process:

- **Attention**: this is the first stage in the learning process and refers to the attention necessary before you can begin learning. What did you need to do to attend to the position of your fingers on the guitar fretboard and position of your fingers ready to be ready to play a bassline? Can you watch the YouTube video and at exact the same time place your fingers/hands in the correct positions ready to play?
- **Acquisition**: this refers the initial stage of acquiring the new skill – likely to have high error rate and typically very tiring for a student. How did you manage to generate a bassline for the first few times – a simple series of notes for example Gmin7, Dmin7, Fmin7, and Gmin7 that sounds clear and accurate? Have you got it?

- **Application**: this refers to using the new skill/practice accurately and as per the 'rules'. Have you connected your guitar lead, turned on the bass amplifier, and carefully adjusted the bass amplifier volume and if you need to, adjusted the volume control on your guitar before starting to play?
- **Fluency:** a student can automatically or accurately carry out a task. Can you now play the bassline smoothly without watching the YouTube instructional video and with minimal preparation?
- **Maintenance**: a student can maintain their learning, often involving practice through doing/time delay/practice and review again. What do you need to do to make sure that you can maintain the perfect bassline and play it forever without forgetting?
- **Generalisation:** a student can recognise where a learned skill can be used somewhere else. Can you now use your knowledge of how to play another perfect bassline? Could you adapt these skills and apply them to play some or all of this bassline on a piano?
- **Mastery:** could you now perform confidently in front of an audience? Could you sit and pass music (bass guitar) examinations?

Questions

1 Apply the Stages and behaviours in the learning process to the last time you learned something new (e.g. a new hobby or skill).
2 Reflect on any emotional difficulties or barriers to success you experienced in your new learning and how you overcame them.

   Apply to 'Jackie'. To focus this reflection here are three stages in the learning process often affected by problems. Jackie has problems exactly in these three areas.

   - **Attention:** you miss the purpose of the learning or instructions necessary to complete it. In the steel guitar example you didn't listen to the YouTube instructional video because your mind wandered or it simply didn't make sense due to interruptions as text messages are coming in or your phone.

3 What strategies could a teacher suggest helping Jackie attend to this new learning? What environmental changes might assist with this focus?

   - **Acquisition:** you get 'stuck' at this initial stage of learning and simply can't produce the correct result. In the steel string guitar example, this would involve playing a note which sounds 'muddy' or simply sounded different from the instruction given in the

YouTube instructional video. Inaccurate finger position, insufficient pressure on the strings could cause this outcome.

4 What strategies could a teacher use to help, for instance, Jackie in this stage of her learning, e.g. in learning the meaning and spelling a new word?

- **Maintenance**: you have forgotten all or much of the techniques and processes necessary to reproduce your previous successful result. In the bass guitar example you might, for instance, not be able to remember the correct finger positions necessary to hold down strings in the correct pattern to produce the bassline you are learning.

5 What strategies could a teacher use to aid Jackie in this stage of learning, e.g. in maintaining knowledge of the meaning and spelling a new word?

Evidence-based strategies for students with disabilities

Evidence based strategies for students with disabilities are the same as those used with students without a disability. HITS (High Impact Teaching Strategies), for instance are '10 instructional strategies' recommended by research as effective (DET, 2019).

Weblink

Education Victoria – HITS

Here is a link to further information about HITS:

https://www.education.vic.gov.au/school/teachers/teachingresources/practice/improve/Pages/hits.aspx

For students with disabilities, any difference is in terms of the **intensity**, **frequency** and **duration** of strategies used and the labelling of the support infrastructure used to deliver these strategies in schools.

Response to Intervention (RtI) is one important support infrastructure whose purpose is to efficiently guide the intensity, frequency and duration of strategies used. RtI, overviewed in Chapter 7, is highly relevant to Jackie's case: indeed better meeting the *specific* needs of children with learning disabilities who struggled to learn to read and write, like Jackie, was a driver in the US for the development of RtI in the first place (Vaughn *et al.*, 2010).

In Jackie's case, the routine, classroom teaching, known in RtI as 'Tier 1' has not succeeded in helping Jackie overcome the difficulties she faces with study. Jackie faces problems with attention, acquisition and maintenance in her learning, like many students presenting with dyslexia (Armstrong and Squires, 2014).

What follows, which outlines what Tier 2 and Tier 3 responses might be, therefore assumes that Jackie has been exposed to well-delivered, carefully differentiated and engaging 'Tier 1' teaching to the whole class. This is a big assumption however and the reader may, critically, reflect whether Jackie's difficulties are partly generated by the delivery of an un-personalised 'one size fits all' education previously – a poor approach to teaching noted by some research studies based in Australia and internationally (Armstrong, 2018).

Jackie's case is typical of many children with learning disabilities in Australia and beyond. A delay in responding to Jackie's need driven by the need for formal labelling and associated funding, has led to her increasing distress, demotivation and disengagement. Research into this poor outcome in the US with children with has dubbed it 'the wait to fail' approach and highlighted the flow on negative impacts for students with learning disabilities when bureaucratic, school system requirements hold up timely support or educational interventions for individuals in distress. In these circumstances the social model of disability discussed earlier in chapter would suggest that the disabling effect of Jackie's literacy difficulties are socially produced and stem from this 'one size fits all' schooling together with the application of educational norms in the school system about what level of reading performance is acceptable at what age.

In Jackie's case, immediate intensive support is needed. Under RtI, this is described as Tier 2 (see Chapter 2) and would involve Jackie working in small groups of three to four children who also receive intensive instruction (see implementation below for further detail). Although Jackie is working in a small group at Tier 2, it's important that her individual needs are noticed and known and that meeting these is planned for in a more through and individualised way using data. To identify these needs and plan for individualised learning, the following process which can be given the acronym of NDPIR is useful.

Notice, plan, document, implement and review (NPDIR)

The NPDIR process is described in what follows.

Notice. Notice the child's difficulties and/or distress. Be receptive to any changes in a student's behaviour e.g. increased irritability or withdrawn behaviour when asked to write and behavioural patterns such as avoidance of in-class activities (e.g. unnecessary pencil sharpening and off-task behaviour on Monday pm double maths). Often these changes can indicate the need to act quickly – as in Jackie's case. Assessment of need, consultation and observations (see Plan response next) can be used to develop a plan of action.

Plan response. Use data to plan interventions or targeted support. Gather new data (or access existing data) about the child's strengths, areas of need and interests – this will inform the selection and implementation of interventions or support which precisely target individual needs. Assess need and knowledge if necessary: existing summative assessment data disclosing student knowledge and skills can be accessed to plan response. This data needs to be high-quality and recently gathered (within last 2 months). To understand a child's general level, standardisation assessment data that has gone through a robust production process is best because it enables you to precisely understand how a child compares with their peers. In terms of literacy and numeracy, the Wide-Ranging Achievement Test (WRAT) is excellent and examines single word-reading, numeracy and spelling (as a proxy for writing).

Weblink

Wide-Ranging Achievement Test (WRAT)

https://www.pearsonclinical.com.au/products/view/599

Assessing prior knowledge can be used to determine what a student understands (prior learning) and identify any gaps in learning which can be detailed in the Individual Learning Plan (ILP). Carefully targeted questions can be used to assess a students' prior knowledge:

What do you know about nouns...?...What about proper nouns can you tell me some...? Where would the noun go in this sentence? Show me...

Images and age-appropriate objects can be used to prompt a response and explore knowledge especially with younger children or those with barriers to communication. Assessment of a student's prior knowledge can be done via quiz, concept maps and by using other techniques as well as by skillful questioning. Ask the child questions about hobbies or interests to identify any opportunities to tie in curriculum-based learning. For example, Jackie's interest in music would be a low-hanging fruit for the teacher to use to ensure progress in reading, writing and motivation to study. Songwriting, reading about her favourite performers (reading comprehension), completing music practice diaries, and writing presentations (show and tell) about her hobby would all be sources of motivation through which progress in literacy could be achieved. Next, **Consult** parents, teachers, teaching aides, wellbeing/welfare support, school counsellors and/or allied professionals as is practicable and who might know the student's social, emotional, psychological or medical needs. A friendly, professional phone call is often more useful than purely email contacts. Allied professionals (e.g. psychologists, social workers, occupational therapists) often have insights into a student's family background which can help gauge the amount of support that child has at home for their learning and can be used to adjust the implementation of an ILP or IEP. Finally, *Observe* the child's behaviours carefully and around their learning if there is an indication that this could be the issue. For Jackie, for instance, the anxiety provoked by literacy lessons disrupts acquisition of new information and impacts on maintenance of this new knowledge and skills. Attention is difficult when Jackie is worried she is failing in study. Although Jackie is yet to be formally assessed it's highly likely that she has weaknesses in working memory: a common problem affecting many students with learning difficulties.

A Functional Behaviour Assessment (FBA), which was outlined in Chapter 9, **Behaviour: building and maintaining calm and productive classrooms,** can assist with identifying any behaviour which interferes with learning and which could be an avoidance response by the child to underlying difficulties in an area of the curriculum (Armstrong *et al.*, 2015). Timely, supportive conversations with students and their family should occur making them aware that the child's difficulties and/or distress have been registered and that timely action to support them is underway. In Jackie's case her increased demotivation and crisis with a meltdown are signs of the urgent need for timely action by the school to better support her needs.

> **Connection: successful learning support and interventions in the classroom**
>
> Students with disabilities often receive additional learning support or interventions to ensure positive progress in school and to enable a timely response to the difficulties or educational barriers they face in the classroom. On IEPs, teachers will often record an array of acronyms or titles which stand for additional support or interventions/programs which students are receiving: Alpha to Omega, PATHS, Good Behaviour Game… Peer Mentoring…DISTAR Program. Research in this area has pointed to great variability in the quality of interventions/programs which are used in schools with students who have disabilities, suggesting that careful selection is important to avoid highly marketed but otherwise unproven interventions. See Social and Emotional Learning (SEL) in Chapter 15 for further discussion.
>
> Strangely, in teacher education and in school practice, minimal attention is given to differences between support and intervention/program. As with many issues in practice this could be because this distinction is tacit knowledge with the assumption that everybody knows what the acronym stands for. Interventions/intervention programs and support

> are however different, with implied differences in the time-scale and intensity of delivery (Durlak *et al.*, 2011).
>
> Support refers to an ongoing background process; whereas intervention implies, in comparison, an initiative involving greater intensity and intended impact, on a student. Interventions are typically also time-limited (Humphrey *et al.*, 2020). Jackie for instance, qualifies for a timely intervention to raise up her literacy and avoid greater risk of disengagement or even school dropout (Squires, 2020). Interventions typically boost skills and knowledge in an area of identified need. To make this more confusing universal interventions exist e.g. a whole-school anti-bullying, as well as targeted interventions which are done with specific groups of students i.e. a social skills program focusing on students with ASD (Daley and McCarthy, 2020). How an educational intervention is put into practice is an important and growing area of focus for research and in schools. Dosage (how much) frequency (how often) fidelity (following recommendations from those who developed the implementation) and timing of implementation can all have an impact on whether or to what extent the intended befits occur in reality (Durlak *et al.*, 2011).

This chapter has highlighted how important it is that teachers notice and respond in a timely manner to a student's needs. Although loosely based on real students, for the reader's interest here is an update on what happened to **Ely, Jackie, and Zac,** after the cases described and according to the author's knowledge:

Ely attended an inclusive mainstream primary school and, six months later, was diagnosed as having ID. Ely had many challenges in his daily learning at the school and received an individualised curriculum. Ely has a friendship with one other boy at the school but often feels incredibly lonely.

Q1. Was this outcome an inclusive one for Ely? What factor(s) led to this outcome?

A1. Mixed. Ely is included physically but not socially.

Q2. What actions, supports or interventions might have improved this outcome?

A2. Many were possible. Pre-school identification of Ely's difficulties and timely support from the early intervention team for Ely and his foster family; more effective pre-school social skills support; greater pre-school-school-school transition planning; social-emotional learning program (SEL) for Ely; Tier 2 (small group) supports for Ely in his academic work; greater support from Ely's teacher/school for his social skills/friendships. Ely is also a candidate for attendance in a nurture group (see Chapter 9, **Behaviour: building and maintaining calm and productive classrooms**).

Jackie remained in mainstream school. A new teacher, with experience of teaching children affected by learning difficulties, gave Jackie eight months of intensive 1:1 support with study skills and literacy on Tuesdays and Thursdays after school. Over the next year, Jackie's confidence and academic performance improved as she learned to overcome some of the problems with reading comprehension, spelling and effective study. This teacher used praise in a targeted effective way to build Jackie's self-esteem and celebrate her progress (Gable *et al.*, 2009)

Q3. Was this outcome an inclusive one for Jackie? What factor(s) led to this outcome?

A3. Yes. The skills, intervention and persistence of the new teacher led to success for Jackie and renewed success.

Zac was withdrawn from the setting by his mother after 18 months. Zac's anxiety levels reached a crisis point, and he attended an alternative education program similar to Flexible Learning Options (FLO) to complete his school-leaver qualification (see Chapter 7). It is not known whether he completed these. Mr Armstrong was sad that Zac had to be withdrawn on mental health grounds despite efforts to meet his needs and scepticism from the school principal about whether Zac could be included.

Q4. Was this outcome an inclusive one for Zac? What factor(s) led to this outcome?

A4. No – but with a complex twist. Zac's withdrawal by his mother was to protect his mental health and wellbeing, but meant that Zac was outside of the mainstream schooling system, which put him at risk of social isolation and of leaving school without qualifications. Supporting Zac's mental health in school would have been a less risky option. This complex issue is discussed in Chapter 2.

Q5. What might have improved this outcome?

A5. A change in attitude by the school principal toward inclusion and support for Zac's continued attendance: support from the senior leadership for Mr Armstrong's professional role and advocacy; greater engagement by the school with Zac's mother; and an effective school-wide behavioural strategy.

Bringing it together

This chapter has been practical in its focus, providing examples of students affected by disability (Ely, Jackie, and Zac) and illustrating how inclusive practices and inclusive systems of support might apply in each case. Some of the complexities and dilemmas of real practice have also been suggested with the purpose of offering readers confidence through a deeper understanding of inclusion in real practice. Knowledge gained in this chapter about the learning process is the start of exciting pathway into becoming a developmentally informed teacher, an essential foundation for meeting the varied educational needs of all students in your classroom.

5 Differentiation and Universal Design for Learning (UDL)

> This section will help you learn how to:
>
> - Understand what differentiation consists of.
> - Explore how to apply differentiation in practice.
> - Understand what Universal Design for Learning (UDL) involves.
> - Appreciate how differentiation can be seen as one element that sits beneath the wider educational umbrella of the UDL framework.
>
> Australian Institute for Teaching and School Leadership (AITSL) Graduate Teacher Standards covered by this learning include:
>
> *Differentiation:*
>
> 1.5 Differentiate teaching to meet the specific learning needs of students across the full range of abilities.
> 1.6 Strategies to support full participation of students with disability.
> 2.5 Literacy and numeracy strategies.

What is differentiation?

Differentiation can be defined simply as *teaching and learning which accommodates the varying ability levels of students*. It is important to appreciate that differentiation is the *outcome* of a range of professional practices by the teacher and/or school. Sousa and Tomlinson (2011), for instance, encourage teachers to constantly check the match between a student's existing 'level of knowledge, understanding and skill and what he or she will be asked to do today' (p. 85) in a classroom. Sousa and Tomlinson (2011) also prefer the term 'readiness' to the term 'ability' (or capability), following the logic, which we agree with, that 'readiness' denotes an individual's distance from proficiency in the skills or knowledge taught. Emphasising distance in this way is helpful because it aligns with considering learning as a process of travel rather than one fixed

DOI: 10.4324/9781003669630-7

point. Chapter 4 adopts this approach with respect to the learning process, and we recommend that you read The Learning Process in Chapter 4 in conjunction with what immediately follows. Classroom practices aimed to generate differentiation can also be understood as classroom-specific elements that exist underneath the umbrella of a larger UDL approach.

One of the most common practices generating differentiation is a teacher deliberately designing in-class or online learning activities which accommodate the varying ability levels of learners. Differentiation can also be built into learning resources, such as the range of readings and worksheet instructions given to students. Whatever the exact context, accommodating the varying capabilities of students generates differentiated learning and, by doing so, maximises the chance that students of all abilities can engage in the classroom and progress educationally. As this emphasis upon engagement suggests, differentiation is necessary for quality learning by students and for delivering inclusive teaching in practice. The following section, Connections: differentiation in practice, unpacks this concept further.

Connections: differentiation in practice

Skilled practitioners and researchers in differentiation suggest that differentiation can be broken down into three distinct but related components. These are given in Table 5.1.

An excellent, accessible article by Jarvis *et al.* (2018) focuses on the challenge of how to differentiate in physical education (PE). As the authors (whom are experts in applying differentiation) note, PE is often regarded (incorrectly) as a curriculum area which can be defy differentiated pedagogy by teachers. Jarvis *et al.* (2018) comprehensively set out the considerations facing teachers when delivering the PE curriculum.

Table 5.1 Connections

Component	Explanation	Example
Content	What the teacher intends to teach/what the students need to learn. Content is typically specified by the relevant educational curriculum, mapped to subject and year level or age.	Victorian Curriculum F-10. National Curriculum.
Process	The activities students will use/engage in to acquire knowledge.	Small group work, individual study, or complete a reading.
Product	Methods used by students to demonstrate their learning, typically these are assessed.	Individual or group presentations, worksheet completion, an examination or test, or an essay.

Points to consider from differentiation

- *Process.* Small boxes on the left, e.g. 'Develop clear learning objectives', detail what a teacher should consider in terms of the broad *process* for planning differentiation – this is cross-curricular and therefore not specific to PE. Jarvis *et al.* (2018) suggest that learning objectives are broad guidance according to philosophical principles.
- *Practical and curricular application.* Note the highly practical application in the grey boxes (centre) and which is unpacked on the right. This content examines questions related to taught skills and knowledge, and questions about how this is practically best achieved, e.g. through grouping and knowing each student's existing (prior) knowledge when selecting and designing learning tasks to extend this knowledge.

The scenario below is offered to help readers further unpack and understand the knowledge about differentiation provided in this chapter.

Scenario: the worksheet from hell

Marie is a dedicated casual relief teacher (CRT) covering a Year 7 class at an urban high school in West Melbourne. The topic is a 'history of the calendar' which helps students to understand the historical and cultural origins of measuring time from a Western and First Nations perspective. This topic is part of the Geography curriculum in the Victorian Curriculum F-10. It is mapped to First Nations 'knowledge about the climate including Geography Factors that influence the decisions people make about where to live and their perceptions of the liveability of places (VCGGK111)' (Victorian Curriculum F-10 https://victoriancurriculum.vcaa.vic.edu.au/overview/cross-curriculum-priorities). Lessons are typically delivered using a mixture of short teacher-led instructional presentations followed by activities where students complete worksheets or participate in activities designed to assess their learning or rehearse new knowledge.

Using clear and explicit verbal instruction, Marie asks students to complete a worksheet provided by the usual class teacher who is on sick leave.

Young people in class 7a dutifully begin to complete this worksheet, displaying varying levels of interest. Marie observes that most students in 7a write *something* in both columns of the worksheet. After further monitoring of worksheet completion, Marie also notes that a significant number of students (around 30% of the class) hesitate when completing it or write little – some appear disengaged and engage in petty, disruptive behaviour.

Marie speaks to Jason, a student in 7a who has an attention-deficit/hyperactivity disorder (ADHD) diagnosis, and who appears to be having difficulty completing the worksheet and is becoming increasing distracted. It becomes clear that Jason does not know the order of the months of the year and is trying to cover up this gap in his knowledge. Jason presents as an articulate and thoughtful student otherwise and achieves high grades in English Literature and Art.

Q1. What could Marie do to improve this worksheet so that a greater number of students in 7a engage and demonstrate their learning? What might help include Jason and other students in 7a who have diverse needs?

Q2. What are the risks and downsides of doing nothing and leaving the worksheet as it is?

Suggestions for improving the worksheet from hell

Here are some suggestions and observations from our perspective in response to **Q1,** and with reference to what Jarvis *et al.* (2018), Sousa and Tomlinson (2011), and other researchers suggest for enabling differentiation. We will leave the reader to speculate on answers to **Q2**. Our suggestions for improvement are:

A1.1. Provide scaffolding on this activity for the whole class, which will benefit all, but most particularly Jason.

- **Explanation:** Images involving how First Nations seasons correspond to months of the year are available to aid engagement and understanding. Marie could ask students to complete the worksheet to help students match First Nations seasons to months of the year. To self-assess understanding, Marie can also ask students to cover the image, add their entry in the worksheet, uncover the image and check their answers against the terms used.

A1.3. Design for a range of abilities. Explanation: In its current form, the worksheet pictured in the worksheet is not designed for the different levels of 'readiness' for learning referred to by Sousa and Tomlinson (2011).

Some students will complete the worksheet relatively quickly and likely be bored, whereas others, who have a lower readiness to learn, will take much longer to complete it or might switch off attention along the way, leaving an incomplete worksheet. Designing a simple extension activity would enable students who are learning ready to extend their learning, and also provide further time to complete the worksheet for individuals who need a longer time to read and process instructions.

A1. Consider process, product, and content.

- **Explanation:** Recall that 'product' means methods used by students to demonstrate their learning, typically these are assessed. In this case, activities could be used to achieve 'product' and could involve, for example, students using their worksheet answers to complete an exit quiz given by Marie.

Graham et al. (2020) reviewed existing research about differentiation in the classroom published between 1999 and 2019. The authors note that many teachers appeared to have a patchy adoption of differentiation in practice and that 'most teachers {are} differentiating in only one domain (e.g., process or content).' Graham et al. (2020) added that 'Only two studies reported that teachers were differentiating across the three most central domains (process–content–product)' (p. 184).

Pause and think: different learners with different needs

Differentiation arises from a highly practical driver: how can Australian schools accommodate the *different academic capabilities* of students?

In any classroom, students have a range of abilities. Consider your own learning while at school. It is highly likely that your own ability, to your mind, varied across curriculum areas and that certain areas of the curriculum were, in your view, 'easy' or 'difficult'. This variation is often unique to individuals and is driven by a host of factors, including academic self-perception – how we perceive and label our academic performance, based, often, on feedback given by adults. For children with a disability, research has consistently indicated that negative feedback from adults and from peers can establish a damaging academic self-perception which generates distress and anxiety in the classroom (Armstrong and Squires, 2014).

The contemporary education system in Australia frames two distinct groups of children along a spectrum of capabilities. The first group include children with 'additional needs' or a disability and are catered for with special curricula and programs, many of which are delivered in special schools. The second are students considered as gifted and who excel academically, performing significantly above expectations for their age. Gifted students, like those categorised as having 'additional needs', a disability (or in some contexts 'special needs'), have devoted educational programs to cater for them.

In Victoria, for instance the Victorian Curriculum F-10, contains foundation levels A–E. These curriculum levels enable progress by students in this group to be recognised and acknowledged. Many special schools follow this foundation curriculum or aim toward it for students with disabilities which significantly affect their daily life, such as the ability to communicate in speech. Victoria has a recently reformed public schools 'accelerated program' in place state-wide for students who perform significantly above expectations and are regarded as gifted. Victoria also has a small number of public schools which specifically cater for gifted students. Talented students (not to be confused with gifted) have sports academies which cater for their status as elite athletes (e.g. Maribyrnong Sports Academy).

In Australian school systems, the identification of students with additional needs and, also, of gifted students rests on test performance as well as a range of other data streams. These streams include ongoing (formative) assessment. Most students in any given classroom exist in the space between either

Table 5.2 Differentiation is and is not

Differentiation is	Differentiation is not	Teacher role?	Student role?	Any other thoughts about differentiation

polarity/group. **Learning Activity 5.1** below helps the reader unpack what is (and is not) differentiation in practice.

Learning activity 5.1 what differentiation is and is not (Dr Carol Tomlinson)

Suggested time: 60 minutes.

Aim: this scoping activity is designed to help you understand what differentiation consists of and also what is *not* differentiation.

Procedure

1. Please view the video below (introduction to Differentiation) featuring Dr Carol Tomlinson, who is known internationally as a researcher on differentiation in the classroom.
2. While watching, take personal notes on content related to what differentiation is and *is not*.
3. Consider Table 5.2 while referring to suggestions made in the video and referring to your personal notes. What would you write in each column of this table, considering the video?

Weblink: https://youtu.be/X6d_gFawCmk

Using learning resources to enable differentiation

Differentiation should occur in planning lessons but should also be considered in the selection of learning resources for use in the classroom. Worksheets and reading materials provided by teachers can aid or impede differentiation to the extent that they are accessible for students operating at different levels in reading development. This logic applies to the physical layout and structure of worksheets and other activity-based handouts, with growing evidence that simple adjustments can reduce the cognitive load that these documents generate and can also aid engagement and performance on tasks by a student (Graham, 2020).

Ensuring that written instructions on worksheets are clear and structured in a logical sequence of steps is one important way to enhance the accessibility of learning activities where a student is asked to write. If a student can understand what is required, then they can perform and make progress. The reverse of this logic also applies: inaccessible instructions in learning materials can prevent engagement and reduce motivation when students struggle to understand.

Designing or acquiring written handouts or readings in 'easy read' format can also help engage kids with different needs or levels of reading ability, including students with disabilities which impair communication and/or understanding.

Activity 2: differentiated reading

Suggested time: 20 minutes

Aim: to explore differentiation in learning resources provided to students by a teacher.

Procedure:

1 Please read the executive summary in the standard Disability Royal Commission (DRC) report below:

   https://disability.royalcommission.gov.au/system/files/2020-10/Interim%20Report.pdf

2 Please read the executive summary in the 'easy read' version of the standard DRC report below:

   https://disability.royalcommission.gov.au/system/files/2020-10/Interim%20Report%20-%20Easy%20read%20-%20An%20Easy%20Read%20guide.pdf

3 Compare the standard with the easy read version. What differences can you note? For example:

   - How are the images used?
   - Anything else you think is important when comparing the regular executive summary and the easy read version?

Q. How can you bring this knowledge into your professional practice? Who can help you achieve this? What resources do you require?

Universal design for learning (UDL) and differentiation

Calls for Australian teachers and schools to adopt UDL have grown over the last decade. For instance, Chen *et al.* (2023) confidently claim that 'The universal design for learning (UDL) framework provides the basis for establishing an inclusive pedagogical learning environment in classrooms.' (p. 1). Less optimistically, Chen *et al.* (2023) immediately add: 'However, implementing such an inclusive pedagogical framework continues to be profoundly challenging across all countries, including Australia. Teacher attitude is the most important construct in efforts to create inclusive educational contexts.' (p. 1). Differentiation can be seen as one important aspect of UDL which focuses on classroom practices and lesson planning by a teacher.

Introduction: what is UDL?

UDL is an inclusive approach to the whole learning experience for a student, encompassing the design of teaching and assessment practices, learning resources, activities planned, and the wider environment, including school systems such as enrolment, student support, and the school's physical environment. In UDL, inclusive experience is 'designed in' from the very start of the process rather than added afterwards as an accommodation. A benefit of the UDL design in approach is that it reduces the number of often imperfect modifications to teaching practice, school systems or the physical environment necessary to enable inclusion. Although, as Jarvis *et al.* (2018) point out, even UDL cannot ensure that no modifications are required whatsoever (p. 49). A powerful feature of UDL is that it considers the whole educational experience of a student and often involves the participation of end-users (students with a disability) in the design or re-design of classroom practice, educational services, or school environments. To illustrate the superiority of UDL when compared with an approach emphasising modifying learning environments, please see the case study below. This case study is based on a real example.

Case study: anxiety in the yard

Western Thornbury Primary School (WTPS) serves a socio-economically varied area of a major Australian city. In the local community and beyond, this school has a positive reputation for effective inclusion of students with a disability. In 2024, school yard areas and doors in school buildings were modernised, enabling better access for students with a physical disability or visual impairment. Ramps and automatic doors with electronic touch pads were installed to aid access, together with modernised toilets wide enough to accommodate a wheelchair turning circle. These changes were intended to enhance the inclusive experience of students at WTPS and also ensure that the school met obligations under the Disability Discrimination Act (Australian Government, 1992).

WTPS has an effective student voice forum attended by students from Year 5 and Year 6. At the term three student voice forum, a Year 6 student representative, Danny, highlighted how several younger students appeared confused about how to operate the new automatic doors with electronic touch pads in the yard and had become anxious about using the yard at recess. Several students affected had disabilities affecting their understanding and communication and had been seen anxiously circling the automatic doors.

The school principal listened carefully to Danny's input, and they devised a plan together. The plan had two components, one was immediate and the other was short-term. With immediate effect, teachers on yard duty were quickly asked to ensure that the door was open whenever needed. Over the next school week (short-term), students across Year 5 and Year 6 were invited to devise accessible, inclusive signage which the school would pay to be laminated and permanently fixed to the door trigger panel. Designing this signage was introduced as a learning project with a book voucher as a prize. Jenny, a Year 6 student who had visual impairment, became interested in the project and tested out the resulting signage for end-user approval. Once the immediate access problem was solved, the school principal reflected on how accessibility should have been designed into the installed doors and panel trigger before installation – as part of a UDL approach in school renovations.

Principal's reflection on anxiety in the yard

'A great solution here to the door access problem in the yard, *but* a well-designed door trigger panel which was, from the outset, accessibly signed and intuitive for all students to use, would have been even better.'

Critical questions

Here are two critical questions which we think arise when a teacher considers applying UDL in their classroom:

Q1. Is UDL something that one teacher alone can choose to implement?

A1. No, but a teacher can work within their influence to ensure that learning environments follow principles of UDL as far as is practicable.

Q2. If UDL is, by definition, a setting-wide approach to deliver an inclusive student learning experience, then does it require buy-in from the whole school community (teachers, school leadership, parents, and state education officials)?

A2. Yes. A teacher can, however, with the support of colleagues, start these conversations with the senior leadership team.

Bringing it together

Differentiation in teacher professional practice and UDL across the school environment has been explained and explored in this section. As you will have gathered, how to achieve differentiation and UDL requires the teacher and colleagues to, respectively, apply knowledge about students' needs to instruction and in the design (or modification) of the school learning environment. Skilled application of practices necessary for differentiation and UDL grows with professional experiences. The principles and examples outlined, however, provide a clear pathway to success in meeting the varied academic learning needs of students.

6 Feedback and effective praise

This section will help you learn how to:

- Expand your repertoire of practical strategies to use when working with a range of students within an inclusive classroom.
- Understand what counts as effective feedback, including effective motivational praise.
- Reflect on your own professional learning needs and practice.

Australian Institute for Teaching and School Leadership (AITSL) Graduate Teacher Standards covered by this learning include:

1.6 Strategies to support full participation of students with disability.
3.1 Establish challenging learning goals.
3.5 Use effective classroom communication.
4.1 Support student participation.
5.2 Provide feedback to students on their learning.

Introduction

Differentiation, effective feedback on a student's academic performance, and praise are distinct but connected skillsets that are central to teacher professional practice in the classroom.

The capability to design learning activities pitched at the varying ability levels of learners is an important practical skill for an inclusive teacher and a simple, but clear, definition of differentiation. Providing targeted and motivating feedback on academic progress is also a vital aspect of professional practice, and research indicates that teachers often require support in becoming proficient (Caldarella *et al.*, 2020).

Praise is a vital issue when considering how we motivate students via the feedback process and is a vital ingredient for achieving a positive and productive classroom environment. From a behaviourist perspective, praise is a

DOI: 10.4324/9781003669630-8

reinforcer of desired behaviour: ideally, praise, if delivered well, should increase the chance that the student repeats the desired behaviour in future (Bayat, 2011). This logic is clear from the perspective of behaviour science but requires further unpacking when applied to the school classroom.

Pause and think: what do teachers require from students?

Before considering how to use praise, or any other technique, to generate a specific response from a student, being clear about what counts as success, based in turn on what we value and prioritise as a teacher, is important. Pausing and thinking about these questions aids clarification of desired behaviours:

Q1. What behaviours should teachers require from a student?
Q2. What attitudes towards learning should teachers encourage amongst students?
Q3. What counts as clear academic progress for a student in their learning?

Here are what we think are the answers to the above three questions. Research exploring problem or 'disruptive' behaviour and in-classroom management literature highlights what desired behaviour presents as in a classroom for many teachers and governments (Armstrong, 2018):

- Uninterrupted attention and focus on learning tasks and activities.
- Compliance with instructions – immediately and consistently.
- Evidence of effort and engagement.
- Demonstrable and smooth progress through the curriculum across all core subjects/subject areas.

Conservative views about teaching and learning often stress the value of discipline, compliance, and academic performance in terms of desired behaviours. These views often stay silent, however, or gloss over the psychological aspects of what behaviours they promote and the implications for children of professional practice which exclusively promotes compliant, on-task behaviours by students. A major problem with this one-dimensional, compliance-led view of teacher interactions with students is that some children and young people will wish to please adults at all costs. The vignette below (Karlia) illustrates how this dynamic can be to the detriment of a student. As with other vignettes in this book, this is based on a composite of several real students known to the authors.

Vignette: Karlia

Karlia is a quiet and compliant Year 6 student who is preparing to transition to high school. Karlia rarely, if ever, communicates her personal or learning needs at school. Teachers have a favourable view of Karlia because she appears engaged and is 'easy to teach'. In terms of what this vignette teaches, there are children who appear very similar to Karlia in many, if not most, school classrooms.

One Tuesday in term three, the class (6E) are taught by a casual relief teacher (CRT) because the usual teacher is unwell. Unannounced, the CRT asks Karlia to present her knowledge to the class about long division. This decision is convenient for the teacher because Karlia is a compliant and apparently engaged student. Within the first minute of the presentation, Karlia freezes and begins to sob uncontrollably. The CRT quickly intervenes. Members of the school senior management team are subsequently involved, contacting the student's family. After investigation, it transpires that Karlia is experiencing major problems with mathematics and that anxiety over this academic 'failure' is blighting her desire to learn across all subjects. Stalled academic progress and rising distress have been masked by Karlia's 'easy to teach' reputation and anxious compliance. The reality is that Kalia has major gaps in mathematical knowledge (including number bonds) and is at risk of poor academic outcomes or even school refusal.

Connections: what is effective praise?

Delivering praise in the optimal way for a student, at the ideal moment for maximum impact, requires skill and careful judgement. At the time of writing, there have been over 60 years of research into praise in the disciplines of psychology and behavioural science. Many questions remain, however, about praise and how best to apply it in the classroom. A study into classroom praise by Jenkins *et al.* (2015) notes, 'The use of teacher praise in the classroom has been the subject of empirical research since the 1970s, but despite more than four decades of research on the use of teacher praise, large gaps continue to exist in the literature.' (p. 263). These gaps in knowledge are accompanied by debate about the application of praise. There are concerns, for instance, voiced in the media, over the excessive use of praise by teachers working from the position that excessive praise rapidly loses its motivational effect and is lowering school standards by 'rewarding' behaviours which should be expected as a minimum (Harris, 2019). Some researchers have indicated that praise is most effective when used sparingly (Dweck, 1999).

Despite these gaps in knowledge and uncertainties, numerous studies indicate that praise is greatly underutilised in schools (Floress *et al.*, 2018; Reddy *et al.*, 2013).

Several studies also reveal that the use of praise by teachers tends to decrease as students age (Floress *et al.*, 2018; Jenkins *et al.*, 2015). Other research has consistently indicated that students with disabilities often receive less praise than their typically developing peers (Flores and Jenkins, 2015; Hawkins *et al.*, 2011). These insights counter the views often expressed by teachers and parents that students receive excessive praise in contemporary schools.

Using praise with students who have a disability

One important observation is that praise is related to the relationship which a teacher has with a student: indeed, praise can be used, very effectively, to build and strengthen student-teacher relationships (Gable *et al.*, 2009). This has an implication for delivering inclusive professional practice and has been suggested as effective in reducing problem behaviours, including aggression in the classroom (Gallagher *et al.*, 2019).

Research into children with disabilities and other forms of disadvantage suggested that, for them, the quality of student-teacher relationships is even more important than for their typically developing peers (Armstrong and Squires, 2014). Logically, any improvement in this relationship is likely to have a disproportionally beneficial effect on their psychological welfare in the classroom.

A major qualifier is required when considering praise and with respect to students with disabilities which impair social understanding, such as, for example, Autism or intellectual disability. Students in these populations might not easily, immediately, or routinely recognise the connections between praise and the positive learning behaviour that generated praise from a teacher or other adult.

Axe and Laprime (2017) in their experimental study of praise with students who have Autism therefore recommend, 'It seems to be best practice to vary praise statements in educational/clinical settings, though practitioners may attempt to pair one praise statement with reinforcement to determine if that praise statement starts to function as a reinforcer.' (p.325). In other words, teachers should try out different tactics when delivering praise to students with Autism or similar developmental disabilities and evaluate when praise seems to work to reinforce a desired behaviour. Adjusting tactics may be necessary for maximum impact. Practically, teachers should also factor in any differences in the speed of response to praise amongst students with communication barriers affecting their verbal or non-verbal response – individuals may take longer to show that they value the praise delivered.

Recommendation for praising students who have autism or intellectual disability

When delivering praise to students with Autism or similar developmental disabilities, if the praise strategies recommended in this section do not work, then experiment with different tactics. Note when praise seems to work to reinforce a desired behaviour for a student. Adjusting tactics as necessary for maximum impact.

Connections: reprimand ratio: the power of praise to raise student concentration

Praise is connected to its opposite, reprimand: where the teacher provides negative feedback on a student's behavioural and intended to act as a behavioural modifier, meaning that the student is (hopefully) less likely to repeat that negative behaviour in the future. A high-quality research study in the United States (US) by Caldarella *et al.* (2020) sheds light on the praise-reprimand relationship. The Institute of Education Sciences, part of the US Department of Education, funded this major, important study.

Caldarella *et al.* (2020) found that praise, if used effectively, could boost student on-task focus by up to 30%. Caldarella and colleagues examined the use of classroom reprimands ('Stop doing that!') by teachers in a follow-up study involving 149 teachers in 19 different elementary schools across three states in the US. As the authors explain, 'Reprimands are meant to stop misbehaviour.'. And they summarise the main finding: 'In the current study, teacher reprimands did not appear to help decrease future classroom disruptions or increase future engagement of students at risk for Emotional Behavioural Difficulty (EBD).' Finding from published research by Caldarella *et al.* (2020) align with an existing body of robust evidence indicating that teachers should focus their energy on motivating students to learn and avoiding punishment wherever possible (Armstrong *et al.*, 2015).

As with many important educational issues, the problem, however, is whether schools will be receptive to this recommendation. Evidence from research about the benefits of carefully used praise is clear, but changing existing customs, culture, and underpinning attitudes in some schools can be challenging.

Recommendations for effective praise

Literature about praise is now extensive, although often in disagreement and debate about how teachers should use praise in practice. Recommendations for how teachers should offer praise have, however, emerged from applied research and are summarised below.

- *Create a virtuous circle:* increasing a student's opportunity to respond and respond correctly can result in higher rates of academic engagement. In turn, this positive event generates greater opportunities to acknowledge successful student performance (Gable *et al.*, 2009; Sutherland *et al.*, 2002). Example: set clear structures during lesson planning with regard to how students indicate they have finished a set task and communicate this via a correct response.
- *Praise for effort, not academic output:* this rests on the logic that social comparison (where students compare their performance with that of others) is detrimental for most students' sense of self-efficacy. Negative self-comparisons can lead to tentative efforts at a task, which increases the chance of further negative feedback, further corroding a student's motivation in a negative pattern called the demotivation cycle. Research into the school experiences of students with disabilities, such as dyslexia, for example, highlights how praise was a rare event, often because individuals

could perform at a level sufficient to trigger praise from a teacher (Gibby-Leversuch *et al.*, 2021).
- *Be specific:* behaviour-specific, contingent feedback in which the teacher precisely describes the behaviour is usually more effective than general praise (Gable *et al.*, 2009).
- *Praise by describing the behaviour:* avoid praising the person or attributes ('Aren't you clever?') (Bayat, 2011).
- *Avoid giving attention to students immediately after they display an aggressive or negative behaviour:* this attention, even if it is corrective, can reinforce the aggressive or negative behaviour. Offer attention, instead, to any students adversely affected by the behaviour ('Are you ok?'). Only praise the aggressor when a student returns to acceptable behaviour (Bayat, 2011).
- *Acknowledge and celebrate:* praise pro-social behaviours including displays of empathy, compassion, and teamwork (Armstrong *et al.*, 2015; Bayat, 2011).
- *Think developmentally:* deliver age-appropriate praise which matches the level of receptive language held by the student.

Gable *et al.* (2009) offer an excellent overview of effective versus less effective praise, including examples of how a teacher might phrase each variation.

Feedback

Feedback and praise are connected but distinct behaviours within professional practice. Praise has a strong emotional (affective) component and is, by definition, positive – designed to increase the chance that the student repeats the desired behaviour (e.g. a student displays active listening behaviour when the teacher is talking). Feedback is a more general and elastic concept and, usually, refers to an emotionally neutral response from a teacher about a student's performance.

Voice box feedback

This emotional neutrality and emphasis on performance as part of a process of learning is captured by educational researchers like John Hattie, who discuss how teachers might consider feedback at different levels, ranging from 'self-level' to 'task level'. Levels are detailed in Table 6.1 with examples of teacher feedback based on our understanding of what Hattie suggests:

Video: Effective, student-centred classroom feedback

Video Link: https://youtu.be/CXGt53AGGng

Suggested time: 30 minutes.

Table 6.1 Feedback Levels

Feedback levels	Example of teacher feedback to student
Teacher feedback at the self-level	'You should focus on learning X as this will help you make sense of what you already know about Y'.
Teacher feedback at the self-regulation level	'You remained calm when learning X despite X being completely new learning and out of your comfort zone'.
Teacher feedback at the process level	'Now you have learned X, you should turn to Z next, as this new learning builds on what you now know about X'.
Teacher feedback at the task level	'You obviously read the task instructions carefully before trying this task, that's why you did so well in Z – remember for next time!'

Procedure

To learn more about Hattie's advice on feedback, please:

1 Access and view this video featuring Prof. John Hattie.
2 While watching this video, please consider how each level of feedback would be delivered by a teacher and the language used in delivery.

Bringing it together

To extend and apply your new or enhanced knowledge about praise and feedback, please consider what language and behaviours are necessary to motivate students and provide explicit, actionable feedback on a student's performance. The topics of praise and feedback connect with an understanding of the learning process, which is explained and unpacked in Chapter 4, and we suggest that you activate your knowledge gained here when you read about the learning process there.

7 Establishing routines in the classroom

> This section will help you:
>
> - Understand the importance of routine, predictability, and structure for establishing and maintaining a calm and productive classroom.
> - Expand your repertoire of practical strategies to use when working with a range of students within an inclusive classroom.
>
> AITSL Graduate Teacher Standards covered by this learning include:
>
> 4.1 Support student participation.
> 4.2 Manage classroom activities.

From time to time, politicians and educational commentators call for teachers to prioritise the teaching of routines, often referring to students at the start of primary school. This section outlines how teachers can establish and maintain routines but highlights common misconceptions and confusion around his topic. What follows counters these common problems and provides a solid understand of habits and routines which is informed by developmental psychology and behavioural science. Readers who teach, or who aim to teach, in the secondary education sector will find that most students they encounter will already have established many of the routines discussed: reading this section can still be of benefit to them, however, because students who are developing atypically are likely to have areas of routine which are still insecure or missing stages in the process.

What are routines? Some myths

In response to calls for teachers to place more emphasis on teaching routines, the Australian Educational Research Organisation (AERO) has invested in a no-cost classroom management guide available for teachers to download.

Weblink: https://www.edresearch.edu.au/practice-hub/classroom-management.

In the description for this guide available via the above weblink, AERO comments:

> Classroom management maximises students' on-task learning time by minimising disruptive behaviour and disengagement. It involves establishing routines to actively engage students in their learning, consistently applying rules and explicitly modelling appropriate behaviour so students know what is expected of them and establishing high expectations for students learning.

This description sounds reasonable but is an example of the misunderstanding, simplifications and confusion which often exists around mention of classroom routines.

Voice box: myths around routines

Table 7.1 presents two distinct myths which often appear when routines are discussed.

Two examples are given below to illustrate the realities of routines in the classroom.

Tidy Mara

Mara is a Year 3 student who diligently hangs up her coat and bag outside the classroom each morning and sits at her desk, smiling. Mara consistently takes out her pencil case and neatly places it in the upper right-hand corner of the desk at which she sits. The class has a 'learning ready' tick reward system on a visual chart, which is prominently displayed in the classroom. Mara walks to the 'learning ready' chart each morning and adds a tick next to her name.

After that, Mara spends much of the class daydreaming and finds it hard to start learning tasks, often preferring to procrastinate and talk about her pet rabbit called Apple rather than academic topics. The overworked, stressed-out

Table 7.1 Routine myths

Myth	Reality
Myth 1: Teachers should establish routines to actively engage students in their learning.	Classroom routines are the foundation for readiness to learn *but do not themselves* typically promote engagement or involve academic learning.
Myth 2: Classroom management maximises students' on-task learning time by minimising disruptive behaviour and disengagement, or similar, routines prevent disruptive behaviour and disengagement.	Routines are behaviourally neutral; students (like all humans!) have 'routines' which can be positive or negative for their learning and wellbeing.

class teacher, Mr M, has been too distracted to notice Mara's procrastination. At the end of the day, Mara is always the first to volunteer to tidy away, neatly packing away her pencil case and collecting her coat, hat, and schoolbag, which hang outside the classroom.

Q1. Is Mara learning through the 'learning ready' set of routines successfully completed each morning?

A1. No. The routines provoke procrastination by Mara and could be a cover for a range of deeper problems with motivation, attention, and focus.

Q2 What motivates Mara to show her proficiency in routines to adults?

A2. Mara wishes to please adults and stick to the rules because Mara has learned that adults like children to stick to rules and will offer praise. Complying with the 'correct' behaviours which adults like to see also acts as a cover for the difficulties with learning affecting Mara.

Pete's pencil sharpening

Pete is a sociable Year 5 student who has Down Syndrome and attends a 'regular' classroom in a primary school near his home. Routines are explicitly taught and valued at the primary school which Pete attends. Ensuring that students have equipment ready for learning is a school priority, especially with respect to younger students. After a problem with students coming to school 'unprepared', teachers model appropriate routines to students, such as bringing at least one working personal pencil and pen to school each day, together with a school exercise (topic) book.

Over the last two weeks, Pete has progressively spent more time selecting pencils from his pencil case, walking over to the opposite side of the classroom, and sharpening them in the recycling bin. Pete is clearly enjoying the pencil-sharpening routines, and his classmates have noticed his jolly demeanour while pencil shavings cascade into the recycling bin; they find his behaviour amusing. In the middle of this morning's pencil-sharpening routine, the class teacher walks over to Pete, attempting to address the behaviour. Pete ignores the teacher and turns away when they try to speak to him, laughing. Exasperated, the teacher grabs the offending 2B pencil, watched by the whole class. Pete stands very still and starts to cry.

Q1. Is Pete learning via the pencil-sharpening routine, which has been promoted to him by the school's campaign to ensure that students are 'learning ready'?

A1. Pete is following the 'rules' as far as he can, and this makes him feel secure and included. No academic learning is involved in pencil sharpening; however, having pencils that are sharp is a foundation for learning, e.g., writing words to add to a personalised vocabulary list, but not learning itself.

Q2 How might the teacher have better handled this situation?

A2 Students with a disability which impacts social understanding, particularly understanding of 'social rules', may need explicit guidance on how to interpret the rules. Students with Down syndrome, intellectual disability, and Autism spectrum disorder (ASD) can be affected. Teachers should always be ready to clarify and model how students should interpret rules around routines in schools. For instance, Pete's teacher could have explained before the school campaign that once a day is usually enough to maintain a sharp pencil and pre-corrected Pete's pencil sharpening by providing a sharp pencil with the words 'Ready to learn!'.

Pause and think: teaching routines

Routines are an important foundation for learning in school, especially in the primary school. Given below are some common core routines in many Australian primary schools at the start and in the afternoon/end of a typical school day. Readers focussed on the secondary education sector or higher might consider how young people or adults have learned routines as part of the socialisation process that is schooling.

Activity 7.1 teaching routines across the school day

Aim: to help the reader identify routines across the school day of a typical primary school and unpack how each routine can be taught, if necessary, by the teacher. This activity also asks the reader to reflect on what students might require to maintain a new routine over time.

Suggested time: 40 minutes.

Procedure

In the centre and right columns, you are invited to consider how the routine detailed (far left) will be taught if this is required, e.g., how will the teacher model the correct behaviour and check that the student has adopted the correct behaviour? Consideration here should be given to any resources or actions necessary for the teacher to use to establish and maintain each routine (see Tables 7.2 and 7.3).

Recommendations for establishing routines with students who find them difficult to learn

A wide range of issues can prevent many students from effectively learning routines and habits (please see 'The Learning Process' section in Chapter 4 for further explanation). Students from any demographic can be affected.

- High levels of distress and anxiety can interfere with learning new information, including establishing new habits.

Table 7.2 Start of the day routines

Routine at the start of the school day	How can this routine be established?	How can this routine be maintained?
1 Hanging coat and bag outside the classroom.		
2 Enter the classroom on time and in an orderly manner.		
3 Sitting at a desk/down before the lesson/day starts, ready for the roll (register).		
4 Administration: hand in any written communication from parents, notes, permissions, etc.		
5 Bringing out pencils, paper, and other resources necessary.		
6 Attention to the teacher for the start of the day.		
7 Activate prior learning (un-park the car). Dedicated time to identify existing learning and understanding, relating to this morning's learning.		
8 Logging into a computer or equivalent device.		
9 Tidying away for recess.		

Table 7.3 End of the day routines

Routine in the afternoon and end of the school day	How can this routine be established?	How can this routine be maintained?
1 Return to the classroom post-lunch on time.		
2 Tidy away hat, coat, etc.		
3 Attention on the teacher for the new lesson/return to the activity pre-lunch.		
4 'Park the car'. Dedicated time to identify today's learning points and 'park' learning ready for next lesson on this topic/tomorrow.		
5 Tidy away at the end of the day.		
6 Exit the classroom in an orderly manner. Access coat and school bag.		

- Disabilities impacting social understanding, such as Down Syndrome or autism, can be a barrier to mutual understanding of 'the rules' and routines a child needs to learn.
- Parents can struggle to help their child prepare for school and commit to effective homework routines.
- Some teachers can themselves be chaotic and struggle to provide a predictable class time for students to gain and maintain routines.

Often, simple actions of support, empathy, and extra scaffolding or modelling by teachers can make a big difference. Patience and avoiding judgment can also be powerful strategies. Working in concert with parents to help students establish and maintain routines can be helpful or even essential.

Strong and transparent relationships by schools with parents or family of students can be a vehicle for offering support and advice in establishing positive routines and habits at home. Consistent bedtimes and clear boundaries around homework, including ringfenced family time after homework is completed, can be discussed with parents by their child's teacher. As highlighted in this book's discussion of establishing parent-school partnerships, this approach should be clearly visible to parents as an open-door, non-judgemental approach, coming from a position of partnership rather than superiority: 'with parents, not to parents'.

Connections

The reader should note that, once securely learned, most of the above routines are automatic, that is, not involving conscious thought and deliberate effort by a student. Motor memory is the term associated with these automatic behaviours. Procedural learning is a term associated with motor memory (Tallet et al., 2015). Students with dyspraxia, formally called Developmental Co-ordination Disorder (CDC), have difficulty gaining and maintaining motor routines as part of motor memory and can struggle with activities involving procedural learning. Schedules and prompts by teachers or other students can assist individuals affected. Sport and physical education, which are heavily dependent on motor memory and gross motor skills, can be challenges. From the standpoint of behavioural science, routines are classified as 'operant behaviour' delivered by operant conditioning. Recent research literature with a slightly different developmental emphasis refers to learning behaviours and habits as forms of adaptive behaviour (Armstrong and Armstrong, 2021; Burns et al., 2019).

As Staddon and Cerutti (2003) note in a landmark article on this topic, operant behaviour is 'what most people would call habit', adding that 'Any well-trained "operant" is in effect a habit.' (p. 115). Behavioural science has long associated schooling with the use of operant conditioning to institutionalise children around the school day. Public schools can be understood as an exercise in human routines since the birth of public education in the 19th century and as a part of a process of socialisation for children. Queuing, classroom seating plans, bells to signify the end of lessons, school uniforms, daily schedules, procedures for students accessing the toilet (yes, really), organised curricula, and a host of other 'routines' are embedded in the fabric of school life (Armstrong *et al.*, 2015). Prizing these behaviours seems strange when few schools actively investigate young children's grasp of habits and routines, other than the award of stickers, badges, or other secondary reinforcers for obvious compliance in the early phase of primary education.

Task analysis

Typically, adopting the above recommendations, plus careful praise and explicit modelling of routines by teachers across home and school, is sufficient for most students to gain and maintain routines. Other, more specialist programs, supports, and interventions exist, however, for use with students who have not responded well to these efforts.

Task analysis has been used with students with sustained and deep-seated barriers to learning routines and habits. Task analysis breaks down a routine or habit-related task into its constituent skills parts, enabling micro-teaching of each small part of the task, for instance, important self-care routines such as oral hygiene (teeth brushing) or dressing (Burns *et al.*, 2019). The overall goal of task analysis is to 'increase adaptive behavior in individuals' (Burns *et al.*, 2019, p. 235).

The weblink below links to a video resource on Task Analysis from the Virginia Commonwealth University (VCU) Autism Centre for Excellence at Virginia Commonwealth University. Please note the examples of students using task analysis to complete their work.

Weblink: https://youtu.be/mIAJ8SKLkGY?si=gAT6z7fgDIxSOR17

Self-care routines, together with effective money management habits, exist beneath the larger umbrella term of daily living (DL) programs, which are often directed at students with autism or intellectual disability (Duncan *et al.*, 2020). Ongoing research is investigating whether video prompts can assist young people with autism, for instance, in learning daily living routines necessary for long-term independence going into adulthood (Cruz-Torres *et al.*, 2020).

Voice box

Hope Valley College is a progressive and inclusive large public secondary school, which welcomes all students across a regional town catchment. Students with a disability or who face other forms of disadvantage are included as fully as possible in all aspects of school life.

Students with impairments affecting their cognition, communication, or senses have a dedicated lounge, fully equipped domestic kitchen, bathroom, and 'chill out' area. Hope Valley High School offers DL programs in this area and where students, in consultation with parents, can learn how to independently make hot drinks, hot meals, engage in effective self-care, and, where appropriate, manage personal finances.

Q1. Please look carefully at the cupboard doors, tea, coffee, and sugar containers – note the labels attached – why are these present?

A1. To help students who have communication or cognitive barriers understand what the containers and cupboards hold.

Q2. Is there another purpose to the labels?

A2. Yes, to support daily living activities held in this space, specifically to support students' learning routines through task analysis.

Bringing it together

Routines are an important foundation for learning in a school setting. Here are some take-home key points about routines and habits:

- Most typically developing children successfully learn foundational routines and habits early in their school life as part of developing adaptive behaviour.
- Gaining and maintaining routines and habits do not imply that a student will be less disruptive and more compliant; routines and habits are often neutral in effect, or a student can learn routines and habits which are detrimental to their wellbeing, behaviour, or learning.
- Some students, however, have great difficulty in gaining and maintaining age-appropriate routines and habits. Often, but not always, many children with disabilities find habits hard to learn and maintain. Empathy, patience, and support from teachers for affected students are a vital ingredient for success in this circumstance.
- Task analysis, when used, for example, as part of a daily living campaign, can be useful for some students in learning routines and habits necessary for functioning at school, especially when a student does not respond to repeated explicit modelling of routines by a patient teacher.
- Habits and routines are an incomplete and limited view of what learning is, especially the academic learning prized by parents, employers, communities, and society. Employers are unlikely to ask whether a potential employee can exit their workplace in an orderly manner.

As highlighted at the start of this section, habits are important for learning, but they are not learning; this limitation is important for teachers to recognise.

Cross chapter connection. Routines and habits involve the student adopting behaviours which are essential to the learning process, which is covered, in greater detail, in this book within Chapter 4, **Disability: becoming a developmentally-informed teacher.**

8 Building strong parent-school partnerships

> This section will help you learn to:
>
> - Identify sound principles for working effectively, sensitively, and confidentially with parents/carers.
> - Identify and evaluate strategies for working effectively, sensitively, and confidentially with parents/carers whose child has a disability or additional needs.
> - Recognise that barriers to parental engagement exist and learn about how to overcome them.
>
> Australian Institute for Teaching and School Leadership (AITSL) Graduate Teacher Standards covered by this learning include:
>
> 3.7 Engage parents/carers in the educative process.
> 7.3 Engage with parents/carers.

Teachers and parents

Teachers are expected to be able to initiate and sustain parent-school relationships. Regulation of the profession at the federal level is explicit about this expectation. For instance, AITSL Teaching Standard 7.3 consists of 'Engage with parents/carers' (Australian Institute for Teaching and School Leadership, 2011). Engaging parents with the school and with their child's education is a wider goal of education policy of all kinds in Australia (Saltmarsh et al., 2014). Connecting parents with their child's learning is a practical necessity for a teacher because information from parents of a child with a disability can be vital for determining what classroom adjustments are required and in the collaborative completion of an Individual Education Plan (IEP) – see Chapter 2 for more about completing IEPs. From a legal perspective, the Disability Standards for Education (Australian Government, 2005) are explicit that parents must be consulted 'when determining what adjustments will be made to support a child's access to school.'

Activity 1: AITSL Video Illustration of practice

AITSL Teaching Standard 7.3 Engage with parents/carers.

Suggested time: 40 minutes.

Procedure

Access video. Please access and watch this video:

https://www.youtube.com/watch?v=S8m3EGJtKuc

Answer Questions. Now, please answer the following questions:

Q1. What practices and behaviours did the teacher recommend for engaging parents? Can you identify two or more?
Q2. How would you characterise teacher-parent interactions?
Q3. How did the assistant principal support the teacher and communicate with parents?
Q4. The video is based in a primary school: are there any differences in how to engage with parents in a secondary context? If so, what are these differences?
Q5. Is this resource helpful? If so, how? If not, why? If not sure, why?

Barriers and obstacles to parent-school engagement

Barriers to parent-school engagement exist. Many disabilities (e.g. autism, dyslexia, and attention-deficit/hyperactivity disorder or ADHD) are heritable (parents and their children have the same disability), meaning that parents of students with disabilities may have had a difficult or traumatic experience at school (Collings and Llewellyn, 2012). This negative prior experience can, unsurprisingly, damage parents' view of teachers and of schooling. The case of Jackie in Chapter 7 illustrates this common problem with parental perception. Some schools and some teachers are also less than optimal in their interactions with parents and can adopt a position of authority, which can inhibit school-parent partnerships. The current cost-of-living pressures in Australia should also give the reader pause for thought here. For example, it could be the case that a parent really wishes to have greater involvement in their child's education but is simply overloaded with work commitments necessary to pay for essential food, rental costs, and utility bills.

Advice from Parents Victoria

Parents Victoria (PV) is the peak body representing the interests of parents whose children are enrolled in Victorian schools. They deal with many, many concerned, frustrated, or aggrieved parents every day of the week. PV are also trusted advisers to the Victorian Department of Education and Training

(DET). PV are experts at conflict resolution between schools and parents and in understanding how teachers can connect with parents to work together.

We asked the Chief Operation Officer (CEO) of PV what key messages they wish to share with you as pre-service teachers about how to engage parents, and the advice is given below.

Advice from the CEO of PV to pre-service teachers

Together is better when it comes to families and schools. When it comes to effective communication, it needs to be with parents, not to parents. It must be relational, not transactional. **WeFirst culture** vs **MeFirst** culture – See Pages 10 & 11 in the Relationship-based Education Booklet at this link.

Weblink: https://www.parentsvictoria.asn.au/wp-content/uploads/2021/10/Relationship-Based-Education.pdf

---

Connections: evidence on the benefits of parental engagement

An important, open-access, evidence-based report published in England by Axford *et al.* (2019) synthesises 'the best current international evidence on parental engagement in children's learning from the early years through to secondary school' (p. 161). This report was funded by the United Kingdom's (UK) peak educational research funder, Education Endowment Foundation (EEF), and offers some important insights for teachers and schools in Australia.

Findings by Axford *et al.* (2019) support emphasis on the *general benefits* of parental involvement promoted by AITSL, (Australian Government, 2005), and successive Australian Federal Governments. The researchers find that 'Parental engagement in children's learning is associated with improved academic outcomes at all ages. The association is strongest when parent engagement is defined as parents' expectations for their children's academic achievement.' (p. 174).

In contrast, the research team indicate that 'The evidence is weak by comparison on the best approaches that schools, and early years settings can take to influence what parents do in a way that improves children's learning, especially in the UK.' (p. 174).

- So, parental involvement in a child's learning is beneficial, but there is no clear evidence about what works to achieve this.

In reviewing the evidence, Axford *et al.* (2019) also move the emphasis away from parents to schools, emphasising those changes to teacher work conditions, school processes, and culture (such as active rather than passive communication). A summary of key points is given below.

Recommendations for schools about engaging parents from Axford et al. (2019)

Recommendation for schools:

- Adopt a more holistic and sustained model;
- Provide the support, resources and time required for school staff to support parents;
- Build positive and trusting relationships with parents;
- Use more sustained and intensive approaches to support parental engagement for children who are struggling with early reading, from disadvantaged backgrounds or displaying behavioural difficulties;
- Make concerted efforts to engage so-called 'hard-to-reach' parents;
- Plan, monitor and evaluate parental engagement activities (what seems to be working?);
- Train teachers in how to engage with parents, but also schools should via trained allied professionals [e.g. social workers and psychologists] (Axford et al., 2019, p. 175).

Reading: Open access report available at: https://ore.exeter.ac.uk/repository/bitstream/handle/10871/39347/Parental_Engagement_-_Evidence_from_Research_and_Practice.pdf?sequence=1

Engaging so-called 'hard-to-reach' parents

Most parents will engage with teachers and with schools about their child's learning if settings present an open-door, positive, and non-judgemental external face to the community, adopting the approaches set out in this section. Despite this positive conclusion, in any school, a minority of parents do not engage despite phone calls, emails and official letters requesting meetings. We recommend that you adopt a curious and open-minded attitude in these cases and avoid jumping to conclusions or blame positions. The phrase 'hard-to-reach' is unhelpful (but widely used) in adopting a curious and open-minded attitude. The case study on Jenny below explores the issue from an attendance and well-being (mental health) perspective.

Case study: Jenny (part 1)

Jenny attends Wilonga State High School, Year 8, which is based in regional Western Australia. Teachers know Jenny as a quiet student who, on a one-to-one level, has advanced social skills and is regarded as a committed, pleasant student. Jenny also has some struggles with study, particularly maths. Problems with staffing have meant, however, that Jenny has not had a consistent maths teacher for over a year. Jenny's parents, May and Jay, met with the school at the start of Year 8 to discuss their concerns and request additional support for Jenny. The deputy principal recommended to May and Jay that they needed to pay, privately, for an assessment and then meet with the school to start the process for creating an IEP.

Last month, Jenny's well-being sharply declined, and the form teacher, together with the school well-being coordinator, invited May and Jay for an urgent meeting, leaving phone messages and via email. Jenny has been absent for most of last week, and there has been no reply from May and Jay.

Questions

Q1. Given no reply from Jenny's parents, what response should Jenny's form teacher and the school well-being coordinator make? Why?

A1. Jenny's form teacher and the school's well-being coordinator should formally escalate their concerns to the school's senior management. This step is important because school senior management has the authority and contacts necessary for further action, including, for example, contacting the school engagement team provided by the state's education department.

Case study: Jenny (part 2)

Jenny attends for several days but appears anxious and unwell. The form teacher and well-being coordinator meet with Jenny to offer support. The next day, Jenny is absent, and this continues for another two weeks with 'parent choice' as the reason given in the school electronic communication system (Compass).

The deputy principal, form teacher, and well-being coordinator met privately to discuss progress in Jenny's case. The deputy principal (Ria) shares news that the state-wide school engagement team have asked to meet with parents on multiple occasions and that due to no response, has dispatched a letter threatening parents with legal action. Ria comments, 'I can't believe that some parents can be so neglectful and let their kids remain at home every morning'. The form tutor and well-being coordinator stay silent.

Q2. Is threatening Jenny's parents with legal action at this point the right approach?

A2. No. Threatening legal action is alienating Jenny's parents, May and Jay, reducing the chance that they will engage with school in future.

Q3. Is Ria's attitude helpful?

A3. No. Parent blaming is unhelpful and often incorrect. Most parents only withdraw their child from school as a last resort.

Q4. Are there any underlying factors in this case which might help explain what is happening to Jenny's attendance?

A4. Here is one: severe school-based anxiety causing distress.

Bringing it all together

Engaging parents in their child's learning has many potential benefits. Engaging parents requires sufficient staff and time to gain and maintain a relationship with parents; however, the time and effort required should not be underestimated. An open-door, non-judgemental, and open-minded attitude by professionals is beneficial for connecting with all parents and is essential for connecting with parents who have barriers to school engagement.

9 Behaviour

Building and maintaining calm and productive classrooms

This section will help you:

- Identify learners who present with behaviours of concern (BoC).
- Recognise that behaviour in schools is a complex occupational issue.
- Develop teaching approaches to support positive conduct in classrooms.
- Identify several evidence-based strategies to ensure positive behaviour in the classroom.
- Understand that behaviour belongs to everybody in settings – conduct is not just about student behaviour.

Australian Institute for Teaching and School Leadership (AITSL) Graduate Teacher Standards covered by this learning include:

4.1 Support student participation.
4.2 Manage classroom activities.
4.3 Manage challenging behaviour.
4.4 Maintain student safety.

This section connects with **Safety in schools and bullying prevention.** We recommend that you read Chapter 12, **Safety in schools and bullying prevention** after reading the content here.

Introduction

Behaviour in schools is one of the most important educational issues according to teachers. Surveys about behaviour conducted by professional organisations often highlight dissatisfaction with how students conduct themselves in school, and research has linked poor behaviour in schools with the number of teachers quitting the profession (Billingsley and Bettini, 2019, p. 719). To add to this concerning picture, lurid headlines detailing aggressive, disruptive, or disturbing behaviour by students in classrooms often appear in the media in Australia and other English-speaking countries, such as the United Kingdom (UK) and the United States (US) (Armstrong and Armstrong, 2021; Graham, 2020). Given the emotive aspects of this topic, this chapter discusses the merits and drawbacks of several evidence-based strategies to ensure positive behaviour in the classroom.

- Advice on effectively delivering praise to students is focussed upon as an example of professional practice by a teacher.
- An evidence-based whole-year or whole-school intervention called Functional Behaviour Assessment (FBA) is explained and illustrated.
- Three strikes, positive behavioural support (PBIS), and other 'whole-school' strategies focussed on behaviour are explained and evaluated for the reader.

The practical purpose of this chapter is enhanced by a brief summary of the psychological theory of behaviourism, which is a fundamentally shaping current school practice and customs but is rarely, if ever, discussed by teachers (Armstrong and Armstrong, 2021; Hart, 2010).

Greater awareness of current customs and practices in Australian schools is helpful to deepen understanding, as is an openness to 'doing things differently' in professional practice (Sullivan *et al.*, 2014). This chapter, like others in this book, illustrates the fundamental point that delivering a calm and productive classroom is entirely complementary to delivering an inclusive environment, benefitting all students but, at the same time, offering a nurturing environment that particularly aids students at risk of behavioural difficulties. Students who express more extreme or concerning behaviours in the classroom may be in distress, and the worrying behaviours we observe as a teacher could be due to a mental health condition. What action we, as teachers, take in response should be informed by considering this possibility, without resorting to amateur diagnosis of a mental health disorder (Armstrong *et al.*, 2015). This chapter should be read alongside **Chapter 14 Mental Health and Wellbeing in Schools**.

Who are learners at risk of behaviours of concern?

Let's break down what we mean by student behaviour. To do this analysis, we need to think more carefully about groups (or 'populations') of students in our classroom and what severity of behaviours we are referring to. Severity is important to consider. For perspective, most behaviours by students in class regarded by teachers as a problem are relatively minor, involving infringements of what the teacher or the school regards as acceptable (Westling, 2010). In literature, the umbrella term 'disruptive behaviour' is used to categorise these types of student conduct and stresses its disruptive effect upon a student's learning and an orderly classroom environment (Armstrong and Armstrong, 2021; Sullivan *et al.*, 2014).

Disruptive behaviour

Studies about disruptive behaviour cite the following as examples: students calling out or making inappropriate noises, inattention to the learning task, irritating others/peers, dropping litter, chatting with other students excessively, unauthorised movement around the classroom, work avoidance in class, and sarcastic comments aimed at the teacher ('Oh yes Sir, *of course* I will return to my seat!') (Armstrong *et al.*, 2015). Research into disruptive behaviour indicates that it is a common occupational problem affecting teachers in Australia and can reduce student learning (Hepburn and Beamish, 2019).

Disruptive behaviours commonly affect schools of all types and across all age ranges. Teachers suggest that these behaviours 'wear them down' psychologically over months and years in the classroom (Clunies-Ross *et al.*, 2008). The reader should note that what is regarded as 'disruptive behaviour' by teachers varies and that research has highlighted the disproportionate use of severe sanctions by schools, such as educational suspension, with students affected by a disability (Graham, 2020; Skiba, 2014).

Challenging behaviour

Challenging behaviour refers to difficult or dangerous conduct which threatens the well-being and/or safety of peers, the teacher, or the student. It is an umbrella term referring to more serious misdemeanours by students. Studies about challenging behaviour cite the following as examples, according to Armstrong *et al.* (2015):

> Physical aggression toward other students or teachers, including kicking or punching; maliciously breaking school property in open acts of defiance; verbal aggression, including threats ('I am going to kill you, stab you' etc.); intentionally dangerous behaviour (setting fire to desks, gas taps, waste bins); the threatened use of a weapon (knife, gun) and severe bullying of others, including younger peers. Use of mobile phones or tablets to film pre-arranged dangerous or aggressive acts toward others has emerged as a new type of challenging behaviour. (p. 5)

Challenging behaviours are often a feature of critical incidents – events which involve classroom evacuation and/or cause serious disruption across a school as the incident is dealt with. Critical incidents involving challenging behaviour can also lead to serious consequences, including the suspension or expulsion of those involved, hospitalisation of students, and the traumatisation of staff and/or students who witnessed the event (Westling, 2010). Challenging behaviour presents in dangerous, aggressive, or violent actions by a student and can be categorised as 'occupational violence' or OV. This topic is discussed in detail in Chapter 12, **Safety in schools and bullying prevention**, in this book.

Who's at risk? Populations most affected by challenging behaviour

Not all individuals have the same risk of presenting with what teachers regard as challenging behaviour. Over the last 50 years, numerous studies have charted the relationship between a range of disabilities and behaviours considered as challenging by professionals (Lory *et al.*, 2020). Developmental disabilities, such as Autism Spectrum Disorder (ASD), genetic disabilities, such as Down Syndrome, and also intellectual disabilities make it more likely that a student will face challenges in behavioural development (Lory *et al.*, 2020; Rzepecka *et al.*, 2011).

Practice recommendation

Caution is urged when interpreting this finding from research about the connection between behaviour and disability: students without any known disability, learning, or development issue can present with behaviour of serious concern to adults.

US-based research indicates that challenging behaviours are relatively uncommon in schools, occurring only occasionally in most mainstream settings (Westling *et al.*, 2010), a view supported by at least one Australian-based study (Graham, 2020). Discussions about incidents of aggressive behaviour by students, however, tend to dominate consideration of behaviour in the media and could be described as part of 'behaviour folklore' affecting schools (Armstrong and Armstrong, 2021), but which not every teacher might uncritically accept.

A widespread focus on aggressive and/or dangerous behaviour in schools is arguably a product of media bias. Many students who are behaviourally challenged are not actually aggressive but nonetheless express social, emotional difficulties or profound psychological distress, which can frighten adults and other students (Elliott and Place, 2012). According to Armstrong *et al.* (2015), the conduct presented in many cases of challenging behaviour is actually a symptom of these difficulties or distress and includes behaviours such as:

> Head-banging, self-scratching/gouging; emotional distress (crying, screaming); hiding under the table/from sight; extreme anxiety; obsessive behaviours; and elective mutism (persistent refusal to talk); self-exclusion and disengagement; sexualised-behaviours (e.g. self-stimulation); amusement at others misfortune and callous disregard for peers/others. (p. 5)

Although not aggressive, the reader might reflect on how challenging and disruptive to learning the above behaviours are in a classroom setting. Such behaviours are relatively common sub-types of challenging behaviour affecting students with disabilities (Westling, 2010). Students with autism, for instance, are particularly at risk of self-injurious behaviours (head-banging, self-scratching/gouging). In research literature, students referred to here as having challenging behaviours are technically described as experiencing behavioural difficulties (Oldfield *et al.*, 2016). As suggested, both simple categorisations have limitations when considering students with a disability and should be treated with caution. Asking whether the behaviour observed in a classroom can, however, be a starting point when considering the severity of behaviours presented by a student and most importantly, how to proceed in response.

The behaviour management perspective

When discussing behaviour in schools, an inescapable historical baggage exists around behaviour. This history shapes how behaviour is currently understood in schools and how student conduct is approached by teachers in classrooms across Australia, the UK, and the US. Many of the recognisable core, stereotypical features of schools, including bells, fixed lesson times, school uniforms, and punishments, such as detention and the authority figure of the Principal or Head, are intended to instil desired, compliant, on-task behaviours from students (Armstrong and Armstrong, 2021). These iconic features of schools and associated beliefs about behaviour are drawn from the theory of behaviourism and often reproduced daily in school customs across the English-speaking world, typically without any critical awareness of their import or origin (Armstrong and Armstrong, 2021). Behaviourism is an important theory of learning in the history of psychology. It is based on several claims about how best to understand human conduct, expressed in two forms: methodological behaviourism and psychological behaviourism.

Behaviourism became the dominant theory in psychology in the 1950s onwards and became famous for its salivating dogs and pecking pigeons: animals which had been conditioned, mainly using food, to respond on demand to specific stimuli such as bells or whistles. Experimental, laboratory-based studies applying these insights to humans highlighted how specific behaviours could be predictably controlled in humans through a process of conditioning, which involved incentives or disincentives. Readers interested in the history of behaviourism should read Guercio (2020), who discusses how behaviourism was applied to humans after its development in studying animal behaviours. Programs using Applied Behaviour Analysis (ABA) still use these powerful techniques to reduce dangerous or aggressive behaviour in children or young people with disabilities (Gable *et al.*, 2009).

Weblink: This video from the Autism Behavioural Intervention Association illustrates how an ABA therapist works with and encourages Daniel, a young boy with autism, to verbally ask for the things he needs to play a game.

https://youtu.be/V9YDDpo9LWg

Teachers rarely discuss the theory of behaviourism. However, it shapes the typical school environment across the English-speaking world and beyond, in fundamental ways. For example, the emphasis on managing a student's behaviours in the classroom is one important manifestation of behaviourism in schools and requires further explanation. Since the 1970s, a large amount of literature has emerged which emphasises the merit of using behaviour management techniques in classrooms and is often built from aspects of behaviourism without explicitly referencing this theory. The techniques promoted could be described as 'behaviourism lite' because they presented a watered-down, or in some cases simply incorrect, application of behaviourist theory (Westling, 2010). The view that teachers can manage children's behaviour became, however, a popular, established idea and *behaviour management* entered professional language, signifying a practical skillset which teachers could learn and perfect to achieve orderly classrooms (Armstrong and Armstrong, 2021).

While behaviour management became a dominant way of thinking about children's conduct, educational trends emerged which threaten this dominant position in the education community, and posed troubling questions which challenge its tidy assumptions (Graham, 2020). These disruptive trends include the increasingly popular idea that educational practice should be based on research evidence like medicine, and the emergence of literature which highlights that behaviour management as practised in many schools is simply not supported by underpinning research studies (Armstrong and Armstrong, 2021).

Many, if not most, psychologists would be very sceptical of the idea that teachers can manage children's conduct because they would regard all behaviour as, alternatively, communicating, social, emotional, or physical needs: something teachers should listen to and respond to rather than manage (Hart, 2010; Parker *et al.*, 2016). Other researchers have critically drawn attention to how behaviour management has been used to justify punishment and exclusion of students with disabilities or who experience mental health difficulties (Graham, 2020).

These critical views about behaviour management should not be taken to imply that every book, resource, or piece of advice given in the name of behaviour management is incorrect or unhelpful for teacher practice. It must be acknowledged, however, that many, if not most, of the books, resources, and advice given to teachers in the name of behaviour management are not based on published research in reputable, peer-reviewed journals, which might count as essential for claiming that they are based on evidence (Adey and Dillon, 2012). Further evidence highlighting flaws in behaviour management comes from research into teacher preparation and from studies of teacher behaviour management in classroom practice. O'Neill and Stephenson (2014), for instance, in their study of coursework content in Australian teacher preparation programs, highlight the missing evidence in the behaviour management component of many teacher preparation programs.

Short Answer Questions

Q1. Can children's behaviour be managed by a teacher or parent?

A1. No, this is the wrong approach: behaviour communicates needs.

Q2. What might be described as the current dominant discourse on behaviour in many Australian schools?

A2. Behaviour management.

Q3. Can you name challenges to this dominant discourse identified by research?

A3. Ineffective, flawed application of behaviourism in Australian schools or behaviour management used to justify punishment and exclusion of students with disabilities or who experience mental health difficulties.

Behaviour of concern (BoC)

'Behaviour of concern' is recommended as a useful phrase for teachers because it conveys the adult evaluation of concern and suggests the need for action (Armstrong *et al.*, 2015, p. 5). As this discussion about 'challenging behaviour' and 'disruptive behaviour' suggests, both terms, although widely used, have limitations – for one thing, neither term includes disengaged and withdrawn behaviours, which can be highly damaging for students in many respects (Bills *et al.*, 2020). What is classed as 'disruptive' or 'challenging' behaviour also varies significantly in professional practice – a point aptly made by Sullivan *et al.* (2014) in their South Australian school-based study of the use of discipline and punishment.

Considering the above discussion, we recommended that readers take a critical attitude wherever disruptive behaviour or challenging behaviour is referenced in educational settings. Readers are encouraged to ask deeper questions about what behaviour presented communicates about a child's unmet needs – prompting efforts to help a student change their behaviour for the better. This approach is consistent with the evidence-based cognitive-behavioural interventions and approaches discussed later in this chapter.

Challenges faced by children with BoC

Students who present with BoC in school often also experience a wider set of educational challenges and face disadvantages made up of multiple issues. Pioneering research has suggested that this mechanism is two-way and that risk factors are additive (mental health condition + disability + behavioural difficulty = major risk of poor educational outcomes), mutually reinforcing the overall educational disadvantage produced and experienced by a student

(Oldfield *et al.*, 2016). Areas of disadvantage are presented in a simplified form below, but the reader should remember that, in reality, these factors mutually reinforce each other and overlap in their influence on a student's presented conduct (Oldfield *et al.*, 2016):

- *Relationships*: gaining and maintaining positive relationships with peers and with teachers can be a challenge (Nicholson, 2014).
- *Inclusion*: affected students face increased risk of suspension, exclusion, and expulsion (Graham, 2020).
- *Participation in school*: increased risk of absenteeism and truancy due to low motivation to learn and attend (Bills *et al.*, 2020).
- *Learning and achievement:* students with problem behaviours face reduced expectations from teachers about the quality and quantity of their learning and achievement (Sullivan *et al.*, 2014).
- *Mental health and wellbeing:* BoC are often psychological distress and signify poor coping (Elliott and Place, 2012).

Teaching approaches and practices to address challenging behaviours

Let's start by breaking the myth that there is one classroom professional practice, system, approach, or behavioural intervention that will work with all students. This statement is necessary to make because commercially motivated or simply naive claims are often directed at schools claiming that a new behaviour program, professional practice, or software application will transform behaviour in your classroom (Armstrong and Armstrong, 2021).

There are effective practices, systems, approaches, or behavioural interventions, which are outlined shortly in this chapter. Still, even the most robust of these can be undone by poor application in setting or can be inappropriate for an individual student due to their unique needs (Durlak and DuPre, 2008). One size does not fit all. In this situation, practical necessity means the selection of a range of practice, system, approach or behavioural interventions and their careful application in the setting based on data, as well as what is ethical in the circumstances (Odom *et al.*, 2019).

Scale matters

Scale is essential to consider in how to select and apply practices or programs designed to address student behaviour (Armstrong *et al.*, 2015). The following section of the chapter is therefore organised, loosely, at the individual scale, classroom/whole year scale and, finally, whole-school scale.

Scales of intervention. When considering classroom-scale and whole-school scale, it is important to recognise that this is a two-way street. What happens at the whole-school scale (interventions adopted to support student behaviour, school policies on behaviour) influences what occurs in the classroom. In turn, classroom events (events and professional practices used by teachers) can influence whether, for example, the school changes or even discontinues school-wide interventions or systems designed to support student behaviour.

Individual, classroom level (teacher to student)

Most, if not all, teachers will be forced to respond to one or more BoC by students over the course of a school week, if not every day, often prompting concern and other negative emotions experienced by teachers. Over the long term, and without effective support, negative interactions have been connected with 'burnout': a state of psychological exhaustion coined by Susan Maslach in 1974 and Lawrence *et al.* (2019), which is a serious occupational issue affecting teachers in Australia.

A common error sometimes made by inexperienced teachers is a focus on the student behaviour, often accompanied by unrealistic goals and unhelpful patterns of thinking about behaviour, according to findings from a UK-based study by Armstrong and Hallett (2012) and which are set out below in Connection 8.1.

> **Connection 8.1 Unhelpful patterns of thought about children's behaviour**
>
> - I control behaviour in my class by applying special technical skills (technocratic view), including surveillance.
> - Some kids are just bad (moralistic view).
> - Behaviour doesn't matter/what behaviour? (self-protection).
> - There's nothing I can do, I give up (resignation, burnout, demotivation).
> - If students misbehave, they will pay (revenge, anger).

These patterns of thought can lead to the following unhelpful practices by teachers, including but not restricted to:

- Applying sanctions to the whole class or group because of the behaviour of one or several individuals.
- Confronting students and escalating minor issues, such as non-compliance, into conflicts.
- Passive response to unacceptable behaviours in the classroom/setting, such as bullying; failing to intervene and/or offer emotional stability for students.
- Shouting, crying, or uncontrolled anger by the teacher toward students because the adult is having a 'bad day'.

- Lack of warmth and empathy, failure to show unconditional positive regard for students.
- Demeaning students in public or being sarcastic in response.
- Manipulative behaviours designed to undermine children psychologically.

Effective preparation for teaching starts by considering our reaction to the everyday challenges of classroom practice: how can we moderate and self-regulate our response when the inevitable irritating disruptions occur? This provokes the query: how can we remain calm, consistent and caring in the face of these challenges? How can we prevent disruptive behaviours 'getting under our skin'? These questions are vital for teachers because research into the impact of these interactions with students suggests that they can impact negatively on teacher psychological welfare (Armstrong *et al.*, 2015).

One recommendation from research is for teachers to adopt authoritative but not authoritarian professional conduct in classrooms (Elliott, 2015). We aim to gain the respect of children by consistently acting as the authoritative adult who has high expectations – a caring professional who is also a rock of emotional and psychological stability in their life at school. Helpful ways for teachers to think about children's behaviour are suggested below.

Connection 9.2: Helpful attitudes for teachers to hold about student behaviour

- I can help my students express behaviours which are positive for their welfare and that of others around them (student self-efficacy).
- Teachers are a key model for good conduct (we are influential).
- Behaviour is part of learning, relationships, and life.
- Behaviours can change for the better and are not fixed in students (or adults).
- I care about the welfare and future of all students I teach.
- All behaviours convey a need; they are messages. Understanding the triggers and purpose of behaviours is key to selecting an appropriate and targeted response from the teacher or school.
- Punishment is often ineffective; positive incentives are preferable.

The need for Australian teachers to adopt helpful attitudes about behaviour by students is driven home by Australian-based educational inquiries such as the Disability Royal Commission (2020b), highlighting the 'inappropriate and disproportionate application of disciplinary sanctions to a student with disability' (Disability Royal Commission, 2020, p. 3). This conclusion is further reinforced by a recent Australia-based research review, which recommends 'deeper "understanding of problem behaviour" by teachers as part of ongoing professional learning and in avoiding reactive, punitive practices toward students' (Hepburn and Beamish, 2019, p. 92). Furthermore, applied research in cognitive-behavioural psychology suggests that modifying unhelpful patterns of thought is a powerful tool to change behaviour for the better amongst teachers and students (Armstrong and Squires, 2014, p. 105).

Teacher self-efficacy and behaviour when interaction with students

Research into teacher efficacy supports recommendations for how teachers can adopt psychologically helpful, sustainable attitudes toward student behaviour. Teacher efficacy here refers to an individual teacher's estimation of how they can affect change around them ('I can make a difference') and personal effectiveness. An influential but bland definition of teacher self-efficacy is given by Davis (1998) as a 'teacher's belief in her and his ability to organise and execute the courses of action required to successfully accomplish a specific teaching task in a particular context' (p. 233). Over 60 years of research into teacher efficacy has highlighted its importance for ensuring confident, effective and motivated teachers. As Pfitzner-Eden (2016) summarises, 'Researchers have identified a multitude of meaningful associations between teacher self-efficacy (TSE) and a range of sought after outcomes for in-service and preservice teachers, as well as for students.' (p. 1486). Occupational research into why teachers leave the profession early has, for instance, indicated that those exiting the profession often have low self-efficacy ('I don't make a difference') and are typically dissatisfied ('I hate my job') with feeling of indifference or resignation ('I don't care, what's the point?') (Jamil et al., 2012; Madigan and Kim, 2021). This relationship appears two-way and is associated with reduced academic motivation amongst students impacted by teacher burnout according to a methodologically robust systematic review of research by Madigan and Kim (2021).

The helpful attitudes detailed in Connection 8.2 are designed to bolster teacher self-efficacy, promoting realistic positive views that children are capable of behaviour change without resorting to punishment or attitudes which damage teacher self-efficacy and optimism over the long term (Armstrong and Armstrong, 2021).

This approach is supported by numerous studies which highlight how teacher self-efficacy is a central factor in effective, sustainable, professional practice around student behaviour (Armstrong *et al.*, 2015; Jamil *et al.*, 2012; Tsouloupas *et al.*, 2010). Critically considering whether the beliefs we hold as teachers are helpful 'rules for living' out our professional lives in the classroom is an approach to teacher self-efficacy which is supported by cognitive-behavioural theory (Armstrong *et al.*, 2015; Armstrong and Squires, 2014). As highlighted later in this chapter, cognitive-behavioural theory has a strong evidence base for school-based practices and programs (Cooper, 2011; Johnson *et al.*, 2019).

Pause and think

Q1. What messages about behaviour by children and young people are promoted by the Australian media?

A1. Australian media often focusses on extreme examples of behaviour, e.g. physical violence in schools or communities, conveying negative impressions about children and young people

Q2. What view of student behaviour is helpful for teachers to adopt?

A2. Teachers should consider reflecting on their personal attitudes toward student behaviour and consider to what extent these support compassionate and research-based professional practice.

Q3. To what extent is personal-professional self-efficacy linked to effective classroom practice?

A3. Personal-professional self-efficacy is connected to effective classroom practice and in establishing a calm and productive classroom.

Teacher expertise

Effective teaching requires the application of a complex set of interpersonal skills and behaviours in the classroom. One problem is that many of these interpersonal skills call on tacit knowledge, which is notoriously difficult to describe in writing but nonetheless exists in practice (Polanyi and Sen 2009). Following Kounin (1970), Elliott (2015) highlights that 'withiness', 'overlapping', and 'group alerting' are important for demonstrating the teacher's role as the authoritative adult, a key ingredient necessary for a calm and productive environment.

- **Withiness** refers to the teacher's ability to be aware of everything that is happening in the immediate environment and to signal this awareness to students.
- **Overlapping** is the ability to focus on more than one event and the effective management of the many events that are simultaneously taking place in the classroom.
- **Group alerting** describes the capacity to use various means to keep children alert, attentive, and engaged. (Elliott, 2015, p. 91).

Withiness delivers the authoritative message 'I am aware of everything in this environment as the professional'. Overlapping enables monitoring and necessary responses by a teacher to ensure that issues are swiftly dealt with before they escalate, anticipating demands, ignoring interruptions, and juggling competing demands for attention from a teacher. Group alerting is an essential skill set involving regular changes in voice tone and volume as well as the use of age-appropriate vocabulary to gain and maintain focus; priming students with questions and careful lesson planning can be used to aid overlapping (Elliott, 2015, p. 93).

While it is not possible to outline every skill or behaviour used by skilled teachers to deliver a calm and productive classroom, establishing strong and supportive relationships with students is a bedrock of good general practice, especially benefitting students with behaviours which elicit adult concern (Armstrong *et al.*, 2015).

Consistency of teacher behaviour and predictable structure in lessons are also very important for students at risk of behavioural difficulties, providing calm predictability and reducing the off-task spaces where problems can often arise. Simple practices, such as having learning outcomes at the start of sessions and clear summaries at the end, can help enormously in providing predictability and structure in lessons (Mitchell, 2014). Together with the consistent use of rewards (Gable *et al.*, 2009), a predictable, clear structure in lessons which aid retention of learning are inclusive teaching practices which encourage student engagement, reducing the frequency and severity of off-task, disruptive behaviours (Armstrong *et al.*, 2015).

Evidence-based strategies and behaviours of concern

Praise, withiness, overlapping, group alerting, and evidence-informed thinking about behaviour are all elements of strategies developed at the level of individual professional teacher practice and with the purpose of delivering the optimum behavioural environment for all students in your care. Students with behavioural difficulties and/or with disabilities are likely to benefit even more when a calm, supportive, and structured environment is delivered by a teacher (Cooper, 2011).

Whole-class strategies, supports, and interventions operate at the next level of scale-up from individual teacher practice. While they involve teacher expertise to deliver effectively, they often operate across a whole year level or even a whole school level. Multiple teachers are typically involved in delivering these types of behavioural interventions and often in concert with school psychologists. Given the emerging preference for evidence-based practice and highlighted earlier in this chapter, there are surprisingly few accessible research reviews of evidence-based behavioural interventions suitable for use by teachers (Armstrong, 2017).

Table 9.1 below is based on research given in Armstrong et al. (2015) and was presented to the Disability Royal Commission in 2020 (Disability Royal Commission, 2020, Exhibit, p. 10)

Cognitive-behavioural interventions are the most effective interventions which can be applied in the classroom, according to research (Cooper 2011;

Table 9.1 The evidence base for effective behaviour interventions, programs and supports

Theory	Evidence Base	Approaches within this topic
Cognitive-behavioural	STRONG	**Functional Behavioural Assessment (FBA):** established a strong evidence base for identifying possible interventions. **Applied Behaviour Assessment (ABA)** is an approach to understanding learning and behaviour. It has a strong evidence base. **Good Behaviour Game** is a teacher-delivered program that has been found to reduce emotional and behavioural problems with an established, strong evidence base. **Cognitive-behavioural therapy (CBT)** is a 'promising' approach, which is not yet widely known or tested in education to date (no controlled studies are yet available).
Transtheoretical model (TT)	STRONG	Established in medicine/clinical practice – very promising for education. This model appears suitable for education, but has not yet been applied to that context.
Family Therapy	STRONG	This approach involves a therapeutic setting aimed at repairing family relationships and models positive interactions with children. This is intended to complement interventions in the school environment.
School-wide positive behavioural support (PBIS, PBIS)	STRONG	Established, but requires whole setting commitment and is prone to a lack of sustained implementation. Suitable for education.
Nurture (attachment) models	PROMISING	Promising – very few large swale studies. Suitable for education.
Social Emotional Learning	PROMISING/MIXED	This approach involves a variety of interventions (some targeted, some general), which have given mixed results. It is generally suitable for education, but issues have been identified with poor implementation.

Gable *et al.*, 2009). Students who have disabilities with or without behavioural difficulties appear to benefit most from strategies or interventions classed as cognitive-behavioural (Cooper and Upton, 2017), and it is these students, often with more complex psychological needs, who receive this type of intervention (Burns *et al.*, 2019). The common purpose of cognitive-behavioural interventions or programs is to change patterns of behaviour underpinning an individual's difficulties, which positively impact that child's emotions and psychological welfare. Individuals are taught to understand patterns in their behaviour, identifying triggers in the environment for problem behaviours and developing an understanding of how to have greater control over their response to these triggering stimuli (Armstrong *et al.*, 2015).

Weblinks

Educate Autism – Functional Behaviour Assessment

Website: http://www.educateautism.com/functional-behaviour-assessment.html

Autism Hub and Reading Centre, Queensland Government – Guided Functional Behaviour Assessment Tool

Website: https://ahrc.eq.edu.au/services/fba-tool

Functional behaviour assessment (FBA), which is described shortly in more detail, is a prominent type of cognitive-behavioural tool used in schools with students who present challenging behaviour (Anderson *et al.*, 2015). The Good Behaviour Game, which is aimed at primary age students, is also best categorised as cognitive-behavioural (with the emphasis on behavioural) and has received support from several research studies as effective (Kellam *et al.*, 2011). However, one very recent, robust study has contradicted this positive evaluation from research (Ashworth *et al.*, 2020).

Functional behaviour assessments (FBA)

One basic challenge facing teachers is how teachers respond proportionally to student behaviours, using the most appropriate strategy or program available. This potential problem arises partly because of the logic that a good fit between response/strategy or program chosen is most likely to have an effect and change student conduct for the better. Professional practice with students who have more complex or ingrained BoC is particularly affected by this problem. If we don't use the right strategy or program, then behaviours can continue and lead to student suspension, or even lead to a student's permanent exclusion (also called expulsion) on safety grounds (Graham, 2020). In many cases, these types of behaviours are also resistant to change, exacerbating the need for excellent, targeted practice which responds to the psychological or other needs driving conduct.

FBA addresses this problem by identifying what underlying needs are most probably generating a negative behaviour. Practitioners can then use this knowledge to select the most effective response (classroom strategy, support service, program or combination) in the situation, removing guesswork about what is most likely to reduce or eliminate the BoC.

The FBA process

FBA is a problem-solving method. It begins with the assumption that if a learner repeats a problem behaviour, it must be serving an important purpose. This negative behaviour is known as 'the target behaviour', which requires change. Some universally relevant purposes of behaviour include:

- *Attention ('look at me everybody.... help me, help me...notice me...').*
- *Power ('I have power over you.... You will do exactly as I say.... I don't need to do this work...I feel empowered').*
- *Revenge ('the teacher will pay, they will pay').*
- *Escape ('I wish I were shopping, somewhere else, out of this classroom, escaping literacy, escaping maths').*

Data about student behaviour is collected by a teacher over a five-day school week, typically, recording the frequency and severity of negative behaviour. Collection should be done by careful observation and recording of the number and severity of behaviours across different school environments, and by consulting other professionals. FBAs are flexible and can be used at the individual teacher level, but work best when adopted across a whole-class or as a whole-school policy. The following questions should be asked when collecting this data:

- Where and when does the target behaviour occur over the week?
- Who is present in the classroom/situation when they occur?
- What *exactly* do these behaviours consist of/who are they directed at?
- Are these behaviours minor misdemeanours, e.g. disruption, inattention, or are they more serious in effect?
- Do they impact the child, e.g. self-injurious, self-handicapping ('I can't work now because my pencil is broken!'), or directed toward the teacher or other student (s)?
- Do they occur in one particular class/situation or are they generalised across the week? Speaking to parents/carers can also add vital context to this investigation: do the problem behaviours also occur at home? If so, behaviours are 'generalised', indicating that they may have a deeper root

and potentially require a multi-agency response, including the involvement of a school psychologist.

Using data gathered, antecedent conditions ('triggers') for an individual student are often analysed through an Antecedent Behaviour Consequences (ABC) observation and analysis.

- Antecedents – what happens just before the behaviour occurs (people, events, environment).
- Behaviour – what the student does (exactly).
- Consequence – what happens as a consequence of the behaviour.

The practitioner then looks for patterns in the behaviours we observe and makes predictions based on this 'hypothesis': an informed guess they make based on the data of which purpose the behaviour observed is serving (or a combination of behaviours). Consultation with a psychologist or behaviour specialist can be helpful at this point in the FBA process (Johnson et al., 2019).

To confirm this hypothesis (or suggest a new one is required), experimental manipulation of a key variable is done to test the working hypothesis of what is driving the undesirable target behaviours (Gable et al., 2014). FBA is typically used with students who have disabilities or trauma and to address ingrained or challenging behaviours previously 'resistant to various intervention efforts' (Strickland-Cohen and Horner, 2015, p. 83). Guidance on FBA practice reflects this and typically refers to students with ASD, intellectual disability or complex needs, e.g. autism + mental health difficulty + self-harming. Emerging research studies have suggested that FBA can be very effective when used with students without a disability in a variety of contexts. Here is a real case titled 'Adam' from the authors' practice to illustrate this point.

Case study 9.2 Adam

Adam, a student at the end of primary school, has presented over the last month with increasingly disturbed, disobedient and defiant behaviours on Mondays. Puzzled, Adam's class teacher asked other staff whether they had any information about this behaviour, as he was regarded as a diligent and compliant student. The teacher spoke to Adam's mother, who disclosed that Adam has started to stay with his father on Sunday nights and because of a prolonged custody dispute. On these Sundays, Adam often bonded with his father by playing video games until 2 am.

Working hypothesis

Adam's teacher created the following working hypothesis:

Control: Adam was responding to stressful home circumstances and asserting control through disobedient and defiant behaviours.

An ABC assessment was done by Adam's teacher:

- Antecedent = Adam stays with his father, leading to distress and anger.
- Behaviour = Adam exerts control through angry defiance and disobedience.
- Consequence = Adam feels in control of the situation at school.

Adam's teacher also spoke by phone to a school psychologist about Adam and the conclusion reached. The school psychologist came to the same conclusion as the teacher.

Experimental manipulation

Experimental manipulation in many circumstances simply involves removing the triggers which appear to generate the problem behaviours. For some students, triggers constitute a person (teacher, a peer/peers), in other circumstances, triggers could be a part of the curriculum (maths or literacy). Where triggers occur provides strong clues as to what is generating the problem behaviour, and this can be used to design targeted support or interventions. If a student displays escape/avoidance behaviours in literacy lessons/sessions, for instance, then this can signify boredom or difficulty, which should instigate further investigation to determine whether, for example, more effective differentiation is required by the teacher.

> To test this hypothesis *(Control)*, the teacher asked Adam's mother whether there was any forthcoming Sunday when Adam did not stay with his father as usual. Sure enough, the following week, Adam did not stay with his father. Adam's teacher carefully observed Adam's behaviour in class on the following day (Monday), and it was exemplary. No behavioural incidents were recorded with Adam that day. This 'manipulation' of the variable (Adam staying at his father's) confirmed the hypothesis: Adam's negative behaviours seek greater control of his life.
>
> On the following day, Adam's teacher contacted his mother and father and invited them to meet at the school to discuss Adam's behaviour. After discussion, it was agreed that Adam would stay with his father on Saturdays to minimise the impact on his behaviour at school. Adam's father also promised to change his behaviour and add clear rules when Adam stayed, e.g. appropriate

bedtime. Adam's father added that he would like some support as he was finding Adam's behaviour difficult.

Outcomes

After this agreement, Adam joined the meeting. An individualised learning plan (IEP) was completed. The teacher, Adam's parents, and Adam himself agreed on specific goals about changing Adam's behaviour with specific targets set on the IEP. Clear indicators of progress, i.e. no negative behaviours for a week at school, were set together with appropriate incentives for positive behaviour at school: Adam gets to help choose one leisure activity on a class trip. Adam was also referred to the school counsellor for guidance on how to positively deal with his emotions, specifically anger. Adam's behaviour was monitored daily over the next month, and a follow-up review meeting with Adam and his parents, and his teacher occurred in order to review the IEP targets. Positive, specific, age-appropriate praise was given to Adam, and Adam's behaviour was substantially improved. Working to address this issue also improved the relationship between Adam's estranged parents.

Teaching replacement/coping behaviours

Conducting an FBA should be an opportunity for teaching and learning and should never just identify a problem with a student's development or capabilities. The underlying social, emotional, or physical needs driving problem behaviours cannot be extinguished. Still, it is vital to help students learn a response that is less harmful for them and/or those around them and when triggers (antecedents) appear at school or at home. Rerouting all emotions (including negative ones like frustration or anger) into positive attitudes and actions is central to teaching replacement behaviours (Armstrong and Armstrong, 2021).

In the case of Adam, the target (problem) behaviours described were triggered by the family situation and did not arise because of any gaps in learning or development. Even for Adam, however, the FBA was an opportunity to learn strategies to self-regulate his own anger and this goal was detailed on his IEP.

For many children like Adam, problem behaviours such as social withdrawal, irritability, or anger occur because of poor (maladaptive) coping to potentially stressful experiences in their lives. Teachers might not be directly 'teaching' children the strategies or skills needed to better cope; this might be the school counsellor, psychologist, or behavioural specialist, but it is vital that professionals support this learning and support the student when applying this new learning and embedding positive changes in conduct (Johnson et al., 2019).

Teacher support consists of reinforcement of new behaviours in class via effective praise, working collaboratively with the school counsellor, psychologist, or behavioural specialist, reporting the progress of behavioural change to parents, and adaption of academic workload for students considering their extra learning, if necessary (Armstrong and Armstrong, 2021; Stevenson *et al.*, 2022).

For children with disabilities which can profoundly affect oral communication and development, such as, for example, ASD, learning to overcome behavioural difficulties via self-regulation is often a key aspect of their lives. Learning to communicate more effectively through language and non-verbal, non-threatening body language is vital and often the focus of allied professionals working in concert with teachers. In these situations, the replacement behaviours taught are clear: problem behaviours associated with needs (hunger, tiredness, boredom) are replaced by appropriate forms of communication using language and gesture (Armstrong *et al.*, 2015).

Short Answer Questions

Q1. Why might an FBA be undertaken by a teacher?

A1. To better understand the underlying function (purpose) of problem (target) behaviours presented and so that appropriate, proportional and targeted responses can be made in response.

Q2. What does ABC stand for in the FBA process?

A2. ABC stands for **Antecedent** = Adam stays with his father, leading to distress and anger; **Behaviour** = Adam exerts control through angry defiance and disobedience; and **Consequence** = Adam feels in control of the situation at school.

Q3. Can replacement behaviours be taught?

A3. Yes, it is vital to teach replacement behaviours so that a student adopts a more positive behaviour, replacing the problem one.

Pause and think

When bored or demotivated with an activity, what behaviours do you present with? What behaviours might an observer note in your behaviour?

Zero Tolerance, three strikes, PBIS, and other whole-school strategies

Let's start with Zero Tolerance whole-school strategies and their three strikes variant. These whole-school strategies have become increasingly popular in the US (and elsewhere) because they stick to fixed rules about conduct which can be clearly communicated in school marketing and are attractive to some parents and socially conservative politicians (Graham, 2020; Skiba, 2014). Disciplinary sanctions typically accompany these fixed rules: suspensions, for example, where a student is removed from school for a temporary period (Graham, 2020). Zero Tolerance and similar effective in reducing problem behaviours in schools in the limited sense because they simply remove students from the classroom or school. Bear (2013) summarises that 'the zero-tolerance approach is effective if one's aim is to remove students who violate school rules' (p. 321). As was highlighted in Chapter 2, Flexible Learning Options (FLO) was designed as a solution to accommodate excluded and often highly vulnerable students excluded from the mainstream. Zero Tolerance and three strikes, therefore, create a problem somewhere else in the system. Furthermore, the disproportionately high number of children with disabilities or mental health difficulties who are excluded or expelled as a result of these policies makes them unethical and in opposition to an inclusive education system (UNICEF, 2017). So, Zero Tolerance whole-school strategies and three strikes have no ethical credibility and are not sustainable.

In contrast, **Positive Behavioural Interventions and Supports (PBIS)** features explicit support across the whole setting for good (positive) behaviours by students and in place of punishments.

PBIS was developed in the US in response to the need to reduce exclusion and expulsions due to behaviour and as part of US legislations which mandate that data-driven, evidence-based interventions should be used first with children who have disabilities and before resorting to suspension or expulsion from school. PBIS aims to reduce disciplinary referrals in mainstream contexts and thereby reduce the risk that students with disabilities are required to be referred out of mainstream into specialist provision (Gable *et al.*, 2009). As part of PBIS, positive behaviours and explicit behavioural expectations are promoted across a whole setting at many levels, with pro-social behaviours recognised and encouraged throughout. In the classroom, negative behaviours are minimally rewarded through being ignored or by the withdrawal of privileges. Strong environmental motivators are ideally put in place across multiple levels to encourage and sustain positive behaviour.

Practice recommendation: the PBIS classroom

Positive teacher-student interactions

Teacher-student interactions should be overwhelmingly positive and encouraging. This point is important because if teacher feedback to a student is predominantly negative, then the student is conditioned to expect negativity and will disregard teacher feedback, internalise negativity ('I am a bad student') or push back against the teacher (Armstrong *et al.*, 2015).

Active supervision. This element of a PBIS classroom connects with in a, group alerting, and overlapping, which were discussed earlier in this section. When activities or tasks are set, the teacher should tour the classroom, proactively checking on student understanding and monitoring progress in an encouraging and authoritative way.

Redirection. For example, if a student is becoming visibly frustrated by a task and irritable, the teacher suggests, 'Why don't you move on to the next task and come back to this one later?'. As another example, if a student is running in the hallway to class, the teacher can say, 'It's time to walk now'.

Here is an excellent resource for redirection across a range of ages:

Weblink: https://familyvio.csw.fsu.edu/sites/g/files/upcbnu1886/files/2018-11/March-2018-E-Press-Final-Part-2-1.pdf

Pre-correction. The teacher anticipates a situation where a student might and prompts the 'correct' desired behaviour. For example, if a student wanders around the classroom immediately after an activity is set (is 'off-task'), then at the end of the activity instructions, the teacher prompts the whole class, 'Let's make sure we return to our seat/table right now to start the activity'.

Effective academic instruction. This point connects to the topics of differentiation and clear, explicit instruction. Students need to understand what is expected of them and the procedure to follow to perform in the classroom. To avoid demotivation and/or disruptive behaviour, academic work needs to be set at a level which is neither too easy nor too difficult. Effective academic instruction is, in our experience, overlooked in classrooms when considering student behaviour.

PBIS is also matched to a three-tier system, whole-school support, whereby the intensity of response by the school increases. Starting at Tier 1, 'practices and systems establish a foundation of regular, proactive support while preventing unwanted behaviours. Schools provide these universal supports to all students, school-wide' (Liasidou, 2024). Before moving to Tier 2, 'practices and systems support students who are at risk for developing more serious problem behaviours before those behaviours start.' (Liasidou, 2020). Finally, at Tier 3, 'students receive more intensive, individualised support to improve their behavioural and academic outcomes' (Liasidou, 2024).

In practice, these high-intensity Tier 3 supports, for students with serious behavioural difficulties, are typically provided by a multi-disciplinary team involving, for example, a psychologist as well as a teacher (Armstrong et al., 2015, p. 65). A teacher's role in this team is often modified by the severity of the needs of the child they are supporting. Learning curriculum content may be less of a priority for children at Tier 2 and Tier 3: simply attending school at all and without major incident over the course of a day are greater priorities for many children in this population (for further discussion see Chapter 10, Case Study 2: Project X and the case of 'Jimmy').

The recommendations given in this chapter regarding praise at the level of individual teacher practice and for FBA at a whole class/year level, complement PBIS, where it operates across a whole school setting as a system-wide policy. FBA provides teachers with the tools to identify and target BoC, which are resistant to the overall environmental supports put in place by PBIS – see the Weblink below.

FBAs are used with individual students, but they have an important connection with school-wide PBIS, as is explained by Dr Tim Lewis from the University of Missouri in this comprehensive video presentation:

Weblink: https://youtu.be/C_AKrr_mCJ8

Social emotional learning (SEL) programs detailed in Chapter 10 also fit well with the approach used by PBIS because they commonly teach children to self-regulate emotions and pro-socially support the development of relationships with other peers (Humphrey *et al.*, 2020)

Practice recommendation: good practice

The following are evidence-based strategies to encourage positive behaviour from students:

- *Team response.* Teachers need support from every member of the school community, including senior leadership and parents, in collaboratively building a calm and productive classroom.
- *Information.* A data-driven understanding of what is driving persistent/major behaviours of concern is key to targeted, proportional response. This understanding underpins timely identification and referral for students whose behaviour is of major concern ((Rouf *et al.*, 2004).
- *Fair rules.* Clear, fair rules applied consistently (Armstrong *et al.*, 2015; Sullivan *et al.*, 2014)
- *No blame.* Avoid 'blame' or within-child explanations (Cooper, 2011).
- *Identify behavioural needs.* Any behavioural needs should be specified on a Behaviour Support Plan (BSP) connected to academic requirements set out in an Individual Education Plan. These documents are a core component of the evaluation and monitoring process (Hanbury, 2011).
- *Praise.* Effective use of praise (Caldarella *et al.*, 2020).
- *Motivational state.* Consider a student's motivation and willingness to change a BoC before action: this understanding is core to reducing 'disruptive' behaviour and promoting engagement (Armstrong *et al.*, 2015; Sullivan *et al.*, 2014). Students need to understand what 'good behaviour' looks like and be invested in making these changes.

Motivating children to replace negative behaviours with positive alternatives can be a challenge. Table 9.2 outlines some practical strategies which a teacher can use in their classroom to aid behavioural change based on Armstrong *et al.* (2015, p. 120) and the 'stage of change' the transtheoretical model (TTM) theory outlined earlier.

Table 9.2 Practical strategies to motivate students to replace negative behaviours with positives

Stage	What you can do
Pre-contemplation	Introduce doubt: raise the child's awareness about the risks of their current behaviours and its negative effect on them and others.
Contemplation	Tip the balance: help the child understand that no change involves risks and negatives.
Determination	Help the child pick the best route to achieve change for them.
Action	Help the child make concrete steps: what actions and decisions should they take?
Maintenance	Assist the child to avoid and prevent relapse by learning strategies to maintain their new state.
Relapse	Encourage the child to renew the process of contemplation, determination and action, without becoming demotivated.

Conclusion

Helping children and young people to achieve positive behaviours at school is core to their educational inclusion (Armstrong and Armstrong, 2021). Providing a calm and productive classroom environment which identifies and encourages positive, pro-social behaviours is therefore essential for teachers to provide as part of their professional practice. The whole school environment, however, together with effective behavioural support programs, enables or disables teacher efforts at an individual level, suggesting the need for settings to support positive behaviours at every level. Behaviour in schools is everybody's responsibility, as with mental health and wellbeing in schools, which are further explored in Chapter 10

Bringing it together

This chapter has highlighted how important behaviour is as an educational issue for the occupational welfare of teachers and for the educational inclusion of students. Here are some final questions, plus a scenario (Maggie and Mr Goh), to help reinforce your learning from this chapter and also designed to reinforce this chapter's core messages about behaviour in schools

Q1. Can you name any problematic outcomes associated with students who present behaviours of concern?

A1. There are numerous problematic outcomes associated with behaviours of concern. For example: the educational suspension and/or exclusion, particularly affecting students with disability and who are Aboriginal or from Torres Strait backgrounds; risk of lowered educational attainment; student disengagement and risk of drop out (early school leaving). For teachers, problematic outcomes include: negative impact on teacher psychological welfare, culminating, potentially, in burnout and impacting on occupational satisfaction. For society, this topic is associated with the failure of educational inclusion and the flow on health and undesirable educational impacts of teacher burnout.

Q2. Is teacher self-efficacy connected with student behaviour in schools

A2. Yes, teacher self-efficacy is connected in several ways, according to research. How we perceive our professional practice as a teacher, and especially with regard to student behaviours, has a complex relationship which impacts our effectiveness in building a calm and purposeful classroom.

Scenario: Maggie and Mr Goh

Maggie, a lively six-year-old, is always keen to engage in any whole-class conversations with class 2B and eagerly puts up her hand when the teacher, Mr Goh, asks for answers. One day, Maggie bursts into tears when Mr Goh does not select her to answer a question. Maggie refuses to complete any schoolwork all day and is distressed.

Based on reading this chapter and your own thoughts, how would you advise Mr Goh to respond to Maggie's behaviour?

Q1. What should he do?
Q2. What should Mr Goh teach Maggie about how to respond in future situations?

There is no standard 'solution' or 'response' to cases like this. But this chapter provides the framework to develop your own solution by thinking critically.

- A starting point would be for Mr Goh to consider what need is being communicated by Maggie's behaviour.
- Next, Mr Goh should consider what actions and approach he should take in response and briefly consider whether there are any deeper issues at play (e.g. home-based issues) or if this is a lesser, temporary issue. Parents and other colleagues can be discreetly contacted for this information. A working hypothesis (best guess) should be produced by Mr Goh about what is causing Maggie's behaviour and inform planning on next steps.
- Finally, Mr Goh should start planning actions and decisions to respond to Maggie, testing and monitoring what works to help Maggie have improved coping behaviours in whole-class conversations. Considering Maggie's

capacity to adopt improved coping behaviours and whether Maggie may need to learn social and emotional skills via a program or intervention is appropriate (see Chapter 12, **Mental health in school: noticing, responding, and providing ongoing support**).

We recommend that you also read Chapter 12, **Safety in schools and bullying prevention.**
In this article, we meet Kerry White, a highly experienced high school principal in Adelaide who has never suspended or expelled (permanently excluded) a student, gaining an insight into how this has been achieved. This article also discusses the issue of suspension and exclusion across Australian schools and highlights how exclusionary practices are rising, but do not work to improve a student's behaviour.

- **AERO**: Australian Educational Research Organisation (AERO) is Australia's peak independent organisation for sharing research evidence pertinent to learning and teaching. This resource on 'focussed classrooms' is designed to offer guidance on providing structure and is designed to aid teachers in ensuring a productive classroom environment:
  - https://edresearch.edu.au/tried-and-tested-focused-classrooms
- **The Blob Tree** is an excellent practical resource for discussing emotions and behaviour with a student. While this resource is hosted by a website, it is best printed off as a paper copy and used as a basis for discussion with a child.
  - https://www.blobtree.com/

  Here is one suggested procedure.

Procedure:

1 Print off a paper copy. Show this copy to the child in a private, non-threatening environment.
2 Ask the child which character they feel like/most associate with;
3 Ask the child which character they think people view them as and why;
4 ask the child which character they would like to be and why.
5 Discuss what steps are necessary to move between Steps 2 and 4 above, i.e. what would need to happen to make them the successful character.

Challenging behaviour: This UK-based documentary, *Britain's Challenging Children*, focussing on challenging behaviour, outlines some of the common issues for primary school teachers on this topic in the US, the UK, and Australia:
https://youtu.be/n9JEIgX_Q9U

Further Resources

Suggested Reading:

Armstrong, D., Hallett, F., Elliott, J., & Hallett, G. (2015). *Understanding Child and Adolescent Behaviour in the Classroom*. Cambridge University Press. This book is designed for pre-service and in-service teachers and offers an evidence-based alternative to outdated behaviour management approaches.

Branley, A. (2020) 'Meet the school principal who has never expelled or suspended a student' *ABC News*. Available at: https://www.abc.net.au/news/2020-08-23/school-suspensions-expulsions-rise-student-engagement-education/12447104

10 Mental health and well-being in schools

This section will help you learn how to:

- Explain key concepts in the field, including: 'school-based mental health promotion', 'mental health difficulties', and 'mental health literacy' and 'childhood trauma', enriching an understanding of systemic responses to student need.
- Have a practical understanding of risk (and protective) factors affecting student mental health, which aid identification of at-risk students and what to do next in effective referral and ongoing support for students provoking concern.
- Understand examples of effective practice for students who are at risk of mental health difficulties and also have insights into specialist services provided to students who have a clinically diagnosed mental health disorder.
- Avoid a deficit focus on mental health illness and instead focus on teachers and schools playing a role in ensuring positive mental health as part of inclusion.

The Australian Institute for Teaching and School Leadership (AITSL) Graduate Teacher Standards covered by this learning include:

1.1 Understand the physical, social and intellectual development and characteristics of students.
1.6 Strategies to support full participation of students with disability.
4.3 Manage challenging behaviour.
4.4 Maintain student safety.

This section connects with Chapter 9, **Behaviour: building and maintaining calm and productive classrooms**, which we suggest is a pre-reading to this section. This section also connects with and is a pre-reading for Chapter 11, **Safety in school and bullying prevention**.

Introduction

Meeting the needs of children or young people who present with mental health concerns is fundamental to an inclusive education. Experiencing mental health difficulties compromises a student's psychological well-being and disrupts or prevents learning in school. Efforts to support positive mental health among students are therefore central to effective teaching and a core part of a teacher's role – as well as ethically sound.

Australia has led the way internationally, in many respects, in supporting practitioners to deliver this core aspect of inclusion and high-profile school-based federal mental health initiatives such as *Be You* (Hoare et al., 2020). Australia has also set out ambitious National Mental Health Plans, which guide the overall purpose and specific targets of school-based mental health services (Australian Government Department of Health & National Mental Health Commission, 2017).

Many students with mental health concerns still face discrimination, exclusion and/or a lack of understanding from educational professionals and some individuals in the wider community. Other challenges exist in offering an inclusive education for this population. Teachers in Australia persistently call for greater knowledge about mental health conditions, how these affect children in their daily life and what to do in supporting affected students (Shelemy *et al.*, 2019). In unity with Chapter 8, this chapter advocates for a compassionate, evidence-based response by teachers to students who present with mental health concerns.

Case study 15.1 Maya and John

Here are two cases ('vignettes') to help the reader consider the issues involved in supporting students who present with mental health concerns.

Both cases are intended to spark reflection by the reader as a background to discussion in this chapter and convey the complexities involved in real cases where students presented with mental health concerns.

Maya

Maya is a committed high school student, known to teachers as hard-working and sociable. Over the last six weeks, Maya's form teacher, Casey, has noticed that Maya's demeanour has changed. Maya seems to have withdrawn from social groups and often sits alone eating lunch. Maya often looks tired, and when Casey has spoken to Maya, she has noticed that her personal hygiene has declined, with noticeable body odour. In a science lesson, Maya suggests excitedly to the teacher that she is gifted with the ability to listen in on phone conversations by tuning in to mobile phone masts. The science teacher speaks to Casey in the staff room and relays their concerns about this comment.

John

John is often shy, but also what might be described as an academically 'gifted' student (his parents have high hopes about his musical ability in piano). He has, however, become increasingly withdrawn and, to you, irritable in setting. He often looks tired (fatigued) with poor concentration despite his ability. Yesterday, he confided to you that he feels 'sad inside' but was clearly irritated when you asked him for further details. It does not seem that any other member of staff has noticed these changes in John's demeanour. John has been 'like this' for nearly every day for over a month.

Questions

Q1. Should Maya's teacher, Casey, be concerned? What are the key issues facing Maya? What should Casey do next?

A1. **Suggested response:** Casey should be very concerned. Social withdrawal, a decline in self-care and incoherent (disordered) language are all concerning behavioural changes warranting immediate referral to mental health services

Q2. Should John's teacher be concerned? What are the key issues facing John? What should Casey do next?

A2. **Suggested response:** John's teacher should be very concerned. The low mood displayed, his irritation and change in behaviours are all concerning behavioural changes warranting immediate referral to mental health services

Maya and John are real cases with details changed to ensure confidentiality. John was also used in research with pre-service teachers on attitudes toward mental health (Armstrong *et al.*, 2015).

- Please read below to find out what happened.
- When reading what happened, reflect on what, if anything, might have been done differently by Maya and John's teachers to produce a better outcome – consider what actions, decisions and resources this might involve and hold these thoughts in your mind when reading the remainder of this chapter.

Maya

Maya was supported by David (the author who worked as a senior teacher at the time) and was aged 15. Maya's mental health deteriorated rapidly that year, and she self-excluded from classes, displaying 'odd and disturbing' behaviour in and around the school. David and the school supported Maya's family, advising them to take Maya to the GP and offering their contact details should the GP require further information. The local Child and Adolescent Mental Health Services (CAMHS) teams were also contacted and briefed about the situation, with the family's full consent and support – as well as Maya's consent. Two days later, the GP called David and expressed concern about Maya's mental health, highlighting that further specialist assessments were 'urgently scheduled'. Over the following weeks, Maya's oral language and behaviour deteriorated further, and she was frequently absent from school. CAMHS and the state school wellbeing team were contacted and briefed.

Two years later, Maya visited the school, meeting David and the principal. It transpired that Maya had run away from home and gone to visit her brother at university in another city. While there, she had experienced a major 'psychotic episode' on a university campus, ending in hospitalisation in a secure mental health unit, detained under the Mental Health Act. Maya had slowly recovered since then and was now feeling more positive towards her life and education.

John

John is based on a nine-year-old child referred to David (the author) by a primary school for a behavioural assessment (John was refusing to complete academic work), but who instead presented with mental health concerns. Mental health was not even considered by the school as a possible issue in this case, by the school or by John's class teacher. David advised the school to refer John urgently to CAMHS and speak to John's family if appropriate. It is not known if the school acted on this advice.

John's presentation exactly meets the diagnostic criteria used to identify clinical depression as outlined in the Diagnostic Statistical Manual (American Psychiatric Association, 2022), e.g. low mood every day for over a month; and in children or young people, often irritability. Clinical depression is a serious and common **mental health disorder**, requiring timely identification and treatment.

To ensure accuracy, John's case was reviewed by the CAMHS Psychiatry Team in the relevant state, found to be realistic, and presented to 250 pre-service teachers to gather their reactions to 'John' as part of a research project. One finding to note from student (pre-service teacher) responses was that many did not recognise the severity of John's symptoms. This research and its findings about how pre-service teachers respond to children who present with mental health concerns are detailed in Armstrong *et al.* (2015).

Weblink

Thinking it through: a study of how pre-service teachers respond to children presenting with possible mental health difficulties

https://www.tandfonline.com/doi/abs/10.1080/13632752.2015.1019248

Armstrong, D., Price, D., & Crowley, T. (2015). Thinking it through: a study of how pre-service teachers respond to children who present with possible mental health difficulties. *Emotional and Behavioural Difficulties*, 20(4), 381–397.

Who are learners at risk of mental health difficulties?

According to the United Nations (UN), Worldwide 10–20% of children and adolescents experience mental disorders which compromise a child's positive mental health and well-being, creating distress, negative emotions, and concerning behaviours (Binagwaho and Senga, 2021). The distress, obsessive behaviours, aggression, disorientation, low mood, or irritability which teachers might observe in an affected child and label as 'concerns' are behavioural expressions of the psychological and emotional difficulties they experience. Mental health difficulties here is the collective umbrella term for what students present with and is defined as changes in thinking, mood, and/or behaviours that impair functioning (Child Trends, 2013).

For teachers, this focus on mental health difficulties is more appropriate than focusing on a mental health disorder (although understanding what disorder means is useful). As teachers, it is inappropriate to refer to or discuss whether a child has a clinical disorder such as 'Generalised Anxiety Disorder'; a teacher is not qualified to confer this label. Teachers should, however, be confidently able to **notice** when possible mental health difficulties may be affecting a student and have the capacity to intervene appropriately in this situation.

Thinking back to Maya and John, given at the start of this chapter, this recognition (**noticing**) has not happened at all for John. For Maya, this recognition was, arguably, timely, but, in hindsight, events outpaced the supports and interventions necessary to prevent a decline in Maya's mental health.

The definition of **positive mental health** is a good place to start when considering the population of learners at risk of developing mental health disorders. The UN defines this as: 'a state of well-being in which the individual realises his or her own abilities, can cope with the normal stresses of life, can work productively and fruitfully, and is able to make a contribution to his or her community' (UN, 2018). Mental health difficulties compromise this well-being, and the collective aim of all professionals, including teachers, involved in supporting a young person's mental health is to deal with and, if possible, alleviate their suffering (Fallisardy *et al.*, 2017).

Vulnerability to mental health difficulties also intersects with other forms of disability and educational disadvantage addressed by educational inclusion. Students from First Nations backgrounds who have Autism Spectrum Disorder (ASD), Down Syndrome, or intellectual disability are at elevated risk of mental health difficulties when compared to their typically-developing peers. Robust recent research reveals that high socio-economic deprivation (poverty) is an important background factor for many affected students (Howarth *et al.*, 2021). A disproportionate number of students with mental health concerns attending Australian schools hail from families experiencing economic stress, family or domestic violence. Having an in-depth understanding of the challenges facing affected students is a firm starting point in enabling a research-informed response.

Risk and protective factors for ensuring children's positive mental health

Internationally developed risk and protective factor models are important when considering Australian children's positive mental health and how this can be supported by teachers (Dray *et al.*, 2017). These models highlight what is achievable for teachers and for schools, and also where schools need supports from other professionals and external support services to reduce risk factors and to maximise protective factors for vulnerable students (Armstrong *et al.*, 2015).

A useful overview of risk and protective factors is given by Korkodilos (2016) in their report about the mental health of children and young people in England. This is reproduced below.

An important Australian study by Bayer *et al.* (2011) examined risk factors for the mental health of two cohorts of children until age nine: 5,107 children from age zero to one year, and 4,983 children from age four to five. Research conducted with groups over time is known as a longitudinal study, and this research design type has a reputation for enhancing the quality of studies (Caruana *et al.*, 2015).

Jordana *et al.* (2011) summarise that 'a small number of significant risk factors, situated in the family context and present from a very young age.' (p. 1). How caregivers interacted with children was the greatest predictor of whether the children presented with symptoms indicating a mental health condition. Family distress and social disadvantage, however, were found to be key background factors shaping these parent-child interactions. Bayer *et al.* (2011) found that 'harsh discipline (by parents) was a strong consistent predictor of externalizing symptoms in both age groups, whereas poorer child physical health, maternal emotional distress, harsh discipline, and overinvolved/protective parenting (younger cohort only) predicted internalizing symptoms consistently.' (p. 1). Internalising symptoms are associated with anxiety and depression (Armstrong *et al.*, 2015; Jordana *et al.*, 2020), whereas externalising symptoms are associated with conduct disorders, presenting with aggression and oppositional defiance (Jordana *et al.*, 2011).

Findings from Jordana *et al.* (2011), arguably, highlight the need for schools and for teachers to work with families in an educative capacity – for instance, in learning to parent without the use of harsh discipline and in avoiding overinvolved/protective parenting (Armstrong *et al.*, 2015).

Challenges faced by children or young people who have mental health difficulties

Multiple systemic challenges affect children or young people in school who have mental health difficulties and should be acknowledged. These school-based challenges operate at different scales and, for example, include:

- *Negative or simplistic attitudes toward mental health difficulties, per se, by adults in the school community.* For example, if mental health is thought of as fixed or part of a person's innate make-up, then this undermines efforts by teachers to notice and appropriately respond to students who present with mental health concerns (Armstrong *et al.*, 2015)
- *Incorrect labelling:* distress symptoms resulting from a mental health difficulty are incorrectly labelled as a behavioural 'problem' by education professionals rather than recognised as a product of psychological distress and poor coping (known as 'maladaptive behaviour'). This happened with John given at the start of this chapter. Incorrect labelling often leads to a limited response by teaching staff/the school. If the behaviours observed are not recognised as symptoms of psychological distress and poor coping, then this reduces the likelihood that child and adolescent mental health services will be involved in supporting a student (Cooper, 2017).
- *Education policy:* education policy at the national or state level has been identified as one cause of everyday challenges currently faced by students with mental health difficulties in Australian schools (Armstrong and Armstrong, 2021). High-stakes testing and promoting school accountability on the basis of academic achievement have been highlighted as education policies which have been most detrimental to this population, making schools less inclusive and compassionate environments for affected students (Armstrong and Armstrong, 2021).
- *A lack of specialist support while at school due to under-funding of specialist mental health services.* Without effective support and specialist intervention during the school day, affected students are at risk of worsening symptoms in school, leading to greater harm for them and increased risk of school drop-out, suspension, expulsion, or exclusion (Graham, 2020). Once out of school, children and young people with mental health difficulties face even greater disadvantage with long-term negative impacts on their educational attainment, employability, and health (Thompson, 2017). In Australia, schools in remote or rural communities are often most affected by this issue when compared with their urban counterparts.
- *Teachers and schools feel professionally under-prepared to respond to students who present with mental health difficulties, with a lack of confidence about how*

to respond to students whom they have concerns about. Teacher preparation and also effective, timely referral have been pinpointed as areas for improvement in how the education sector includes students with mental health conditions (Armstrong *et al.*, 2015). To bypass these structural educational problems, helping young people themselves to learn.

- Mental health first aid (MHFA) in schools has been advocated and is defined as 'the help provided to a person who is developing a mental health problem or experiencing a mental health crisis, until appropriate professional help is received or the crisis resolves' (Hart *et al.*, 2018, p. 639).
- *Challenges in the home/family setting and existing in the wider community.* A constellation of adverse factors outside of school present major challenges to children and young people who experience mental health difficulties. Individuals with mental health difficulties, of all ages, are vulnerable to discrimination and stigma due to negative attitudes held by some in our communities, despite efforts in Australia to de-stigmatise mental health (Shute & Slee, 2016). Family or domestic violence can cause, sustain and exacerbate mental health difficulties. Socio-economic deprivation (poverty) appears as an important, but subtle, background factor in generating and sustaining mental health difficulties. Recovery from mental health difficulties can be impeded or even prevented by the influence of these adverse factors, working against the support provided by teachers and the aims of specialist therapeutic interventions.

It should be noted that the vast majority of these challenges arise from factors extrinsic (outside) of affected students: they reside in social attitudes to mental health, unintended negative consequences of national education policy, the resourcing of mental health services, and low levels of **mental health literacy** in some (but not all) schools.

Trauma

Trauma is also a major predictor in the development of mental health disorders months or years after traumatic experience(s) (Danese *et al.*, 2020). Traumatic events can happen at any stage in the lifespan but with most relevance to schools,

> childhood trauma can be described as occurring based on an event that poses a threat, which may be experienced by the child as harmful (physically or emotionally); the child's reaction to the traumatic experience may have enduring effects on functioning and well-being.
> (Chafouleas *et al.*, 2019, p. 40)

Weblink: Here is a very useful overview of childhood trauma by the public service broadcaster SBS.

https://youtu.be/fLqmwU0J1c8

Students who are 'looked after'/in care (Gatwiri *et al.*, 2019), who have experienced abuse (sexual or physical) or neglect (lack of care – physical and emotional), who have witnessed domestic violence and, also those who hail from Aboriginal or Torres Strait backgrounds; are at elevated risk of experiencing trauma (Menzies, 2019). Students from refugee or asylum seeker backgrounds and who may have experienced war, separation from family, and other hardships may also have trauma (Fazel *et al.*, 2012). One recent study suggests, however by Lau *et al.* (2018) suggests that many refugee children and adolescents from refugee backgrounds make remarkably positive psychological adjustments to their new life in Australia (p. 157).

Trauma-informed educational practice

Adverse childhood experiences (ACEs) are often the root of ongoing difficulties for many students in school, with or without a disability. ACEs are an important area of research supporting support, practices, programs, and interventions designed to aid the effective education of students with trauma.

Since 2000, trauma-informed educational practice has emerged as an important, distinct trend. The Berry Street Educational Model has emerged as one promising approach in Australia:

Weblink: The Australian Institute of Family Studies offers more education about The Berry Street Educational Model:

https://aifs.gov.au/cfca/2019/08/22/new-approach-trauma-informed-teaching-teacher-practice-berry-street-education-model

No single, widely accepted model of trauma-informed educational practice currently exists in Australia or internationally (Avery *et al.*, 2021; Overstreet & Chafouleas, 2016). Lack of a common understanding in Australian schools about what trauma-informed practice exactly consists of and its associated goals or benefits does, however, not invalidate the effort to better cater for affected students in schools.

No common understanding here does, though, create the risk that trauma-informed practice is a free-for-all space used to deliver whatever practices or customs are popular with a school or favoured by a teacher, not all of which may be appropriate or based in research evidence. Armstrong and Armstrong (2021) describe problems arising from an uncritical application of several educational trends similar to trauma-informed practice. Research reviews on this topic have, tentatively, suggested what could be features of trauma-informed practice. Here are four examples:

1 **Avoiding re-traumatisation of the student** through, for example, adjustments to teacher-student interaction by ensuring that it is emotionally sensitive (Cole *et al.*, 2013).

2. **Adoption of a student-centred and positive strength-based approach** by teachers, paraprofessionals (i.e. teacher aides, learning support workers), and wider professionals (i.e. school psychologists) involved in a student's education. Venet *et al.* (2021) call this an 'asset-based approach' and recommend its use with students who have experienced trauma.
3. **Professional teamwork and responsibility-sharing** by those supporting a student with trauma (Cole *et al.*, 2013), and to meet the range of academic, social, and emotional needs that individuals have.
4. **Ensuring emotional safety for students in the classrooms** and across the wider school environment has emerged as a focus.

A useful summary of research about trauma-informed teaching by the New South Wales (NSW Department for Education, 2020) suggests further elements of trauma-informed educational practice which teachers can use in the classroom:

> Teachers can provide further emotional safety to students through preventative strategies, such as teaching students self-regulation (for example, breathing and meditation exercises), having clear, firm, and repeated boundaries, rules, expectations and consequences, and, providing advance warning to students when there will be a change in routine. (p. 5)

Recommendations for practice

When applying trauma-informed practice, we recommend careful consideration of whether what is planned is sufficiently detailed and specific to the needs of a student who has experienced or is experiencing trauma. Avoiding vague, general appeals to well-being is best when planning interventions or ongoing supports. Instead, consider and respond to the specific educational, social, and emotional needs of individuals when planning, carrying out, and reviewing learning or teaching practices. Practices by the teacher, such as strong interpersonal communication and establishing trust with an affected student, are important. Communication of clear and fair expectations by the teacher around behaviour, academic expectations and boundaries is important. Some students may be very sensitive to what they perceive as being treated 'differently' on account of traumatic life experiences, and this sensitivity should be considered on a person-by-person basis when providing ongoing support. Establishing a calm and emotionally safe but also productive classroom environment is likely to benefit most students who have experienced or are experiencing trauma. This emphasis on the emotional climate of the classroom aligns perfectly with recommendations made in **Behaviour: building and maintaining calm and productive classrooms.**

Extract 15.1 Adverse Childhood Experiences (ACEs)

Adverse Childhood Experiences (ACEs), such as experiencing domestic violence, are known to place affected children at increased risk of developing mental health difficulties. An important US-based study by Zeng et al. (2019) examined ACEs in relation to estimates of parent-reported suspension and expulsion rates for pre-school children. They examined a large existing dataset of children aged three to five years old (N = 6,100) in the 2016 National Survey of Children's Health dataset. Zeng et al. (2019) report that an estimated 174,309 preschoolers (2.0%) were suspended, and 17,248 (0.2%) children were expelled annually. According to this study, children were more likely to be suspended or expelled if, for example, they had witnessed domestic violence, lived with parents who had a mental illness, lived in a home with adult substance abuse, lived in high poverty, or had parents who were incarcerated. Worryingly, Zeng et al. (2019) also highlight that 'risk factors increased odds ratio increased by 80% for every unit of ACEs increment' (p. 104).

Connection 15.1 Students with mental health concerns and the law

Students with diagnosed mental conditions, e.g. Generalised Anxiety Disorder (GAD), have legal protection in the Disability Discrimination Act (Australian Government, 1992) and are described under the sub-set of 'psychiatric' in legislation (Australian Human Rights Commission). A lesser-known fact about this legal protection is that it applies where an individual is *believed* to have a mental health condition (or other type of disability) (Australian Human Rights Commission, 2022). Under this provision, students who *present with mental health concerns* are already provided with full legal protection in the DDA. In technical terms and as part of a clinical diagnosis, mental health conditions are classified as disabilities in terms of their adverse impact upon daily life for those affected. This is why people with mental health disorders also have legal protection under disability discrimination legislation.

> **Pause and think**
>
> Please pause and consider that students who *present with mental health concerns* are provided with full legal protection in the DDA (1992).
>
> Q. *How does this knowledge impact teacher practice and the actions they must take to support students who present with mental health concerns?*
>
> Suggested response
>
> A. Teachers must ensure that students with mental health conditions do not face discrimination and exclusion in the classroom on account of their disability. This also applies to students that students who are believed to have a mental health condition (i.e. are waiting for clinical assessment).

The mental health sector, jurisdictions, and service models

It is essential that teachers understand some core features of the public mental health sector as a basis for effective collaboration with allied professionals in the sector (Armstrong *et al.*, 2015; Whitley *et al.*, 2018). Understanding the mental health sector has been seen as a valuable part of 'mental health literacy', preparing teachers to better respond to student needs (Rouf *et al.*, 2024), and in efforts to develop 'a common professional language for use in registering mental health needs' in students (Armstrong *et al.*, 2021, p. 340). One challenge of the mental health sector is its complexity: a feature often due to shifting budgets and local historical factors.

Child and Adolescent Mental Health Services (CAMHS) are the key public agency in Australia (and the UK) for delivering mental health services to school-aged students. They are often also involved with pre-school children. Table 10.1 sets out the typical arrangement in Australia in terms of which service caters for different age groups.

Table 10.1 Public mental health services in Australia

Age group served	*Public mental health service responsible*
University, TAFE, Year 11 and 12 (18 years and over)	Adult Mental Health Service
Secondary/high school (Year 7–12)	CAMHS
Primary school	CAMHS
Pre-school settings	Pediatrician/pediatric team, plus CAMHS

Complexity emerges when these arrangements are examined in greater detail and which generates challenges for teachers acting as part of a multidisciplinary team. These challenges cluster around *jurisdiction, effective referral,* and *thresholds/labelling.*

Jurisdiction

Students aged 16–18 could be treated by either CAMHS *or* Adult Mental Health services, depending on their individual needs and circumstances. Similarly, pre-school children might be under the care of hospital-based pediatric services, plus CAMHS. Problems with jurisdiction are a known complication for the sector and have led to major failings in care, where a child, young person, or adult has fallen between the jurisdiction of different services due to their age, e.g. young people aged 16–18 or pre-school children not attending pre-school settings but not under pediatric care. In these situations, bureaucratic wrangling has, in some cases, led to a lack of intervention and treatment, resulting in serious harm.

Referral

How to connect specialist mental health services, in a timely way, with students who present with mental health difficulties is a known challenge in schools; without timely intervention and treatment, many students' psychological welfare can rapidly decline. Referral by a teacher is a key mechanism in the process and therefore deserves illumination. There are, however, several routes through which referral can happen.

Referral route 1: via the family GP

In Australia and the UK, children and young people with mental health concerns can be taken to a registered GP by their parent (s)/guardians. After an interview, the GP can deem the child or young person to be suffering from a mental health disorder and/or make a referral to CAMHS or other specialist public services, typically for further assessment. Eating disorders, such as anorexia nervosa, and psychosis, including schizophrenia, often require specialist assessment. One immediate problem with specialist referrals is that there are often waiting times of weeks or months for children to receive specialist assessment and associated care. During this period, children or young people can be vulnerable to a deterioration in their well-being and an increased risk of exclusion, suspension, or expulsion from school, compounding the harm they suffer. Many affected children and young people also simply drop out (self-exclude) because they cannot cope with school at this time of most need (Bills *et al.*, 2020; Squires, 2020). This problem affected Maya, as described at the start of this chapter.

Referral route 2: via CAMHS

As well as referral through a GP, direct referral to mental health services can be made through a variety of other routes, including, for example, in Australia, direct referral by a school to the CAMHS team, who assess a child's mental health needs. Whether permission by the child or young person is required is a thorny legal and ethical question, but it does not generally arise for students under the age of 18 (Armstrong *et al.*, 2015).

The exact procedure for school referral varies state-by-state/regionally. NSW, for example, has a dedicated 'NSW Mental Health Line for advice, assessment and referral', which 'determines the appropriate service for referral' after speaking to a 'Mental Health helpline clinician' (NSW Department of Education, 2020).

Referral route 3: self-referral help-seeking by young people

Although this chapter is aimed at explaining what teachers and schools should do to notice and refer students who arouse mental health concerns, it is important to note that Headspace which is the Australian Government's National Youth Mental Health Foundation, also accepts self-referral by young people or secondary referral by family or friends, as well referral from a health or community service provider like CAMHS. Self-referral can be face-to-face by appointment, via a helpline or wholly online through chat and can be done independently or, alternatively, with the support of a teacher (Rickwood *et al.*, 2015). The 'young person friendly' Headspace, which provides online and telephone counselling, mental health, and well-being support, information, and services to young people aged 12 to 25 years and families (Rickwood *et al.*, 2015, p. 3). A full list of confidential helplines for students is given at the end of this chapter. It could be provided to students by teachers to aid mental health help-seeking by young people, either independently or with the support of their teacher.

Studies into mental health help-seeking in Australia, however, highlight that fear of stigma and concern about embarrassment by young people often prevent help-seeking (Rickwood *et al.*, 2015). So, self-referral may not always be an effective option for many young people. In addition, self-referral is not appropriate for younger students (pre-high school).

In Australia, Mental Health Care Plans (MHCPs) are produced after an individual (of any age) has been diagnosed by a GP or clinician as suffering from a mental health disorder. This document is a plan designed to support a child or young person experiencing mental health difficulties. It can include, for example, further specialist referrals and other care needed, plus everyday strategies needed to protect their well-being. As with practice for populating an individualised learning plan (IEP), children or young people are expected, ideally, to participate in populating an MHCP and to have a voice in deciding what happens to them. Research suggests this may not, however, happen.

Thresholds/labelling

How students are labelled by mental health professionals can constitute a barrier to effective support, often because it is connected to funding criteria and can result in a delay to urgent support for a student and their family. This is a complex issue. For example, a phenomena called 'diagnostic overshadowing' can occur whereby challenging behaviours by a student with disability, such as, for example, ASD are attributed by family, teachers, and other adults as part and parcel of their disability, overlooking the possibility that these behaviours are, in fact, due to a mental health difficulty (Armstrong *et al.*, 2015).

In thinking about what mental health means in a school setting, it is important to identify how this is addressed for teachers/staff and for students. Mental health programs/interventions and school-based mental health promotion programs/interventions are two different organising models that are important to understand.

Mental health literacy programs/interventions: designed for teachers

'Mental health literacy' refers to teachers possessing the practical skills, confidence, and knowledge necessary to intervene when a student's mental health is of concern (Whitley et al., 2018). According to Whitley *et al.* (2018) effective mental literacy program for teachers would help professionals:

- Understand the presentation and outcomes of a range of common mental health disorders, including anxiety and depression, and how these present in the age group they teach.
- Notice and respond to student behaviours of concern in a timely way.
- Work in an integrated, informed way with a range of professionals.

Mental health literacy programs are therefore delivered as part of professional learning for teachers and other school professionals, such as, for example, well-being coordinators or school counsellors.

School-based mental health promotion involves improving teacher mental health literacy but also provides *children or young people* with the skills and knowledge to safeguard their own mental health and psychological well-being (Askell-Williams et al., 2013). These capabilities are known protective factors against mental health. According to authoritative researchers in the field, school-based mental health promotion involves:

- Increasing what adolescents understand about common mental health disorders and associated symptoms.
- Strengthening the social and emotional capabilities of students, including student-teacher relationships.

- Supporting parents and providing information about child and adolescent mental health.
- Promoting collaborative practice by teachers in multidisciplinary teams (teacher + psychiatrist + social worker).
- Teachers recognising mental health concerns and responding to students who present with early signs of a mental health disorder (Helen Askell-Williams and Murray Harvey, p. 76).

Social and emotional learning (SEL) programs are programs typically used as part of school-based mental health promotion and focused on in the next section.

Students with mental health concerns: evidence-based teaching approaches, strategies, and practices

The idea of 'teaching' needs to be critically unpacked in the context of students with mental health concerns. Teaching and learning may not be viable without first noticing student distress, acting in a timely way via referral to specialist services, effective communication with parents and other professionals, and also a flexible, student-centred approach (Armstrong *et al.*, 2015).

Early intervention (which includes referral to mental health specialists) and timely support for students facing mental health concerns from teachers are known protective factors, reducing the chance of severe mental health difficulties emerging (Armstrong *et al.*, 2015; Cooper, 2017). The two case studies on SEL programs and Project X presented in the next section illustrate effective and evidence-based strategies for attending to students with mental health concerns.

When reading both case studies, it is useful to consider exactly what they add to your existing knowledge about evidence-based strategies for children with mental health concerns: what do you now understand about this topic after reading and reflecting on both case studies?

Case study 1: SEL programs

Education settings in Australia are increasingly using programs, interventions, and practices designed to develop students' social and emotional learning (SEL).

School-based programs which develop social and emotional skills have received support from Australian-based research as particularly effective in maintaining student mental health (Singh *et al.*, 2020). A major international meta-analysis of research studies that examined school-based programs reported a range of positive effects identified, including improved mental health among students and improvement in behaviour (Payton *et al.*, 2008). A later meta-analysis of international research by Sancassiani *et al.* (2015) highlighted that SEL programs appear to most benefit students with anxiety and with depression.

Many schools have specific staff whose role is to help ensure students' well-being, including their social and emotional development. These educators are often called 'well-being coordinators', 'belonging coordinators', 'welfare officers', or have similar titles.

What is social and emotional learning (SEL)?

There are diverse views by researchers and practitioners about what SEL is. Here is one definition by the respected US-based organisation Collaborative for Academic, Social, and Emotional Learning (CASEL):

> Social and emotional learning (SEL) is the process through which children and adults understand and manage emotions, set and achieve positive goals, feel and show empathy for others, establish and maintain positive relationships, and make responsible decisions.
> (CASEL, 2020: https://casel.org/what-is-sel/)

Types of SEL

Following key literature (Durlak *et al.*, 2011; Humphrey *et al.*, 2018), SEL programs can be categorised as:

- *Universal interventions:* all children in settings receive these.
- *Targeted interventions:* children at risk of difficulties with social development, emotional development, and/or behaviour are targeted.

Humphrey *et al.* (2020, p. 5) also explains that there are different flavours in the focus of interventions:

- Interventions emphasising the delivery of a taught *curriculum*;
- Those designed to change aspects of the *school environment or ethos*;
- Programs that involve work with *parents and/or the wider community*; and
- Those that involve some *combination* of these components.

Humphrey *et al.* (2020) also notes that some interventions are *top-down*, providing detailed guidance on how they should be implemented in practice; whereas others are *bottom-up, emphasising flexibility and local adaption in setting* (p. 5 – italics added).

Weblink

Collaborative for Academic, Social, and Emotional Learning (CASEL)

https://casel.org/guide/programs/

The respected US-based organisation CASEL recommend evidence-based preschool and primary school (elementary school) SEL programs. Several programs recommended by CASEL have been investigated by robust research, e.g. Tools of the Mind (Solomon et al., 2018) and PATHS (Humphrey et al., 2018).

Empathy and SEL

SEL programs help children develop skills, for example, in gaining and maintaining relationships and specific developmental abilities connected to relationships. Empathy is one of the specific developmental abilities which underpins relationships and is also strengthened by relationships

Historically, empathy was first described in English by the British critic and author, Vernon Lee, but taken from the German word Einfühlung ("feeling into") and officially translated from German by the pioneering psychologist Edward B. Titchener in 1909. Tong et al. (2012) offer a useful definition of empathy as an 'ability to understand and share another individual's emotional state' (Tong *et al.*, 2012, p. 2457).

The emergence of empathy is very important in a child's development and is connected to the ability to use prosocial behaviour, forming and consolidating relationships with peers and with adults (Eisenberg *et al.*, 2015. Experiencing empathy also contributes to the overall emotional development of a child (de Minzi *et al..*, 2016).

Empathy is closely related to social cognition (understanding social situations) and some mental disorders, as well as disabilities such as ASD, are known to reduce social cognition (Warrier *et al.*, 2019). Targeted SEL programs benefit these groups of students by mitigating these disabling effects and helping students to gain and maintain positive empathetic relationships. In turn, empathetic relationships are, according to research, one important protective factor in preserving positive student.

What do teachers need to know about SEL?

Key questions for a teacher to ask at the start of involvement in delivering a SEL program are:

- Is this a universal or targeted program?
- What's the focus of the program?
- What, if any, flexibility do I have in delivering this program?
- What do I need to know about this program before I take part in delivering it?

Strategies to encourage SEL in children

We suggest the following strategies to encourage SEL in children:

- *Make space*: make children's social, emotional, and behavioural development a key part of the curriculum and make explicit space for it in the timetable (Humphrey *et al.*, 2020). For young, typically-developing children, this means being able to name and recognise emotions, delivering the curriculum using songs, play, stories, and toys. Children with disabilities or who have experienced trauma or neglect may require similar services because

they are operating, socially, intellectually, and emotionally, at a lower level than their age might suggest.
- *Do your research:* find out about the SEL program/intervention used (Solomon *et al.*, 2018).
- *Think about implementation:* How often? To what extent? What kind of SEL program/intervention? What flexibility do teachers have?
- *Know the concepts:* consider underpinning concepts such as empathy and how to encourage their application in everyday professional practice in the classroom.
- *Model it*: practitioners should model SEL in their classroom interactions with learners (McClelland *et al.*, 2017).
- *Prevent first*: preventative rather than reactive SEL programs are best (Humphrey *et al.*, 2020). This also holds true with programs which focus on SEL for addressing students with or at risk of behavioural problems (Armstrong *et al.*, 2015). Targeted interventions, e.g. for students who have experienced trauma (and which tend to be *reactive*), often promote greater change in children when compared with universal programs (and which tend to be *preventative*) (Humphrey *et al.*, 2020).
- *Be critical*: is it working? What gains are apparent? How do I know?
- Remember, *play* and *friendships* are central to children's social and emotional development. Focus on the emotions in, for example, fantasy play and on what makes for positive friendships (reciprocity, trust, care, etc.) are age-appropriate examples for young children (three to five years old).

The evidence base for SEL

As highlighted at the start of this discussion, important studies based in Australia (Singh *et al.*, 2020) and internationally (Sancassiani *et al.*, 2015) have highlighted the benefits of school-based SEL programs for helping students maintain positive mental health.

In contrast, other research has reported more mixed results about school-based SEL programs (Bailey *et al.*, 2019; Humphrey *et al.*, 2018). In their overview of SEL programs for ECE, McClelland *et al.* (2017) summarise:

> Although finding intervention effects is encouraging, the small-to-moderate effects – and sometimes the lack of effects – that we see in some SEL interventions suggest that we still have a lot of work to do before we can effectively promote SEL skills for all children, especially in diverse early childhood education setting. (p. 43)

Studies in SEL persistently suggest that poor implementation is often why SEL programs don't have the intended effects and is a plausible explanation for the reported mixed results (Durlak *et al.*, 2011). This problem is important for teachers who wish to use SEL programs, and it should be emphasised that this does not mean that SEL programs are of themselves ineffective. Indeed, poor implementation is a widespread problem affecting many types of programs and interventions in Australian schools (Armstrong and Armstrong, 2021).

> **Weblink**
>
> **Early Childhood Education – emotional intelligence and ECE**
>
> https://youtu.be/4dPvAo3OMNI
>
> Please watch this video discussion about SEL between Dr David Armstrong and Prof. Jayne White.

> **Pause and think**
>
> Q1. *What specific abilities are necessary for social and emotional learning in children?*
>
> Suggestions: empathy, and the ability to name and identify emotions.

Connection 15.2: what are nurture groups?

The UK-based psychologist Marjorie Boxhall worked in inner-city London in the late 1970s and 1980s with disengaged children and young people who had complex psychological needs and hailed from disadvantaged backgrounds. Boxhall noticed that many of the children and young people she supported had difficulties with establishing and maintaining relationships – problems predicted by attachment theory. Boxhall established nurture groups as safe (nurturing) spaces where children and young people could learn (or re-learn) how to form positive relationships and develop emotional literacy (Boxall and Lucas, 2010). Since then, nurture groups have been identified as particularly beneficial for children and young people with mental health disorders (or who are at major risk of developing them) and have become increasingly popular in schools around the world (see **Support for nurture groups from research** below).

Nurture groups have variations but the classic model is where 10–12 children are taken out of a mainstream classroom each day for a

> certain period each day and for a limited length of time over the course of one school year and, within a small group setting, to model out positive attachment relationships and provide opportunities for social learning and the development of emotional literacy.
>
> (Sloan et al., 2020, p. 2)

To learn more about teacher practice and nurture groups, please access the weblink below.

Weblink: The Nurture Room

This high-quality (1.29 hours) documentary explores nurture group principles and teacher practice as used by one Scottish primary school– note the complex developmental needs demonstrated by 'Jamie' and other children. Note that some of the behaviours captured are distressing.

https://youtu.be/5XFjLdNO4FU

Support for nurture groups from research

Nurture groups have received growing support from research for students with or who are at risk of mental health disorders. Important findings (give in italics) in research about nurture groups are detailed below.

Nurture groups work best for students with mental health disorders and behaviours of concern. Nurture groups have been typically used with populations of children who had mental health difficulties, including presentation of behaviours of concern (Cooke et al., 2008; Grantham and Primrose, 2017; March & Kearney, 2017).

Nurture groups have growing popularity. Nurture groups have a growing status stemming from their increasing popularity among practitioners supporting children with mental health disorders (Grantham and Primrose, 2017). In 2016, The Nurture Group Network (Sloan et al., 2020) identified 2100 groups in operation across Australia, Canada, Malta, New Zealand, and the UK.

There is a growing research base to support best practice in nurture groups. Although still small, a research base is emerging to support best practice in the delivery of services or initiatives that use nurture groups for children with mental health difficulties. Early studies by researcher Paul Cooper et al. have been succeeded by a crop of recent literature. 2017, for instance, saw publication of several important new studies (Cefai and Pizzuto, 2017; Cubeddu and MacKay, 2017; Grantham and Primrose, 2017; March and Kearney, 2017). Cubeddu and MacKay (2017) note that 'the growth of nurture groups has been accompanied by, and indeed has been further fostered by, a growth in the research literature supporting them' (p. 262). In one of the first controlled trials involving nurture groups, Sloan et al. (2020) conducted a non-randomised control group trial involving 384 children from 44 primary schools in Northern Ireland. They report: 'there is clear and consistent evidence of improvements in social, emotional and behavioural outcomes for children attending Nurture Groups compared to those in the control group' (p. 6).

Case study 2: Project X

This is a case study of a real provision that has been adjusted in minor details to maintain anonymity. For background, in 2018, the author was asked by an Australian state government to evaluate a growing nurture group project (Project X) and to assess whether its success had any transferable insights for how mainstream public schools could inclusively support students with mental health disorders accompanied by challenging behaviours.

Project X is based at a hospital school and serves a cohort of 12–15 children aged 5–10 years attending public primary schools across an Australian state. Children attending this project were classified as having complex needs consisting of a diagnosed mental health condition plus challenging behaviour. Approximately 60% of the children attending had Foetal Alcohol Spectrum Disorder (FASD), and many faced violence at home or had suffered neglect. Approximately 50% of the students attending Project X did not live with their biological parent(s); a number of parents of children attending were incarcerated and/or receiving support from drug and alcohol services.

Project X is jointly governed by the State Child and Adolescent Mental Health Service (CAMH) and by the State Department of Education. Staffing consisted of five full-time teachers and two part-time teachers, plus a deputy principal and school principal. The CAMHS clinical team worked closely with all staff providing specialist therapy services, support and advice.

Project X aims

- To reduce the risk of expulsion and/or suspension for a sub-population of primary age children with a clinically diagnosed mental health condition accompanied by challenging behaviour.
- To reduce the harmful behaviours (aggression, manipulation, tantrums) and distress (meltdowns) affecting this sub-population.
- To enhance inclusion for this population using a nurture group model.

- To enhance the prosocial skills of students attending Project X.
- To improve the academic progress of attending children by addressing their social, emotional, and behavioural needs.

Project X delivery

Children attended Project X for two days each week, with the other three days spent in their regular class at a state primary school. Project X provides intensive support (nurturing) to help students gain and maintain relationships with each other and with teachers. Teaching in Project X also focusses on specific aspects for development in terms of a child's academic needs, i.e. reading, spelling, study skills, and mathematics. After an assessment of their social and emotional skills using the Boxhall Profile (Boxhall & Lucas, 2011). Students attending Project X join nurture groups of five to six children with two teachers per group.

Classroom-level practice in Project X

Staff who worked at Project X talked to the author about their daily teaching practice in Project X, and their comments are shared below in italics, with common themes given in bold.

Differentiation of need: '*Sub-clinical kids (children who do not yet present with psychological needs severe enough to receive a clinical diagnosis) need to be separated out from kids with clinical (more severe) behavioural needs. These are the kids that need professional help plus what we offer. For these kids we work closely with therapists and psychologists from CAMHS*'. '*Many of our students operate well below their age, socially and emotionally – in severe cases kids aged 5 who are functioning at the level of a 2 year old*'.

Professional practices used by staff at classroom level: '*Connecting behaviours and feelings*' '*Connecting behaviour with a response by others*' '*modelling relationships for children*' '*regular staff debriefing*' '*caring, non-judgmental interactions by staff with kids*' *Explicit teaching and modelling of skills needed to gain and maintain relationships (student-teacher, student-student)*.

Interactions with students in the classroom: Teachers at Project X emphasised how they '*helped kids recognise and articulate how they have changed for the better*' as a result of progress made in Project X and helped students to grow in confidence, '*Every time a student successfully navigates a stressful experience*'.

Data collection in the classroom:

Staff at Project X were highly committed to the use of data for evaluating student progress, one teacher typically commented:

> We collect real time data on kids' progress in achieving their (developmental) goals (e.g. behaviour and self-regulation) and also their academic progress.

Classroom Philosophy: This was summarised by the following statements *'Nobody has sole responsibility for kids in the classroom – it's everybody's responsibility'* and *'We don't claim therapeutic skills but our practice in informed by therapy – that's the nurture group influence'.*

Staffing model: *'We have 2 teachers rather than 1 teacher and 1 support assistant because there is no delegation'.*

Project-school collaboration model: Children who attended Project X also attended a regular class at a mainstream public primary school for three days out of a five-day week. Staff at Project X collaborated with a mainstream public primary school, offering information and advice about nurture group principles and how they might translate into a mainstream public primary school setting. The Project X Deputy Principal commented:

> Schools are encouraged to establish elements of the nurture group so that kids attending the project can see the nurture group in school. We offer advice and support on how they can this. Most schools take up our offer.

Daily classroom-level practice at Project X: Jimmy

'Jimmy' was given to the author as an example of nurturing practice with students attending Project X, many of whom came from backgrounds featuring domestic or family violence.

> Jimmy turned up at the project in the morning looking fearful and pale. It turned out he had locked himself in the bathroom all night at home, terrified at the domestic violence happening outside the bathroom door.
>
> In the morning he crept out of the house and came to the project. Rather than give him schoolwork (maths) that morning we gave him some breakfast and he curled up and slept on that beanbag (points to beanbag) until just before midday. After a drink and quick wash, he was then ready for learning. He didn't go back home after school that day.
>
> Teacher – Project X

Pause and think

Q1. How did Jimmy's teacher at Project X respond to his needs in this scenario? How would you categorise their response/decisions made?

Suggested response

Jimmy's teacher responded to his immediate needs for emotional safety after a traumatic experience at home. This practice is supported by trauma-informed teaching frameworks (NSW, DFE, 2016). Flexibility, compassion, and pragmatism also informed this response: these qualities might seem standard when responding to, but unfortunately, many teachers and many schools do not appear to be flexible or compassionate toward students affected by trauma, according to the Disability Royal Commission.

Outcomes of Project X

Teachers at Project X outlined several benefits of Project X for attending children. The benefits are summarised below with comments by staff in italics:

Language development

Staff at Project X consistently reported noted improvements in the expressive (speaking) and receptive (listening, understanding) capabilities of attending children:

> We can see a change in kids' language (it becomes) less aggressive and more complex. This emerges after 2-3 months (in the program) for most kids.

Reduced disciplinary referrals in school

Staff at Project X consistently reported:

> A reduction in referrals for behaviours of kids in school and who are involved in the project.

Home and school context

Parents/careers of students attending Project X highlighted positive changes in children:

> Teachers and parents/carers report reduced aggressive incidents and report improved self-regulation.

Improved mental health literacy for partners schools

Mental health literacy for professionals in schools whose students attended Project X appeared improved:

> By working with us schools become more aware of what mental health in kids means – and in some cases this triggers efforts to improve practice in school 'Over a third of schools have asked for input from the team

140 *The Inclusive Teacher*

on how we achieve such successful changes' – these benefits for schools were unexpected by staff in Project X.

Data-driven practice

Staff at Project X emphasised that data gathering and analysis were regularly used to evaluate student progress in each child's emotional, behavioural, and academic capabilities.

'*We don't claim we have an effects size but we do have behavioural and academic data which indicates improvement.*' To explain, effect sizes are statistical measures often used to gauge the impact of an educational intervention, practice or program. For note, following Cohen (1988), effect sizes of around 0.2 are categorised as 'small', those around 0.5 are described as 'medium', and those higher than 0.8 are regarded as 'large' (Cocks *et al.*, 2011; Sloan *et al.*, 2020).

Conclusion

As well as offering insights into evidence-based practice, this chapter has stressed how important it is that teachers show compassion and care towards students, without crossing over into the role of a counsellor or mental health specialist. Teacher conduct, plus the social and emotional climate of the classroom which teachers shape, are factors which protect a student's positive mental health; these are school-based factors which professionals can control, and their efforts can make a difference to outcomes. The programs and practices outlined in this chapter are intended to support a compassionate and caring teacher (you!) who strives to support positive mental health in school for everybody.

Bringing it together

Please re-read Scenario 15.1 Maya and John, given at the start of this chapter.

Q1. In light of your learning from this chapter and existing knowledge, how would you now advise Maya and John's teachers: what actions could/should they take – should they speak to parents?

Suggested response:

A2. John's teachers would benefit from undertaking mental health literacy professional learning and from reviewing school processes for noticing and referring students who present with behaviours of concern, and which could indicate a decline in mental health among students like John. School leadership is required to support this change in teacher practice and school policy. Maya's case is more complex since timely action was taken, but the severity of the mental health condition impacted on events. Ideally, with hindsight, CAMHS might have acted within 48 hours of referral by the school, with a psychiatrist meeting and assessing Maya.

Whether to involve a student's parent(s)/carer(s) when a mental health condition is suspected is a decision that requires very careful consideration and in light of the issue of child protection (mandated reporting). If child protection is not a known issue, and the teacher has a good relationship with carer(s) or parent(s), then a timely referral via the family GP route could be possible. If there is doubt here, school-based referral should be pursued. Each case should be carefully considered by the teacher with involvement by members of the school leadership team.

Q2. *What are the issues affecting Maya and John, and how would you explain these to their teacher, i.e. what language and terms or concepts might you use?*

Suggested response:

A2. Maya and John both have behaviours of concern which warrant timely referral to CAMHS or, with the support of parents, their family GP.

Q3. *What actions could/should be taken by the schools which Maya and John attend? Who might progress these actions in the school staff? Which external agencies might be contacted (and why)?*

Suggested response:

A3. Noticing behaviours of concern should have prompted timely referral and assessment. CAMHS or the family GP should have been involved in this process. For older students, who feel able, self-referral to mental health services (given at the end of this chapter) might be a positive option – but individuals may need support from their teacher or other school professionals (well-being coordinator) to ensure that this happens in a timely way.

Q4. *What are your key learnings from this chapter? Can you name four to five learning points about mental health concerns from this chapter?*

Further resources

- **Suggested reading**: Bennett, H. (2015). Results of the systematic review on nurture groups' effectiveness. *The International Journal of Nurture in Education, 1*(1), 3-7.
- The accessibly written research article *Results of the systematic review on nurture groups' effectiveness* provides expert knowledge on nurture groups. Available at: https://www.nurtureuk.org/wp-content/uploads/2023/07/IJNE_Vol_1-Results-of-the-systematic-review-on-nurture-groups-effectiveness---Dr-Hanna-Bennett.pdf
- **Suggested reading:** Schulte-Körne, G. (2016). Mental health problems in a school setting in children and adolescents. *Deutsches Ärzteblatt International, 113*(11), 183. Schulte-Körne's open-access article highlights what research suggests teachers can do to support positive mental health in schools.
- **BeYou** is the key Australian federal organisation responsible for school-based mental health. The BeYou website contains links to a range of high-quality advice and professional learning resources aimed at the education workforce (teachers, support staff, school leaders). Available at: https://beyou.edu.au/resources Areas of focus for these professional learning resources include: Suicide prevention and support, including a suicide prevention toolkit, available here: https://beyou.edu.au/resources/suicide-prevention-and-response Indigenous mental health, available here: https://beyou.edu.au/resources/always-be-you
- In Australia, **Beyond Blue** is a national organisation devoted to ensuring young people's mental health. Their website is packed with resources for teachers and for young people and has an excellent collection of other useful contacts, specifically for teachers, available at: https://www.beyondblue.org.au/ and https://www.beyondblue.org.au/get-support
- **SANE Australia**, available here: https://www.sane.org and **Lifeline,** available here: https://www.lifeline.org.au/, also offer suicide prevention and suicide response resources for schools.
- **Mental health literacy for teachers:** Headspace Schools is a national workforce that 'supports, engages and partners with education and health sectors across Australia, to build the mental health literacy and capacity of workforces.' Offering Professional development packages for school staff (SAFEMinds In Practice training, Suicide Risk Continuum Training and Skills-based Training on Suicide Risk Management STORM®), available at: https://headspace.org.au/schools/headspace-schools/

Helplines for children and young people

- Lifeline (suicide prevention, crisis support). Call **13 11 14,** 24 hours/7 days a week or chat online.
- Beyond Blue (depression and anxiety). Call **1300 22 4636,** 24 hours/7 days a week or chat online.

- Blue Knot (childhood trauma). Call **1300 657 380**, 9 am to 5 pm, AEST, 7 days a week.
- Headspace (online and telephone counselling, mental health, and well-being support, information and services to young people aged 12–25 years and families). Call **1800 650 890**, 9 am to 1 am, AEST, 7 days a week.
- Kids Helpline (Australia's free, confidential, and private counselling service specifically for children and young people aged 5–25). Call **1800 55 1800**, 24/7 days a week.

Helpline for teachers

Dealing with topics such as suicide and child mental health can be psychologically confronting for all school staff, including, but not restricted to, teachers, impacting on well-being and adult relationships beyond work. Here are some useful helplines if you are impacted by these issues as a teacher/in your professional life in school:

- **Relationships Australia** (relationship support services). Call 1300 364 277 24/7 days a week.
- **Beyond Blue** (anxiety or depression). Call 1300 22 4636, 24/7 days a week, or chat online.
- **Lifeline** (suicide prevention, crisis support). Call 13 11 14, 24/7 days a week, or chat online.
- **SANE Australia** (for individuals living with a mental illness). Call 1800 18 7263, 10 am to 10 pm, Monday to Friday, AEST/AEDT or chat online.

11 Inclusive assessment

> This section will help you *begin* to learn how to:
>
> - Apply principles of inclusive assessment in professional practice.
> - Consider alternative assessment formats.
> - Understand principles of inclusive assessment.
>
> The Australian Institute for Teaching and School Leadership (AITSL) Graduate Teacher Standards covered by this learning include:
>
> 1.1 Physical, social, and intellectual development and full participation of students with disability.
> 3.1 Establish challenging learning goals.
> 5.1 Assess student learning.
> 5.2 Provide feedback to students on their learning.

This reading explains inclusive assessment for students with a disability. This part evaluates whether assessment, as currently practised in Australia, is or even can be inclusive. Senior school examinations and National Assessment Program – Literacy and Numeracy (NAPLAN) are critically reviewed to answer this question (spoiler alert: the conclusion is 'no'). Inclusive alternatives to existing assessment practices are explained, specifically, the 'assessment for learning' approach.

The reader meets Carey, who is a case study student with a disability. What an inclusive assessment for Carey might consist of is detailed. This detail features the use of an assessment for learning approach. A visual journal is outlined and, as an example of an inclusive assessment *format* suiting Carey's needs, enabling Carey to achieve progress, referenced to English level (writing) descriptors at Level C, Towards foundation in the Victorian curriculum. Guidance is given to readers on the equitable use of special considerations in formal summative examinations like NAPLAN or Senior school examinations for students with a disability.

DOI: 10.4324/9781003669630-13

Introduction

Educational assessment commands a major portion of teachers' daily work in the classroom and is vital in judging whether a student with a disability is learning successfully. Cumming and Dickson (2013) capture the educational and *social* value of assessment when they comment:

> Educational assessment plays a significant role in the lives of teachers and students. On a daily basis, it can be used formatively in classrooms to identify students' strengths and weaknesses, and guide future teaching and learning. It is undertaken for summative purposes when, at a point in time, judgement is made about students' achievement, usually for reporting progress to parents or carers. (p. 221)

Definition: In Australia, formal academic 'achievement' typically involves results and qualifications arising from assessment involving examinations and tests. National Assessment Program – Literacy and Numeracy (NAPLAN), for instance, is an 'annual assessment of students in Years 3, 5, 7 and 9' and was introduced in 2008 (Australian Curriculum, Assessment and Reporting Authority, n.d.). This type of *summative*, formal assessment of academic skills and knowledge dominates what successive Australian governments, parents, and wider society think of when the topic of 'assessment' is mentioned (Armstrong, 2018). This bias has also shaped research on assessment for students with a disability, according to Australia-based research by Rasooli *et al.* (2021) about fair assessment and where they comment: 'Research on assessment accommodations has largely focussed on the effects of accommodations on students' academic achievement in large-scale and summative tests to provide fairer conditions (p. 305).

The purpose of assessment: is it just about academic achievement and the grade?

Purpose is a fundamental factor in *considering* any kind of assessment: what is this assessment for, and what are its goals? A question about purpose should be accompanied by the connected query: how do these goals benefit a student educationally and/or personally? Researchers, teachers, and educational leaders in Australia and elsewhere have expressed growing concern that formal assessment of academic skills and knowledge has come to dominate the purpose of schooling and come to be seen as the sum of its value. Trends such as professional practice which 'teaches to the test' (Armstrong, 2018; Rose *et al.*, 2020) and the connected issue of 'curriculum narrowing' (Gleeson *et al.*, 2020) have been identified as damaging outcomes of this increased emphasis upon school as delivering formal academic 'achievement' and as mainstream public schooling a pipeline for results and qualifications arising from assessment of academic performance. Given that many attend mainstream public schools, students with a disability are most disadvantaged by these developments (Armstrong and Armstrong, 2021).

Assessment via senior school examinations for students with a disability

In mainstream Australian public secondary schools, senior school examination results are important outcomes of summative, formal academic assessment. Examples of senior school examinations, typically, taken in Year 12 include: The Victorian Certificate of Education (VCE) in Victoria, the Higher School Certificate (HSC) in New South Wales, the Queensland Certificate of Education (QCE) Exams in Queensland, the Western Australian Certificate of Education (WACE), and the South Australian Certificate of Education (SACE). Across Australia, senior school exams are the primary mechanism for recognising student academic achievement in the Australian school system and are the gateway into tertiary education, Technical and Further Education (TAFE), and/or employment. For many students and their families, completion of senior school examinations is a watershed moment in their education and wider life as a young adult.

Unsettling questions emerge, however, when considering how students with a disability fit with the system of senior school examination and with NAPLAN. Questions arising are highly practical and moral and relate to the goal of providing inclusive assessment for all students.

Senior school exams and NAPLAN are not examples of inclusive educational assessment

The Australian Institute of Welfare and Health AIWH (Australian Institute of Health and Welfare, 2021), which is part of the federal government, presents compelling data on the participation of students with a disability in Year 12 during which senior school exams take place. Data from the AIWH (Australian Institute of Health and Welfare, 2021) reveals that, 'Around 1 in 3 (34% or 1.2 million) people with disability aged 20 and over, and 1 in 4 (27% or 261,000) with severe or profound disability have completed Year 12 or equivalent.' (AIWH, 2022). This depressing and alarming finding reveals that around two-thirds of students with a disability in classrooms will not participate in the most important summative academic assessment in Australian schools. As the AIHW highlights, this number of students is even higher for those with a severe or profound difficulty. Readers interested in further information about educational attainment for young people with a disability can learn more by accessing the AIWH webpage below:

Website: https://www.aihw.gov.au/reports/disability/people-with-disability-in-australia/contents/education-and-skills/educational-attainment#Age%20left%20school

High non-participation rates in NAPLAN amongst students with a disability have been detected by research, with, for example, between '250 and 270,000 annually 2008–2010' (Davies 2012; p. 63). If anything, non-participation in NAPLAN has worsened amongst students with a disability since the dataset reported by Davies (2012). A report published in 2023 by the Australian Educational Research Organisation (AERO) finds an overall national increase in the number of students 'missing the test', and comments that 'Participation rates among students from priority equity groups are much lower, and declining faster, than average' (Lu *et al.*, 2023, p. 3).

This failure in NAPLAN has prompted calls for it to be replaced by 'a fairer, inclusive nation system, which developed in partnership with the teaching profession, so that it supports teachers' professional practice, helps, not hinders, student learning – and is valued and trusted by all' (Wilson and Sahlberg, 2021, p. 18).

The future of NAPLAN and senior school exams is unclear when considering the broad scope of educational reform set out in **Understanding inclusion** earlier in this book. NAPLAN and senior school exams, as currently practised, are clear barriers to the stated goal of this reform, that: 'All Australian governments and educational authorities should address and progressively overcome the barriers to inclusive education in mainstream schools' (DRC, 2023, p.338).

Key point

As currently practised, senior school exams and NAPLAN are *not* examples of inclusive assessment – a conclusion supported by research on this topic (Duncan *et al.*, 2020). This point is important because NAPLAN and senior school exams function as the key formal summative assessment of academic skills and knowledge in Australian schools. Furthermore, senior school exams and NAPLAN, therefore, cannot plausibly provide a model for teachers showcasing how 'inclusive assessment' should be – teachers must look elsewhere.

The role of academic assessment for students with a disability

One immediate question naturally arises when considering inclusive assessment in the classroom and the Key Point above. Q1 summarises this question below.

Q1. Given the unsatisfactory state of summative, formal assessment of academic skills and knowledge, should teachers and schools prioritise teaching and assessing non-academic skills and knowledge, for instance, vocational education, life skills or similar, with students who have a disability?

Teaching, learning, and assessment of vocational knowledge or skills, life skills, and other non-academic vocational areas of the wider educational curriculum amongst students with a disability, has a long and popular history in Australia, like other countries with similar education system, such as the United Kingdom (UK) (Nakar, 2023, Slee, 2018). South Australia, for instance, has a tradition of vocational pathways in schools for students with intellectual disability and Down Syndrome (Carey, 2015). Vocational Education and Training (VET) has emerged as a key curriculum framework for teaching, learning, and related assessment of employment-related skills and knowledge (Meltzer & Saunders, 2020; Nakar & Bagnall, 2024). In VET pathways, teaching, learning, and assessment are geared to preparation for life post-school, as an employee (Department of Education and Training, 2025).

A1. In answering **Q1**, we think that teachers should be mindful of the danger of 'writing off' students with a disability under the assumption that an individual cannot make academic progress, which is assessable and reportable to parents or carers. This advice is given in light of the 'culture of low expectations' identified as a problem in some Australian schools by the Disability Royal Commission inquiry and research studies into this topic (DRC, 2023; Woodcock and Faith, 2021).

Recommendation for practice

We recommend that teachers and other decision-makers around assessment (e.g. the school inclusion coordinator or equivalent) carefully consider each student's academic capabilities across the curriculum, using observation and evidence from what the student can do to plan teaching and learning related to the academic curriculum, including how to assess progress and learning. Further applied advice on this process, known as 'assessment of learning' (Rasooli *et al.*, 2021), is given shortly in this chapter.

Alternative sources for inclusive assessment

Detailing a more inclusive alternative to NAPLAN and senior school exams is beyond the scope of this section and of this book. What follows offers a brief, focussed consideration of one inclusive alternative to formal summative assessment of academic skills and knowledge.

Abilities Based Learning and Educational Support (ABLES)

A range of inclusive assessments has arisen for students with a disability, partly in response to dissatisfaction with existing assessments as often practised in Australian schools. Abilities Based Learning and Educational Support (ABLES) is one of these and is a no-cost online assessment tool available online for teachers via the School Curriculum and Standards Authority website.

Website: https://k10outline.scsa.wa.edu.au/home/resources/ablewa/the-ables-assessment-tools

ABLES assessment tool takes the form of an observational survey that takes 'approximately 20 minutes for teachers to complete for each student', and assesses students' readiness to learn across seven learning domains, which include curriculum areas of English and mathematics. Two learning domains with ABLES, 'Personal and Social Capability' and 'Self-Awareness', are designed specifically for students who have autism.

Recommendation for practice: purchasing educational assessments

Educational assessment is a major commercial venture, involving global publishers and other large commercial organisations which offer a range of products. When choosing which products to purchase for the purposes of assessment. Slick marketing can, in our view, sometimes overwhelm important questions about the suitability of educational products. Research in the area highlights how little regulation of this market in Australia exists for commercial educational products (Armstrong and Armstrong, 2021).

When deciding alternative assessment tools or products, we recommend caution and careful, collegial, cost-benefit consideration of how assessments are based on the needs of students with a disability in the setting. Consulting other local schools with similar student demographics about the positives and downsides of the assessments they use could be helpful in this selection process.

Assessment for learning

Delivering effective, meaningful assessments for students with a disability becomes more important, considering many teachers consistently report that they struggle in this area of professional practice. Assessment for learning is a promising way and overcome this problem, consisting of (Rasooli *et al.,* 2021):

- Assessment of learning: assessment as part of the daily structure of classroom practice and as opposed to summative, once-yearly, tests and examinations such as NAPLAN.
- Issues in assessment specifically pertinent to students with a disability and who, as a group, are under-represented in literature recommending best practice to teachers.

Assessment for learning implies that all assessment tasks set should be closely connected to the *learning priorities of a student*, making assessment likely to be a meaningful process for that student's educational needs and personal goals.

This focus on the student's needs and personal goals highlights that individuals' *agency* in the learning process and recognition of learning through formative assessment by the teacher. In Australia, when assessment for learning is mentioned, the key component of student agency is often not the focus and is used differently from how assessment for learning is used here.

For instance, the New South Wales Education Standards Authority (NESA) refers to 'Assessment for, as and of Learning'. It describes how this informs teacher practice, stating 'Assessment for learning involves teachers using evidence about students' knowledge, understanding and skills to inform their teaching. Sometimes referred to as 'formative assessment', it usually occurs throughout the teaching and learning process to clarify student learning and understanding.' (NSW Standards Authority, 2024).

The case study vignette below is given to further examine assessment for learning in practice. The curriculum area discussed in this vignette is English. Assessment processes represented are the focus – discussion about the aspects of oral language, reading (decoding and comprehension), and writing skills, involved have been simplified for the reader.

Case study vignette: Carey

Carey is a quiet and hard-working Year 5 student at a school in Victoria, attending a school in a regional Victorian town called Warburton. Carey has an intellectual disability and has a communication impairment affecting his speech, reading development, and handwriting. Despite barriers to acquiring literacy, listening to stories is one of Carey's favourite pastimes, and at home, Carey enjoys listening to audiobooks. At school, Carey is supported by the teaching assistant, Jay, who also offers focussed support to three other students in the class. Carey can write his name reliably, but his illegible handwriting is a major barrier. Carey is learning to use the keyboard and can type a variety of one-syllable words, but his typing is slow in speed, and he tires quickly.

Carey is studying English at Level C, Towards foundation in the Victorian curriculum, with hopes to progress into Level D and beyond next year. Carey's father, Joyce, is highly supportive of the school and of Carey's educational progress. Carey's teacher, the teaching assistant, Jay, and Carey and his father have agreed that learning to write stories is an accessible literacy goal. Carey is excited to begin.

It has been a cold winter, and the teachers have planned a class trip to nearby Mount Donna Buang to enjoy the snow. The visit is a great learning experience for Carey and an ideal basis for him to then achieve his goals.

Preparation

In the weeks preceding the trip, Jay assists Carey with preparation for the learning experience itself (things he will learn on the day, or which will spark learning later, e.g. the structure of a snowflake), plus preparation for the assessable story which Carey will write about this trip.

What follows offers an illustrative example of one part of this preparation based around one lesson involving assessment for learning. This lesson has two parts in procedure, providing the teacher with some preparation time between Part 1 and Part 2 to locate and sort flashcards based on the words which Carey selects in Part 1.

Preparation lesson aims

1 To prepare Carey for constructing a story about his trip to Mount Donna Buang.

Inclusive Assessment

2 Reading: to assess Carey's prior knowledge of words connected with the trip and focus on words he needs to learn (word-level knowledge).
3 To encourage Carey's autonomy as a learner by enabling him to self-select the words he wishes to use in the story.
4 To provide praise for adopting the correct learning behaviours and for effort demonstrated.

Resources: Winter flash cards with plus one flash card with the image of a bus and one with an image of soup.

Procedure part 1: selecting the story words

Time: 30 minutes.
Prompt the student. Jay prompts Carey to think about words which he will likely use in his story about the trip to Mount Donna Buang.
Jay: 'What words will you use in your story, Carey?'

Student identifies suitable words for use in meeting the English level (writing) descriptors in the task

Several one- or two-syllable words, connected with the trip, are orally identified by Carey as words which he will probably use when writing the story.

Carey has clear difficulty in recognising Mount Donna Buang and appears uncertain.

Assess that the student understands and can apply each chosen word in context, using prompts

To help Carey contextualise each word and think about the sequence in which they might be used in the story, Jay and Carey discuss these choices, aided by oral prompts:

Jay: 'Carey, why did you pick the word scarf?'
Jay: 'What will you have for lunch on the trip, Carey?'

Procedure part 2

Time: 40 minutes

Present chosen words in image only

- To assess Carey's prior word-level knowledge in reading and focus his learning, Jay presents Carey with a series of images on flash cards that visually represent the words he has chosen. Jay prompts Carey to look at these images.

  Jay: 'Here are pictures of ice, snow, cold, scarf, snowball, bus, and soup'.

Jay asks Carey to look at the words he has chosen.

Jay: 'Look at the words, Carey'.

Student matches the appropriate word with the appropriate image, observed by the teacher or teaching aide

Jay asks Carey to point to each image and place the appropriate word underneath it.

Jay: 'Match the right words with the right picture, Carey'.

Provide praise for effort made and learning behaviours adopted by the student

Jay praises Carey for correctly matching most of the words with the right image.

Identify target words to learn based on this assessment for learning

Jay communicates that he thinks the words scarf and snowball should be the focus of Carey's learning, going forward in planning for writing a story about the trip to Mount Donna Buang, and provides Carey with flashcards to start this process.

Summarise learning and/or achievements, highlight next steps based on any gaps in learning or academic needs

Jay asks Carey to think about what he has learned today.

Jay: 'What have you learned today, Carey? Can you say it?'

    Prompt/clue: 'Words I recognise and can use for this story are...'

Jay: 'Can you say any words you need to learn?'

    Prompt/clue: 'Words I should learn are....(clue – one keeps you warm)'.

Helping students to identify what they know, and future learning are important to assist application, fluency and maintenance phases in the learning process and as highlighted in Chapter 4, **Disability becoming a developmentally-informed teacher.**

Discussion

The lesson presented above to illustrate assessment for learning is simplified, and this discussion unpacks deeper factors that readers should consider in the lesson, including: the benefits of assessment for learning, and unexpected learning opportunities.

Inclusive Assessment   153

The benefits of assessment for learning. This simple formative assessment for learning identifies several insights which are helpful for Jay's teaching and Carey's learning going forward. These are:

Word knowledge level. Carey can recognise and appropriately use many simple one-syllable words, e.g. 'ice'. This is a foundation for Carey learning more complex words (two- to three-syllable words), e.g. 'icicle', and compound words, such as 'snowball'.

Areas for development. Carey did not recognise the compound word 'snowball' and the word 'scarf'. He also did not automatically recognise the uppercase letters in Mount Donna Buang (see below) and had clear difficulties recognising the term. This assessment suggests that learning 'snowball' and the word 'scarf' should be immediate priorities in terms of writing the story about the trip to Mount Donna Buang – a phrase which would be an obvious choice to include in the title of the story. Data from this assessment also indicates that other compound words, e.g. 'football', could be added to Carey's list of wider vocabulary to learn to read. For further explanation about compound words, please see the website below from the online *Cambridge Dictionary*.

Website: https://dictionary.cambridge.org/grammar/british-grammar/compounds

Unexpected learning and assessment opportunities. These unplanned opportunities present in many lessons and should not be simply ignored in favour of sticking to the procedure in the plan for any lesson. One unexpected learning opportunity which could happen in this lesson is around the term Mount Donna Buang. To illustrate the potential of unexpected learning and assessment opportunities, here is one: **Scenario: Mount Donna Buang.**

While delivering this lesson, Carey comments that the place name Mount Donna Buang is 'weird'. In assessing Carey's comment and how it might be related to gaps in his knowledge, Jay uses prompts to help Carey progress his understanding:

Jay: 'What things are weird in Mount Donna Buang, Carey?'
Jay: 'Can you point with your finger to show me?'

To aid communication and encourage the desired behaviour, Jay accompanies his request by pointing his finger, generally, at the written place name 'Mount Donna Buang'. Cards with appropriate images (e.g. a pointing finger) could also be used to support communication for students who require a little more support than Carey.

Carey takes a moment to process this request while Jay patiently waits. Carey points to the uppercase letters given in bold here: '**M**ount **D**onna **B**uang'. Carey also points to the word Buang. This prompts a learning rich discussion about uppercase letters and how they are used in the names when writing places and the names of people. Jay also explains that many place names come from indigenous words for places.

Correct use of uppercase letters in writing and understanding the category known as 'proper nouns' are not stipulated in the Victorian curriculum in The English level (writing) until the foundation level, which states:

> **Writing**
>
> When writing, students use familiar words and phrases and images to convey ideas. Their writing shows evidence of letter and sound knowledge, beginning writing behaviours and experimentation with capital letters and full stops. They correctly form all upper and lowercase letters.

Carey is designated by his teacher as working at Level C, Towards foundation in the Victorian curriculum. Understanding the use of 'proper nouns', the ability to recognise them when reading, and correctly applying this knowledge are therefore academic goals for the future. The unexpected learning opportunity detailed here indicates that Carey may be operating on this topic at least, ahead of expectations. For context, and for those new to teaching, uneven academic development is not unusual: few students progress evenly across the curriculum and in all the skillsets required. Students with disability often have greater variation between capabilities in the curriculum than their typically developing peers.

An assessment for learning approach is ideally placed to exploit unexpected learning opportunities for students with a disability. This strength arises because assessment for learning involves assessment as part of the daily structure of professional practice, lending those who use it an agility and flexibility in response to individual needs and capabilities in the classroom.

Carey's trip to Mount Donna Buang: opportunities for inclusive assessment

Carey had a great trip to Mount Donna Buang.

The focus of Carey's work in English for the weeks following this trip is to represent his learning around this trip in an accessible format, which meets his personal academic goal (writing a story), and exactly meets curriculum descriptors English (writing) at Level C, Towards foundation in the Victorian curriculum. Australian teachers indicate that achieving this balancing act can be difficult.

Research studies back up this point indicating that recognising the academic progress and achievements of students with a disability can be problematic, especially when the curriculum sets out very specific expectations the skills and knowledge which a student can demonstrate – also known as 'standards' (Price and Slee, 2021; Walker *et al.*, 2018). Existing curricula in Australia tend to be based around typically developing students, with the needs of students like Carey added as an afterthought or not at all (Price and Slee, 2021).

Use of an alternative assessment format is one way to evidence student performance in meeting specific curriculum descriptors. There is no proscribed way of using an alternative assessment, but imaginative alternative formats can be used to clearly demonstrate that the student has met standards. Here is one suggestion below.

Visual journal

A visual journal, in educational application, is a journal format (physical or digital) that represents a learning experience using a combination of images and explanatory text (Kulinski, 2023). Representing experiences and thought processes connected to these experiences has a rich intellectual history and has been connected in literature with sophisticated personal reflection and learning (Arnheim, 1997; Ritchhart *et al.*, 2011).

In the context of alternative assessment, visual journals can be used in a more modest application and with the aim of helping students represent their thoughts and learning with the aid of images and an accessible format. Carey's trip to Mount Donna Buang can be used to illustrate this application and with the purpose of creating an assessable.

The procedure used consists of components in sequence: planning, carrying out (construction), and review.

This part of the procedure involved learning centred on *vocabulary* and *story sequence*.

Vocabulary

- **Student identifies suitable words for use in meeting the English level (writing) descriptors in the task.**

As detailed earlier in this section, several one- or two-syllable words connected with the trip are orally identified by Carey as words he will probably use when writing the story. Words which Carey verbalises are:

ice	snow	scarf
	cold	soup
		bus
weather snowball Mount Donna Buang		

Assess that the student understands and can apply each chosen word in context using prompts

Jay makes this assessment using flashcards in the procedure set out earlier where Carey matches a word with the correct image.

As a result of this assessment, it becomes clear that Carey needs to learn the words.

Both words become the focus of Carey's learning pre-trip.

Story sequence

Jay helps Carey consider the narrative sequence of the story. This involves Carey considering the likely order in which he will use the vocabulary chosen in relation to the beginning, middle, and end of a story. 'Start' is an easier word than 'beginning' when reading and learning, so it could be substituted at this point.

The flashcards that Carey already has for these chosen words can be conveniently used here. For instance, Carey intends to have his lunch ('soup') in the middle of the trip, so the flash card with the word soup can be placed in the middle of the day's vocabulary sequence. 'Scarf' is likely to come at the start of the day as Carey dresses with a warm scarf, so the flashcard will probably be placed to the right of 'soup'.

Some words, like 'bus', can be placed at the beginning or end of the story. In the event, Carey chose to place 'bus' at the end (travel home). When placed down here is what emerges is the start of a story sequence.

This sequence also provides guidance for Carey on the position of the words and accompanying image when working on the layout of his visual journal.

Carrying out (construction) of the visual journal

Careful planning before the event aids this part of the procedure. The level at which Carey is operating in English (writing and reading) must also be factored into expectations from Jay and the class teacher when constructing the visual journal. As noted at the start of this case study vignette, Carey has significant difficulties with writing. It is also, at the same time, important that Carey has ownership of the story produced and maximises this opportunity to learn as deeply and as quickly as is possible – particularly the ability to independently write.

Research has identified several potential problems here with the support provided by teaching assistants/aides or teaching-paraprofessionals in their work with students who have a disability. Studies have identified 'unnecessary dependence' (Giangreco, 2010) and a lack of independence in learning (Sharma and Salend, 2016) as outcomes of support which are detrimental to student learning.

In Carey's case, and the production of the visual journal, this boils down to the question of how much Jay should scaffold Carey in the writing process and intervene if Carey is unable to complete written sections of the story. Here is a list of what we think are 'reasonable adjustments' in this case, and which ensure Carey's independence and participation.

Format. Carey can create the journal in a digital format. This enables him to type familiar words and bypasses problems with handwriting.

Vocabulary. Carey must type all of the words he has chosen to use on the trip. Carey can have assistance, if he needs it, with typing additional and or unfamiliar words. This is a learning opportunity for Carey to expand his reading vocabulary.

Sentence structure. Carey will verbalise appropriate sentences containing his chosen words. If required, Jay will suggest any grammatical changes necessary. Carey will aim for simple sentence structures to maximise learning. This is a learning opportunity for Carey to expand his understanding of simple sentence structures, punctuation, and the use of uppercase letters.

Images. Carey will work with Jay to select and add appropriate images to the layout. Jay will also advise on readability and any other visual issues which interfere with Carey communicating his learning.

Review

This consists of a quality check on the grammar, spelling, sentence construction, and other standard elements in a review. For Carey's learning, however, the review should also focus on the learning acquired and the distance travelled in Carey's learning in the process of creating.

As part of Carey's Trip to Mount Donna Buang, a review by Carey of the choices he made when creating this story is important for his progress and in feeling he has agency in the learning process.

Practically, Carey also needs to evidence that he can meet the following criteria to fully meet the writing component in English (writing) Level C, Towards Foundation in the Victorian curriculum:

- Review choices made during shared construction of personalised multimodal texts during shared review *(VCELY091)*.

There are several ways in which this evidence could be created and the learning demonstrated. Advice from Carey's speech and language pathologist/ therapist would be useful in guiding what is most appropriate. A conversation which reviews choices made during the construction of Carey's Trip to Mount Donna Buang could be recorded as an audio file and saved as a copy alongside a digital copy of the story.

Sentence started prompts would be most useful in scaffolding the conversation, however, and in ensuring that they have a clear, predictable structure.

Finally, when completing Carey's learning through writing his story, celebrating this achievement by sharing the visual journal story with carer(s) or parents is an important conclusion.

Special examination arrangement for students with a disability

Readers employed in public schools or state government in an educational capacity will probably be aware that examination assessment practice, rules, and procedures are firmly regulated by state government or associated curriculum and assessment bodies. Student experience of the exam or test situation itself is a key example of how this regulation operates and some of the barriers it creates to an inclusive assessment experience for a student with a disability.

Australia has a long-standing practice of providing additional supports or support services to students with a disability in an examination, and to provide them with an equitable, inclusive opportunity to perform, in light of the impacts of their disability. Parents Victoria (PV), a not-for-profit body who advises and supports parents of students in public education, explains:

> Special Examination Arrangements are available if your child has a disability or long-term illness. The arrangements vary depending on individual needs, but the aim is to help your child access the questions and communicate their answers. The support comes in many different forms, such as taking rest breaks during the exam or being given extra time to provide responses (PV, (2023) special provision for VCE exams). https://www.parentsvictoria.asn.au/special-provision-for-vce-exams/

Special Examination Arrangements (also called 'exam considerations') are usually highly proscribed in public schools around summative examinations, for example, those which occur at the end of high school. Examples of senior high school examinations where special examination consideration is used ('exams') include: the VCE in Victoria, the HSC in New South Wales, the QCE Exams in Queensland, the WACE, and the SACE. Teachers and schools, therefore, must work with these systems and often have little if any agency to work outside them to ensure that a student has an inclusive examination or test experience.

Table 11.1 offers further examples of the type of arrangements and supports given to students with a disability:

The Victorian Curriculum and Assessment Authority (VCAA, 2023) offers exhaustive guidance about types of Special Examination Arrangements and rules around the use of each arrangement pertinent to Victorian schools (VCAA, VCAA (2023).

Website: https://www.vcaa.vic.edu.au/administration/special-provision/special-examination-arrangements-vce-external-assessments

Connections: barriers to inclusive assessment in an examination or test

The VCAA is 'a statutory body' which is 'responsible for developing high quality early learning and development frameworks, curriculum for school aged students and assessment products and services.' (VCAA, 2023a). Policy

Table 11.1 Arrangements and supports

Student	Arrangement/support	Reason
Josey has ADHD	25% extra time Private, quiet room for the exam.	Josey can be easily distracted by others and requires extra time to focus on the exam questions.
Bilan is deaf and communicates by sign language (Auslan)	25% extra time. Private, quiet room for the exam. Extra time. An Auslan interpreter supports Bilan.	Bilan will need extra time to process the exam questions. The Auslan interpreter will coordinate communication between the supervising staff and ensure that Bilan understands what is being asked of him.
Will is recovering from COVID-19 and has periods of extreme fatigue	25% extra time. Extra rest breaks.	Will requires rest periods to prevent or mitigate any extreme fatigue in the exam.

and practice on special considerations for students with a disability in Victoria are determined by the VCAA, which comments, 'The VCAA recognises that some students with a disability, as defined in the Disability Discrimination Act 1992 (Australian Government, 1992), or illness may require Special Examination Arrangements to enable them to access the examination/test questions and communicate their responses in a timed external assessment.' (VCAA 2023b, Special Examination Arrangements). The VCAA communicates several practices, procedures/processes, and conditions necessary for schools to access special examinations. These are:

1 **Process.** That the school must make the application for special consideration, and the application process must be followed and must use VCAA's Special Provision Online (SPO) system.
2 **Approach.** That each student's needs are treated on a case-by-case basis.
3 **Evidence.** That the application should be informed by 'school-based evidence and recommendations taking into consideration any additional academic and educational assessments and independent evidence provided with the application.' (VCAA 2023b, Special Examination Arrangements).

This information by VCAA (2023b) details, for example:

Practices: teamwork to deliver the application and engage in the application process (teacher, school leaders, parents, external specialists, and the VCAA); consultation about a student's needs (between teacher, school leaders, parents, external specialists, and the VCAA).
Procedures: administrative processes sticking to the application process set out (VCAA – School application) and to the timescales involved. Use of the VCAA's Special Provision Online (SPO) system.

Conditions: active support by the school's senior management, independent evidence of the impact of a child's disability on their learning, and likely performance in an examination or test; knowledge of the VCAA's SPO system; up-to-date knowledge of the student's disability, its impact on their learning, and likely impact on performance in an examination or test; and supportive parents/family.

Barriers to an inclusive educational experience in exams/summative assessments

The practices, procedures and conditions detailed above disclose several potential barriers to inclusive assessment involving exam consideration for a student studying for VCE in Victoria. Here are some possible scenarios that could prevent a student from receiving Special Examination Arrangements:

1. **Information.** The school does not have access to the necessary reports from external specialists because parents do not engage with requests to share reports. Given that parents of students with a disability can face systemic barriers to engagement (see Chapter 8: **Building strong parent-school partnerships**), this is an important possibility.
2. **Clarity.** Reports from external specialists are insufficiently clear or applied to the impact of a child's disability on their capacity to sit a test or examination. Research on this topic has highlighted that the lack of educational application is a recurring problem in reports from external specialists (Armstrong, 2018),
3. **Capacity.** School staff do not have the capacity to complete the documentation and coordinate the application in sufficient time. There are insufficient staff available with sufficient expertise and experience (this scenario is increasingly likely given current pressures on school staffing).
4. **Circumstances.** The student and/or family are absent during key periods in writing the application. The school staff member responsible for. Emails from the VCAA are missed or go to the junk folder.

Recommendation for practice: Teachers and school leaders should be mindful of constraints affecting Special Examination Arrangements which arise from assessment regulation. Strong, ongoing relationships with parents of students with a disability to enable information-sharing, timely application for Special Examination Arrangements. Developing and maintaining strong relationships with external stakeholders and writing reports (plus clarity around what is needed for special arrangements) will offset some, but not all, of these system constraints of students with a disability and is often problematic in terms of the stated aim of ensuring fair assessment for such students.

Questions and answers

Here are some questions and suggested answers pertinent to the Preparation Lesson for Carey.

Q1. How might this lesson have been integrated into English writing activities for the whole class?

A1. The trip to Mount Buang could be used, conveniently, to plan and deliver learning in the English (writing) area for other children in Carey's class. The lesson aims and content would simply be *differentiated* so that what is delivered is flexibly able to meet the needs of different students. For example, the words chosen for the story, e.g. 'snow', could be more complex (e.g. 'snowfall') or could even be sentences constructed by the student for assembly into a more sophisticated story than the one produced by Carey.

Q2. How might learning from this lesson be extended?

A2. **An extension task could be set.** Jay sets an extension task for Carey for later in the week: to find out the history of the name 'Mount Donna Buang' using Carey's Chromebook. Carey will need support to search the written information presented. A sentence starter example could also be used to deepen Carey's understanding of the review process and of how to go beyond simple descriptive thought about experiences.

Q3. Is there anything else structurally missing from the lesson that might improve learning for Carey?

A3. Yes. Jay, at the end, could add a structural component to the lesson called 'Connect with next lesson/next learning' and which helps Carey connect learning in this lesson with the next in advancing his story about a trip to Mount Donna Buang. In this section, Jay should use clear, concise language to foreshadow how learning in this lesson will be extended in the next lesson.

Jay: 'Next time we will…'

Highlighting the sequence of learning and how this learning connects across lessons is important for the application, fluency and maintenance phases in the learning process. Students need to identify and be able to recall what they have learned to apply their learning in future.

Resources

Here are some suggested resources for information and inspiration.

Visual journals. Here is an excellent guide to the use of Visual Journals by the collective redesign:

Website: https://www.redesignu.org/creatively-communicating-metacognition-and-meaning-making-art-visual-journaling-learning/

The noun project: an excellent resource for simple but stylish icons and symbols which are free to use under the Creative Commons licence. Users need to sign up to access the range of designs. Remember to mention (attribute) the kind designers who share their designs:

https://thenounproject.com/

Accessible story writing

100 Story Building describes itself as a 'unique organisation for young writers in Footscray, Melbourne. We use storytelling as a tool to foster imagination, creativity and confidence in children and young people'. No-cost resources are available on their website and are designed with disadvantaged students in mind:

Website: https://www.100storybuilding.org.au/about-us

12 Safety in school and bullying prevention

> This chapter will help you:
>
> - Understand what critical incidents are in an educational context and how to prepare for them.
> - Understand how to reduce risks to your safety and that of your students in the classroom due to aggressive, violent, self-injurious or dangerous behaviours by a student.
> - Plan in case a critical incident arises and be prepared.
> - Recognise the impact (s) of bullying and consider your professional response.
> - Meet your responsibilities under Work Health Safety (WHS) and your duty of care.
> - Recognise that ensuring safety is a key aspect of educational inclusion.
>
> The Australian Institute for Teaching and School Leadership (AITSL) Graduate Teacher Standards covered by this learning include:
>
> 1.6 Strategies to support full participation of students with disability.
> 4.3 Manage challenging behaviour.
> 4.4 Maintain student safety.
>
> This section connects with **Behaviour: building and maintaining calm and productive classrooms**, which we suggest is a pre-reading to this section.

Introduction

Ensuring that schools are safe working environments is a key occupational Work Health Safety (WHS) issue for everyone employed in education. State and territory education departments have a legal obligation to ensure that

DOI: 10.4324/9781003669630-14

employees are safe in their workplace. This obligation is reflected in policies which require that all schools have, for example, 'procedures and strategies in place for managing and reporting incidents and for promoting learning environments that are safe and supportive.' (Department of Education and Training, n.d.).

Ensuring safe schools is, however, made even more pertinent for this book to address and for two reasons:

1 **Exclusion and suspension.** Safety concerns on account of aggressive, violent, self-injurious, or dangerous behaviours are a major driver for teachers and schools for the suspension and exclusion of students with a disability (Roy, 2016). Addressing these concerns without resorting to exclusion is a priority.
2 **Safety-disability connection.** Students with a disability, or other differences or facing other disadvantages, are at elevated risk of feeling that schools are unsafe for them, due to discrimination and/or bullying.

As guidance when considering safety as grounds for the exclusion and suspension of a student with a disability, we follow the recommendations of the Disability Royal Commission Final Report (DRC, 2023) and urge you to do the same. The Royal Commission Final Report (DRC, 2023, p. 96) states

- Education providers should avoid the use of exclusionary discipline on students with disability, unless it is necessary as a last resort to avert the risk of serious harm to the student, other students, or staff.
- In considering the use of exclusionary discipline, consider the student's disability, needs, and age and particularly the effects on young children.
- Require steps be taken before exclusion to ensure an individual behaviour plan and reasonable adjustments have been implemented for the student.
- Include a robust review or appeals process for students with disability and their families or carers and supporters.

In this section, we focus on aggressive, violent, or dangerous behaviours by a student in the physical classroom in the physical school setting as a helpful start when considering safety, and we also, more briefly, discuss bullying.

Recommendation for practice: many deeply damaging behaviours occur without the obvious aggressive, acting-out presentation or violence

As highlighted in **Behaviour: building and maintaining calm and productive classrooms,** we urge the reader to avoid assuming that aggression, defiance, or violence is the sum of 'behaviour', especially by students with a disability. Many deeply damaging behaviours occur in students without the obvious aggressive, acting-out, or defiant presentation.

Mobile phones, computers, and other technologies under the banner of 'Information and Communication Technologies' (ICT) and the online environments which they host are a complex, still emerging area where teacher and student safety can be compromised – we encourage the reader to consult the latest advice in their jurisdiction to understand best practice. The Australian Curriculum (v 9) has well-developed educational resources for students about online safety, including easy-read versions:

Weblink: https://v8.australiancurriculum.edu.au/resources/curriculum-connections/portfolios/online-safety/

Prevention is better than having to respond

Preventing an unsafe situation from happening in the first place is far superior to having to respond to an incident impacting teacher or student safety (Cooper, 2015; Stevenson *et al.*, 2022). Many existing policies and recommended classroom practices published by Australian states and territories refer to preventing an event from happening in the first place.

Definition: occupational violence (OV)

Events which involve harm coming to teachers or students from events involving aggressive or dangerous behaviours by a student are collectively known as occupational violence or OV (Stevenson *et al.*, 2022).

Much of the content of this book is devoted to establishing and maintaining a calm, safe, and productive classroom environment, and we suggest that the reader refer to sections on differentiation, establishing routines, effective praise, and mental health when thinking about how to avoid OV from happening. If consistently applied, then the approaches, strategies, supports, and interventions recommended in these sections of the book will help build safe, calm, and productive classrooms, preventing problem behaviours or OV from happening and reducing severity if incidents do occur. Our critical observation about OV is that the OV incident is often focussed upon in schools, without consideration of what could have been done to prevent the incident happening in the first place – a point also picked up by research on this topic (Armstrong *et al.*, 2015; Duong and Bradshaw, 2013; Kor *et al.*, 2023; Leuschner *et al.*, 2017; Stevenson *et al.*, 2022). A recommendation on this point is given below.

Recommendation for practice: focus on what led up to the incident involving aggressive or dangerous behaviours, as well as what happened in the incident itself. In this focus, we suggest that teachers and school leaders ask what could, reasonably, have been done differently by school staff (teachers, support staff, school leadership, psychologists, parents) to prevent it or reduce its severity/any harm caused.

Despite preventative efforts, it is inevitable that incidents involving OV will, occasionally, occur. What immediately follows touches on several specific issues before, during and after an incident occurs, focusing on aggressive, violent, or dangerous behaviours. As such, this content is an extension of **Behaviour: building and maintaining calm and productive classrooms.**

De-escalation: a definition

Many major incidents in school resulting in OV have a small beginning and can emerge out of what adults regard as trivial events. The process of 'raising the stakes' in an interaction is called *escalation*. Health guidelines (National Institute for Health and Care Excellence, 2015) from the United Kingdom (UK) on preventing violence in psychiatric mental health settings define this process:

> The occurrence of a violent incident is generally portrayed as the culmination of a gradually escalating behaviour pattern, starting with restlessness, moving through agitation and irritability, through verbal aggression, gestures, threats, damage to objects in the surrounding area and culminating in an assault' and add 'When such a gradually developing behaviour pattern is seen, it allows most scope for prevention, diversion and de-escalation. (p. 5)

Here is an explanation of The Escalation Cycle, including a discussion of how understanding this cycle and its components can help a teacher select when and where to de-escalate or even, ideally, prevent OV from happening in the first place. Please note that de-escalation is no substitute for prevention via ongoing support to ensure that a student's personal and academic needs are being met in school. This note is especially relevant when a student has a disability because we know from many studies that a lack of reasonable adjustment and ongoing support for such students is a major cause of incidents that are labelled by schools as OV (Armstrong and Armstrong, 2021).

- **Curving line:** The curving line plots emotional intensity over time. The left-hand, steeply rising, sector of the line represents escalation, and the right-hand portion of the line represents recovery, where arousal declines and the student, eventually, adopts a calm state.
- **Crisis zone:** this is the highest point of escalation and the point where aggressive, dangerous, or violent actions typically occur.
- **X and Y axes:** The vertical y-axis indicates the level of emotional arousal – what level of anger is the student experiencing? The horizontal x-axis represents time. For simplicity, no units of time have been given, but this is likely to be measured in minutes.
- **Dotted lines:** meltdown risk; low mood risk; and exhaustion risk. These, approximately, plot risks occurring in the recovery stage of an escalation. Meltdown refers to an uncontrolled state of emotional distress – a student may cry at this point and be overwhelmed by shame at their actions and

distress. Low mood can result from shame or emotional exhaustion. Some students may want to self-harm here, or simply hide away from others. Exhaustion can be the outcome of the escalation process.

Discussion

Pre-correction, distraction, and trigger

There are two points in prevention of escalation: pre-correction and distraction. Both prevention strategies are possible immediately before a child is triggered and can prevent a trigger from generating the steep ascent in emotional arousal, driven by negative emotions (e.g. anger, frustration). The timeframe for use of pre-correction and distraction by the teacher is, however, often small (minutes typically). So the teacher needs to quickly recognise the presence of a potential trigger for a child and swiftly act to avoid escalation (Stevenson et al., 2022). Knowledge of what triggers a student, monitoring and action if any early signs of triggering present are all necessary, but there are major benefits for the student, teacher, and other students in the class if escalation is avoided.

Crisis zone

In this zone, de-escalation is unlikely and the student will be focussed on verbally or physically expressing negative emotions. In the crisis zone, we recommend that the teacher present:

1 **Assess** potential risks quickly and calmly (will this likely escalate to physical violence? Destruction of property? Risk of harm to students? Risk of harm to the teacher?)
2 **Prioritise their safety** and that of others (students, colleagues).
3 **Evacuate the class,** if necessary, block physical aggression by moving furniture to protect you, students, and/or colleagues in harm's way.
4 **Call for assistance** from colleagues immediately.

It is important that the teacher calls for assistance immediately (by phone or verbally), and if this is not possible, then we recommend that the teacher send a trusted member of the class to call for aid from the nearest colleague. If safe to do so, and this depends on the exact situation, wait until the student has expressed these emotions and be ready to support the recovery process.

Recovery

This is usually a lengthier part of the escalation process. For the student perpetrating aggressive, dangerous, or violent behaviour, there is a risk of meltdown, low mood, and exhaustion. The teacher may also feel the physical and psychological after-effects of shock. Literature on OV highlights how important care, compassion and support from colleagues are at this point for teachers impacted by OV (Armstrong *et al.*, 2015; Stevenson et al., 2022). 'Team around the teacher' is the phrase used to denote this support in recommendations for practice given later in this section. Debriefing of the student about the incident can also happen at the end of recovery, but often, it must be done hours or days after the incident. Typically, the school senior management team deal with the end phase of recovery, as parents are notified and asked to collect their child pending investigation and formal reporting of a critical incident.

It is important that those directly impacted have the time and space to recover. In some cases, staff may have to seek medical treatment for injuries sustained and/or go home, emergency services may need to be called in rare incidents. To minimise harm and help-seeking, we recommend that affected teachers be provided with appropriate counselling and mental health support information as soon as possible. What applies to teachers also fully applies to any students who have been directly impacted by the incident, whether the harm caused is unintentional, as illustrated in the vignette later in this chapter involving Darren, or fully intentional. Informing parents of the situation as soon as possible is essential and should be part of the initial response by the school's senior leadership team.

The impact on students who witness the incident is sometimes overlooked. Students may need counselling and support from teachers and other support staff (e.g. school well-being leaders) or may need to take time out to recover from what they witnessed. It is also paramount that recovery involves a return to 'normal' learning at the first appropriate opportunity and requires additional staffing to transition back to scheduled classes.

The process of escalation and recovery is also described as the 'Acting out cycle' by Colvin and Scott (2014) and who argue that it contains seven distinct phases moving from calm to recovery. The United States-based (US-based) IrisCenter have created some excellent video resources about the acting-out cycle and the process by which a teacher can intervene and de-escalate.

Here is an excellent, highly practical video talk-through of ten de-escalation strategies from UK-based specialist teacher Scott McFarnell:

Weblink: https://youtu.be/Py2T-Gsqq7s?si=PYXvInjfs2uTG_ZC

Connections: ADHD, developmental disabilities, and impulse aggression

What is described as 'acting out cycle' in schools and education, is connected to what psychologists call self-regulation and a phenomenon called inhibitory response. To explain, we might want to scream and shout our frustration in frustrating situations, or worse, but well-adjusted individuals self-regulate (most of the time!) and a learned inhibitory response prevents acting on our impulses with aggression or impulse, if we fail to self-regulate then we can present with a behaviour known as 'impulse aggression' (Pawliczek *et al.*, 2013).

Research has established that individuals with attention-deficit/hyperactivity disorder (ADHD) and developmental disabilities impacting behavioural development are particularly vulnerable to 'impulse aggression' and disinhibited behaviour (Puiu et al., 2018; Raaijmakers et al., 2008). Note that 'vulnerable' does not imply that every or even *most* students affected by ADHD and developmental disabilities will present in this way.

Research into self-regulation, with typically developing students, has indicated that self-regulation is present in pre-school children (aged four) and that poor self-regulation in pre-school children, if not addressed, is a predictor of aggression later in adolescence (age 13 upwards) (Robson et al., 2020). This finding highlights the deep roots of aggressive behaviour in many students' lives – with or without a disability. Furthermore, recognising the early origins of aggressive behaviour for all students suggests that pre-school is the ideal place for early intervention to help children learn self-regulation and a solid inhibitory response. When a student cannot self-regulate, recommendations for school-based practice are given below.

Recommendation for practice

We recommend focussed professional practice or support by a teacher, in helping students (with or without a disability) unlearn the use of aggressive behaviours and escalation when interacting with others. The effort and time required to reduce reliance on aggression and escalation for a student should not be estimated and is likely to be months or years (Armstrong *et al.*, 2015).

Explicit teaching of self-regulation and of the inhibitory response to students framed as a smarter, more mature reaction is a way forward when faced with emotionally challenging situations. Social emotional learning (SEL) programs can be used to teach or strengthen self-regulation. Further detail about this topic is given in **Behaviour: building and maintaining calm and productive classrooms.**

A developmentally appropriate explanation of the escalation cycle could be used as an educative tool here to help students start to learn how to control impulses and any negative underlying emotions. Understanding and applying the stages of change (transtheoretical model or TTM) given in **Behaviour: building and maintaining calm and productive classroom** is a key tool we recommend in helping deliver the above recommendations. Table 12.1 is given again below from this chapter to remind the reader about this longer-term (months, years) process of sustained change. Examples of what the teacher might say to a primary-age student are given. Note that the language used in examples below should be varied, considering each child's circumstances and level of development. Technological or other communication aids (e.g. sign language, AUSLAN) may be required to effectively communicate with students with speech and language impairments or other forms of disability, e.g. Autism Spectrum Disorder (ASD), impacting communication.

Table 12.1 Practical strategies to motivate students to replace negative behaviours with positives

Stage	What you can do
Pre-contemplation	Introduce doubt – raise the child's awareness about the risks of their current behaviours and its negative effect on them and others, e.g. 'What will happen if you carry on?'
Contemplation	Tip the balance: help the child understand that no change involves risks and negatives. 'Classmates won't want to be your friend.'
Determination	Help the child pick the best route to achieve change for them. 'Let's agree how you can change.'
Action	Help the child make concrete steps – what actions and decisions should they take? 'Let's figure out what to do if you're angry.'
Maintenance	Assist the child to avoid preventing relapse by learning strategies to maintain their new state. 'You were amazing – you didn't show anger. You kept cool.'
Relapse	Encourage the child to renew the process of contemplation, determination and action, without becoming demotivated. 'Keep this up – look at the new friends you now have – they love the new cool you.'

Case studies Shona, Anj, and Darren are given below to illustrate small beginnings to the process of escalation and offer the reader insights into the sheer variety of incidents which can occur under the banner of safety in school.

Shona: defiance and escalation

Shona is a Year 6 secondary student who has recently moved from another primary school interstate. From speaking to parents, support staff have signalled to Khalil, the teacher, that Shona 'has issues with self-regulation' and 'with anger management'. Shona has strong academic skills in English and can be a gregarious student. In a maths session one Thursday morning, Shona fails to open her Chromebook as requested and stares at the front of the classroom, unmoving. When asked again to begin work by Khalil, Shona is visibly irritated, unsettling nearby peers who begin to physically move away.

Khalil walks over to seated Shona and stands over her. Khalil raises his voice and engages eye contact 'Please OPEN your Chromebook as requested'.

Shona throws down her pencil and maths workbook, pushing her Chromebook (PC equivalent), which immediately falls onto the floor, loudly, breaking the screen. The classroom is silent, with students staring at Shona or the broken Chromebook in shock.

Q1. What should be the next response by the teacher Khalil?
Q2. From the above case study, can you identify a trigger point for Shona's aggressive behaviour?

Q3. What would be a reasonable, fair, and proportional response to Shona (and her teacher, Khalil) by the school in these circumstances?
Q4. Are there any learning points for school policy or professional practice in this case?

Anj: school uniform elopement (leaving school premises without permission)

Anj comes from a single-parent family that has experienced domestic violence. Anj experiences anxiety and is waiting for an appointment with the family GP for a mental health care plan. The school where Anj is enrolled (Year 7) are recently aware of these home circumstances.

The secondary school which Anj attends is on a 'uniform blitz' with the senior leadership team roaming the school at the start of the school day and reprimanding students who fail to wear the required school uniform. One Wednesday morning, Anj is stopped at the school gates by an angry Deputy Principal who says that he must visit the school office for a reprimand on account of his incorrect school uniform. Anj silently walks to the school office as the Deputy Principal remains at the gate on uniform duty.

Anj does not attend his morning form class and disappears, with his whereabouts unknown. The school contacts his mum, who is distraught at this news. The police were called later that day after concerns about his well-being. Anj's classmates overhear a teacher talking about this incident and are unsettled by his elopement.

Anj returns to his emergency accommodation the following morning after sleeping rough in an abandoned building overnight. It transpires that Anj's parent, his mum, was unable to wash his school trousers because they moved into emergency housing at the weekend and are behind on the laundry. Anj grabbed the only clean pair of trousers he could find that morning, which were not exactly school regulation (dark grey with a sports brand logo).

Q1. How should the Deputy Principal have responded?
Q2. From this case study, can you identify a trigger point for Anj's elopement?
Q3. Are there any learning points for school policy or professional practice in this case? How might staff or the school have responded differently?

Darren: injury at Breakfast Club

Darren is a compliant Year 6 Primary School student who enjoys learning. Darren also has an Intellectual Disability and is studying an adjusted, personalised curriculum suitable for his personal academic needs. Darren is a popular member of the class and likes to socialise. His classmate Kerry is a friend and is always happy to clarify anything that Darren is unsure of in his academic studies. Darren also lives in a disrupted home environment and often comes to school in dirty clothes without a schoolbag or having had breakfast. His teacher, Jill, is highly supportive and often discreetly provides him with clean clothes and personal care items (toothbrush, toothpaste). The family receive support from a social worker and Adult Mental Health Services. Darren's family own several large Alsatian dogs which live in their house, and sometimes Darren's clothes smell of dog or even dog faeces.

Darren is attending the school Breakfast Club on Thursday morning and is eating his toast when three members of his class, including his friend Kerry, appear in the Breakfast Club area. A classmate, called Carl, sniggers 'Dogshit Darren' as they approach and is reprimanded by Kerry. Carl laughs at Kerry's reprimand. This interaction is witnessed by Darren, who is shaking with distress and protective anger. He pushes Carl, who pushes back. Darren hits Carl hard in the face, and Carl falls, catching his head on a corner of the Breakfast Club table, sustaining a large cut to his temple.

The Deputy Principal is first on the scene and freezes in shock at the sight of Carl, who is bleeding and semi-conscious on the ground. For several moments, nothing happens.

Q1. Why did the Deputy Principal freeze in inaction?
Q2. How should the Deputy Principal respond to Carl's injury?
Q3. From this case study, can you identify a trigger point for Darren?
Q4. What would be a reasonable, fair, and proportional response to Darren (and Carl) by the school in the circumstances?
Q5. Are there any learning points for school policy or professional practice in this case?

Learning points and recommendations for practice from Shona, Anj, and Darren

Here are some learning points which we suggest from Shona, Anj, and Darren, including recommendations for practice based on these insights.

- **Predictability.** Many, but not all, violent or dangerous incidents can be predicted. Adults often play a key role in escalating the process, either directly (e.g. Shona) through 'upping the stakes' or indirectly through acting as a trigger for the behaviour (e.g. Anj) (Armstrong *et al.*, 2015; Colvin and Scott, 2014). Use of the FBA process described in **Behaviour: building and maintaining calm and productive classrooms** enables a teacher to identify whether they or an adult is an indirect trigger. For instance, the student behaviours are driven by the need for attention from the teacher. Even negative attention can be the purpose for violent, aggressive, or dangerous by some students. Wilful, public destruction of school property (e.g. breaking pencils and hurling them at classmates, or smashing furniture) is often involved in attention-seeking.
- **Know the signs, know the student.** Irritability and negative body language are often signs that violent, aggressive, self-harming or dangerous

behaviours are likely (NICE, 2015). Knowledge of at-risk students is vital in detecting these signs and a basis for defusing the situation *before* it escalates (e.g. for students Shona and Darren). Information sharing about at-risk students is vital, and this is aided by having a secure, confidential, up-to-date, central source of at-risk students in the school.

- **Have a plan.** Working with colleagues, set up a practical, informal plan of action for what to do should a violent or dangerous incident occur. Agree to assist colleague(s) should they require help; for instance, if they need to move some or all students from a classroom in the event of an incident. The critical incident plan, which follows, presents a formal structure for this plan but can be supplemented by informal agreement between professionals.
- **Acknowledge the acting-out cycle**. Have preventative strategies ready for at-risk students (pre-correction, distraction) before they are triggered, and strategies ready to use as soon as possible if a student is triggered.
- **Find your inner calm** but remain ready to act decisively to defuse any aggression or mitigate its effects on you and others present (Shona, Darren). Deep breathing techniques and self-talk ('Keep calm, Dave ... it will pass').
- **Respond quickly.** Prioritise your safety and that of others (students, colleagues) in the immediate vicinity of the event (Darren). Knowledge of basic first aid is desirable.
- **Expect the unexpected.** As in the case of Anj, bear in mind that unexpected incidents can always happen in schools. Self-blame should be avoided, and, as stated at the start of this section, we recommend asking, critically, about what could have been done differently in these incidents as the best approach. This critical evaluation is illustrated further in the critical incident plan, which follows.
- **Take time to recover.** Debrief with colleagues and speak to occupational counselling services if you feel it might be beneficial. School leadership (not you!) have the responsibility to arrange cover for teaching if you are physically or emotionally impacted by an incident. Remember that directly or indirectly impacted students require immediate support too, coordinated by the school senior management.

Recommendations for practice

An Australian study by Stevenson *et al*. (2022) into OV and aggression against teachers recommends that the following two actions be taken by school leaders/the school after an incident has happened:

1. **Team around the teacher.** Ensure professional and emotional support for affected teachers from work colleagues.
2. **Debriefing.** Support debriefing post-event: purposefully discussing with the student what occurred in a way that identifies what exactly happened and encourages reflection.

One clear message given by Sprague and Walker (2021), in their book about safety in US schools, is that it is very important for schools to identify, monitor and share information about students at risk of involvement in a critical incident (p. 52).

Effectively and quickly sharing information on issues affecting a student's well-being or safety outside of school is key to planning and anticipating incidents in school before they happen (Stevenson *et al.*, 2022). Knowledge of this wider context and a student's level of development is a key to a fair, considered, and proportionate response by the school should an incident happen, as is part of the recommendation by recent policy (DRC, 2023). This background knowledge was missing in the case of Anj and led to a situation where he absconded, with concerns over his safety. A classroom escalation based on power or attention is often more difficult for a student to achieve if the other person in the interaction (teacher, parent) does not cooperate in this destructive game. Often, the adult presence can be a trigger for the escalation itself (Colvin and Scott, 2014) something discussed in **Behaviour: building and maintaining calm and productive classrooms**, and can be a focus for emotional development support with a student.

School safety and critical incident response plan

Sprague and Walker (2021) author a thorough and highly practical book about designing a critical incident plan in the context of building safe and healthy schools in the US. The crises they describe, including natural disasters, gang activity on campus, or a 'shooter' in school, when discussing a critical incident response plan, are beyond the more modest focus of this section and of this book but may be of interest to readers who wish an insight into these topics which impact school safety in severe ways. Given below is an example of a critical incident response plan relevant to an Australian context and referring to Shona, Anj, and Darren (see Table 12.2).

Definitions

Here are some definitions of bullying and victimisation for clarity.

Bullying is a student's exposure "repeatedly and over time, to negative actions on the part of one or more other students" (Olweus, 2013, p. 755). Eilts and Koglin (2022), in their Australian study of bullying in school, add that when considering bullying, 'Another important concept that should be taken into consideration is the concept of unequal level of effect meaning that the victim is left traumatised by the victimisation, whereas the perpetrator is left unaffected by their actions' (p. 133). Bullying can also take subtle forms. One type is called 'covert bullying' and consists of indirect social aggression and exclusion, including verbal rejection, spreading slanderous rumours, or deliberate social exclusion (Cross *et al.*, 2009; Moffat *et al.*, 2019).

Safety in School and Bullying Prevention 175

Table 12.2 Critical incident response plan

Stage	Purpose	Example of practice or actions	Who is responsible
1 Risk assessment	To assess how likely it is that the incident will happen.	All teaching staff, including casual relief teachers/temporary staff, are aware of the students they teach who are at risk of problem behaviours or who have risk factors (a disability, mental health condition or who are in the care system).	All teaching professionals in contact with at-risk students, with guidance from the school senior leadership team.
2 Preparation and preparedness	To make reasonable preparations for the incident.	Emergency school contacts are accessible for all teaching staff should they require aid or support. The school has sufficient staffing and expertise to respond to critical incidents. The school has a clear risk reduction plan with risk reduction systems, processes and procedures known to all staff.	The school senior leadership team and the state, territory, or area education department. Students would benefit from knowing what to do in the event of a classroom evacuation.
3 Response	Actions in immediate response to an incident.	The teacher de-escalates a potential incident. Basic first aid is delivered to an injured student; assistance is called for quickly (Darren).	Teaching staff, with support from everyone in the school community.
4 Recovery	Considering how the classroom or school returns to normal operation after an incident.	A member of the senior Leadership Team supervises or assists the affected teacher when a class has been impacted by an incident. Senior leadership sensitively consults with parents and/or students/the school community about an appropriate response in recovering from the impact of a major incident.	The school senior leadership team.
5 Review	Lessons for policy or professional practice arising from the incident.	Did the enforcement of the school uniform policy contribute to the incident? Should enforcement change? (Anj). Do teaching staff need further supports in the classroom, i.e. advice from a behaviour specialist or professional learning about how to avoid triggering problem behaviour? (Shona) or support from wider professionals. Staffing ratio: should two staff always be present at the Breakfast Club? (Darren).	The school senior leadership team and state, territory, or area education department, with input from frontline teaching staff and the wider school community, including parents.

Victimisation is where a student is deliberately targeted by a person or persons and is typically part of the bullying. Physical appearance is one of the weapons often used to cause psychological harm (Frisén et al., 2008) in the process of victimisation. Physical or psychological difference from 'the norm' is commonly directed at students with a disability by perpetrators of bullying (Cross et al., 2009).

Connections

A large-cohort, Australian-based study by Moffat et al. (2019) examined covert bullying of students with a disability in the middle primary years (Years 4–8) who self-identified as living with disability (p. 614). Data was taken from a survey conducted as part of the Australian Child Wellbeing Project (ACWP – www.australianchildwellbeing.com.au) (p. 616) and involved a national sample of 4,753 Australian 8–14 year olds, 490 of whom self-identified as living with disability (p. 613). Moffat et al. (2019) summarise the results of research:

> This study shows that among primary school students, girls with disability experience a significantly higher incidence of frequent covert bullying than girls without disability. Among secondary school students, both boys and girls with disability experience more frequent covert bullying than those without disability. (p. 622)

Although Moffat et al. (2019) report higher rates of covert bullying than other international studies on this topic, these findings are consistent with other earlier studies (Sentenac et al., 2013). The authors highlight how participating high-school students who self-identified as female reported 'significantly higher levels of covert bullying (57% compared with 28%)'. In response to this elevated risk based on gender, Moffat et al. (2019) suggest that 'Awareness training to create belonging for all students within the classroom has been shown to have positive impact on bullying rates overall… and may be particularly valuable in reducing target vulnerability of girls with disability' (p. 624).

Bullying prevention

Bullying is a major safety issue facing all students, but particularly those with a disability or facing other forms of disadvantage (DRC, 2023; Humphrey and Hebron, 2014). A student cannot be included in a school and have a successful school life if they feel psychologically or physically unsafe, and too many students with a disability feel neither.

In terms of scale of harm caused to affected children and young people, evidence from many studies, spanning decades of research, highlights that the harm caused can be lifelong and severe in its impact on a student's psychological well-being (Humphrey and Hebron, 2014). At Hearing 7 of the Disability Royal Commission in 2020, one parent who lived in Queensland gave an example of how her son, Quaden, was bullied at school and its impact. Quaden has Achondroplasia, which is a type of dwarfism:

> Ms Bayles gave evidence about Quaden's experience of bullying at his school. She spoke of incidents including Quaden 'being called names, and pushed on the ground, as well as being isolated and left out...' (p. 12). Ms Bayles emphasised the impact of the bullying on Quaden, noting that 'it got to the point where sometimes he was attempting suicide multiple times in a day.'(pp. 10–11)

Robust research details that students, like Quaden, who experience bullying are at elevated risk of 'Mental illness, suicide, weaker social relationships', with flow-on negative impacts on a student's physical health (Kavanagh *et al.*, 2016). The negative impacts from bullying can often result in students being withdrawn from school by concerned parents – effectively *excluded* on account of inaction or ineffective response by schools (DRC, 2023). Students with a disability are over-represented in this category (Armstrong and Armstrong, 2021), but many students with no known disability are also withdrawn for this reason, according to research. Students who report experienced bullying seem over-represented in out-of-school education provision such as Flexible Learning Options (FLO) (Bills *et al.*, 2020).

The research is clear that whole-school bullying prevention programs are the best prevention, but there is currently limited research on what works best for students with a disability (Houchins *et al.*, 2016; Moffat *et al.*, 2019).

In light of this gap in evidence and with respect to covert bullying of students with a disability, Moffat *et al.* (2019) highlight the value of classroom and schoolwide strategies that focus on reducing social isolation of students with disability, and challenging tolerance of covert bullying among all students (that is, reducing the population of potential aggressors). They also add that 'Structured environments that reduce opportunities for bullying in the context of the routine activities that make up the school day are also important' (p. 623). With respect to classroom structure and routine, the reader may wish to refer to the section **Establishing routines** in this book.

Which whole-school bullying prevention program?

Readers who are teachers or enter the profession in future are likely to find that their employer has already signed up to an existing whole-school bullying prevention program. Choosing a whole-school bullying prevention program to adopt is surprisingly difficult for Australian schools. This choice also needs to be carefully evaluated according to the local needs of the setting. Readers should be mindful that at the time of writing, there is limited research evidence on the most effective program for students with a disability. Details of available Australian whole-school bullying prevention programs are given in Resources.

Bringing it together

Bullying in schools overlaps with OV discussed in this section. Aggressive, dangerous, or violent behaviours in the classroom can, in many cases, be a crisis response by a student to their negative experience of bullying by classmates or by a teacher. Given that students with a disability are often targeted by bullies, it is no surprise that they occasionally respond with aggression. The vignette Darren, given earlier, is an example of this response and where his experience of victimisation triggers anger and violence. Given that students with a disability are at elevated risk of experiencing bullying or victimisation in school, it is entirely predictable that some will respond with aggressive, dangerous, or violent behaviours. In this case, teachers and schools should ask critical questions about whether anti-bullying policies were effective, as well as respond proportionally to victimised students.

Effective differentiation, building a positive classroom culture, and other supports for the needs of students with disability detailed in this book, are essential progressive supports necessary to reduce bullying and OV for a student with a disability and part of the bigger tapestry which makes up a safe school environment.

Further resources

There is a range of non-cost programs, resources, and initiatives publicly available to Australian schools on OV prevention and reduction and on bullying prevention. Prominent examples are given below. On these topics, the readers should note, however, that public schools have often been allocated preferred programs, resources, and initiatives chosen by their local education department or equivalent.

Occupational violence prevention and reduction

Here is an excellent video resource on de-escalation by UK-based specialist teacher Scott McFarnell: **Weblink**: https://youtu.be/Py2T-Gsqq7s?si=PYXvInjfs2uTG_ZC

The US-based Department of Cybersecurity and Infrastructure Security (CISA) has published an excellent one-page guide to de-escalation. The recommendations on changing verbal communication and on body language are particularly good: **Weblink**: https://www.cisa.gov/sites/default/files/2022-11/De-Escalation_Final%20508%20%2809.21.21%29.pdf

Australian schoolwide anti-bullying programs and resources

Kids Helpline

Website: https://kidshelpline.com.au/teens/issues/bullying **Call**: 1800 55 1800

Description: Kids Helpline is Australia's only free (even from a mobile), confidential 24/7 online and phone counselling service for those aged 5 to 25. Kids helpline offers advice and support on bullying to those directly affected, an overview of bullying and which is also useful for teachers or parents.

Description: kids' helpline

NSSF – National Safe Schools Framework

Website: https://studentwellbeinghub.edu.au/

Description: Since 2003, the NSSF has been the official national anti-bullying framework for all Australian schools. Lack of its implementation by schools led, in 2017, to a change and the Student Wellbeing Hub was formed to help implement the NSSF. Respectful relationships education is hosted by the Student Wellbeing Hub and tackles bullying as part of its larger focus on helping students have 'respectful, equal and non-violent relationships'.

Website: https://studentwellbeinghub.edu.au/respectful-relationships-education/

Bullying no way!

Website: https://bullyingnoway.gov.au/

Description: Several states, including South Australia, subscribe to Bullying Now Way – an initiative supported by the Australian Federal Government, and which includes anti-bullying resources and advice for teachers, schools and students.

Friendly Schools program

Website: https://friendlyschools.com.au/

Description: This school-based buying prevention program was evaluated by Le *et al.* (2021) and found to be effective for Australian primary schools. The authors highlight that these findings strongly support primary schools in considering implementing the Friendly Schools Program (p. 24). The National Mental Health Commission funded research by Le et al. (2021) and published an evaluation report (n.d.) (Cross et al., 2011)

The National Mental Health Commission notes that the *Friendly Schools Program* requires significant investment by schools for school psychologists and teachers in learning how the program operates, but concludes that this investment was cost-effective in preventing depression among students affected by bullying.

Part III
Final words

13 Key learnings

This section will help you:

- Summarise key learning points from this book.
- Identify which learning points are most relevant to you.
- Formulate a plan of action relevant to your personal or professional life.
- Identify gaps in learning or personal understanding about educational inclusion of students with a disability, with a focus on how to address these through fact-finding.

The Australian Institute for Teaching and School Leadership (AITSL) Graduate Teacher Standards covered by this section include:

6.2 Engage in professional learning and improve practice.
6.3 Engage with colleagues and improve practice.
6.4 Apply professional learning and improve student learning.
7.4 Engage with professional teaching networks and broader communities.

Introduction

The ultimate learning point from this book is that it is now over to you, the reader, to consider what you have read and how to apply it to your context. What this means exactly and what happens next as a result depends on why you read this book in the first place and your professional interest in advancing inclusion in school or the wider world of education.

To encourage your process of consideration and application, this section offers what we consider to be the key learning points from this book. Yours may differ, and that's fine, but we hope that this section helps to bring together your journey through this book and be clear about what you have learned and how to transfer this knowledge into action. Rather than offer a standard

DOI: 10.4324/9781003669630-16

dot point summary of content in *The Inclusive Australian Teacher Handbook*, here, we offer a less traditional learning journey format, based on storytelling, and which is designed to help the reader recall and make sense of what they have read.

Your learning journey through *The Inclusive Teacher*

Our journey begins set against a crisis in the Australian school system and focused on the complex issue of **declining attendance** by students in the public school system, particularly affecting students with a disability. Against this grim background, we offer the more positive learning point that educational inclusion has a key role to play in combating declining attendance and is a distinctive feature of a well-functioning and sufficiently resourced public school system.

We encounter **myths about inclusion and objections** to its application in practice next along the road. Along this journey, the authors wanted readers to encounter the bad, sad, and sometimes bizarre objections that are levelled at inclusion. We encourage our travellers to take a sceptical but compassionate attitude to these dissenting voices and the half-truths occasionally circulating in staffrooms. To help with the sceptical element of what we recommend, a simple framework was given based on asking two questions about the person voicing the objection:

1. Who is voicing the objection? And
2. For what purpose?

And we recommended that how they frame the 'problem' they object is likely to give you a clue about this purpose if it is not clear and help you decide about whether it is a result of anxiety, a lack of knowledge, or self-interest.

The journey continues by clarifying what inclusion is and isn't in **Understanding inclusion.** We learn about the legal and professional responsibility of the teacher to include students with a disability and examine what the key phrase 'reasonable adjustment' involves in teacher professional practice. Current barriers to the application of educational inclusion in Australian schools are highlighted, such as the practice of gatekeeping. We look ahead at the hopeful future of inclusion in Australian schools as envisaged by important changes and improvements as recommended by the Disability Royal Commission (DRC, 2023). In keeping with our mission to 'make it real' for readers, we offer a thought-provoking case study of a school (School A) which is working hard to be inclusive. In this case study, based on a real school, we uncover some of the external factors that frustrate and undermine this committed work by teachers and school leaders at School A. **Understanding inclusion** ends by framing *The Inclusive Australian Teacher Handbook* as a practical guide for teachers about how to confidently apply inclusion in the classroom. We end on this constructive note by setting out how the content in the book and in your learning journey ahead maps to recommendations by the *Disability Royal Commission Final Report* (DRC, 2023). We provide this map to inspire confidence in the reader that their learning journey ahead is rooted in the best and most recent authority on this topic.

With this confidence established, the second and longest part of the journey begins: the 'how' of making inclusion happen in classrooms and the wider school for students with a disability. In this content about the how of inclusion, we have added a **Recommendation for practice** to help you consolidate your learning and gain confidence as you travel through each section. Look out for this sign and take a moment to note and consider what we recommend in your context.

This stage of the journey guides you through important 'bread and butter' topics in the inclusion of students with a disability in the classroom.

We begin with helping you become a developmentally-informed teacher in **Disability: becoming a developmentally-informed teacher.** This skillset refers to a teacher who understands and responds to each student's developmental needs, whatever these may be. We highlight how, when applied, this knowledge is indispensable when making 'reasonable adjustment' in the classroom with associated classroom accommodations as are set out by the law (Australian Government, 1992) – as discussed in **Understanding inclusion.** To help you achieve these benefits, this section briefly guides you through broad categories of disability and their likely impact on a student's development, education, and daily life. Readers also gain a deeper insight into the topic of disability with an explanation about developmental delay, complex needs, and Intelligence Quotient (IQ) (Roy & Dock, 2014).

Readers meet Ely, Jackie, and Zac as real-world case studies (vignettes) of students with a disability, and to help you unpack some of the complexities and dilemmas affecting professional practice.

To advance this section's developmental approach, we explain and illustrate stages in the typical learning process to students who are developing typically and those who are atypical. Here, you may find that this information is useful in itself and to help readers consolidate their understanding of how learning happens for all students. Readers are asked to apply this knowledge to help Ely, Jackie, and Zac overcome barriers to their learning.

Practically, developmental knowledge about the learning process benefits professional teacher practice because the teacher can help students when they encounter difficulties at a stage in the learning process or become stuck at a stage. Taking this developmental approach, as illustrated, is also far more inclusive and practical than the alternative of learning about thousands of possible types of disability, particularly since a student might not (yet) have a formal label but is still facing barriers to learning.

Differentiation and Universal Design for Learning, next, tackles two concepts central to 'the how' of inclusive teaching and learning. We define differentiation simply as teaching and learning which accommodates the varying ability levels of students but discuss more nuanced ideas about differentiation. To enable confidence about this topic, readers encounter one of the world's leading authorities on differentiation and consider what is, and what is not, differentiation. Through a case study scenario, readers are invited to apply this knowledge to help redesign a 'worksheet from hell' so that it can enable learning for all students in a class. Advice and guidance are also provided on designing resources to be read by students so that these are clear and accessible for all.

In the second half of this chapter, Universal Design for Learning (UDL) is outlined and explained. We note that UDL has attracted increased interest from schools and teachers in Australia. As the authors highlight, UDL asks teachers and school leaders to consider the physical and pedagogical design of the whole school environment (classrooms, corridors, yards, and more) and design-out or remove any barriers to success for students with a disability. By way of illustration, readers are asked to consider a real-world case study example of UDL in action and its benefits.

We travel through the short but important territory of **Establishing routines in the classroom**. Routines are increasingly emphasised in Australian educational policy as important for teachers to establish in all schools. This concise section acknowledges the point and provides guidance on how to establish routines in learning which support effective behaviours and habits for learning. The related concept of task analysis is explained, which has a history of application with students who have deep-seated barriers to learning routines and habits due to a disability. Routines necessary for daily living and self-care, as well as for academic learning, are important. A real-world example, the **Hope Valley College case study**, is provided to help readers see how routines necessary for daily living and self-care have been used. Readers are also encouraged to adopt a sceptical but realistic attitude to the benefits of routines in this section and are presented with some myths that have developed around their value.

Building strong parent-school partnerships guides the reader through this important topic. Many of the sections included in 'the how' section of this book, such as **Establishing routines** in the classroom, are most effective when reinforced in the home environment. Conversely, school-home communication breakdown can undermine learning and progress for a student with a disability, leading, in some cases, to the withdrawal of students by parents from a setting.

Parents of students with a disability have been, we think unfairly, regarded in some schools as one demographic who are 'hard to reach'. This section offers practical advice on how to overcome any barriers to engagement by parents of a student with a disability. We share advice from research evidence and from an industry stakeholder on what schools can do to build strong parent-school partnerships. Readers are invited to consider how to respond to a case study about a student called 'Jenny', which explores this topic from an attendance and well-being (mental health) perspective. Jenny's story connects with the complex and current issue of declining attendance by students in the Australian public school systems raised at the start of the book.

Behaviour by students with a disability is cited by schools as a reason for several practices which prevent their inclusion and are harmful for those involved and their families, as set out in **Understanding inclusion**. Many teachers cite problem behaviour as a major occupational problem in schools and identify improving behaviour in their classroom as a priority. Practically, if a student is not present in the classroom due to suspension or exclusion on behavioural grounds, then this is a fundamental ('existential') threat to what we recommend and advise.

Behaviour: building and maintaining calm and productive classrooms responds to these important issues. Readers are guided through universal and specialist interventions designed to reduce the severity and frequency of behaviours that interfere with learning. The scale of interventions and the research base for different interventions is expertly discussed, with 'Adam' and 'Maggie' given as case study scenarios to aid the reader's learning. In this section, we invite readers to critically unpick their own attitudes to behaviour and envisage how they can build and maintain a calm and productive space for learning. **Behaviour: building and maintaining calm and productive classrooms** has strong connections with the subsequent stops in our learning journey, and we recommend that it pairs perfectly with **Mental health in school: noticing, responding, and providing ongoing support** and with **Safety in schools and bullying prevention.**

Mental health in school: noticing, responding, and providing ongoing support to students extends your learning journey about student behaviour by considering mental health in schools. Here, you might encounter a rare find on your journey through this book. There are limited up-to-date books or book chapters designed for Australian teachers that discuss the practical issues surrounding mental health in the classroom. You meet case study students Maya and John, who experience mental health conditions, and you delve into some of the real-life issues involved with supporting students who have a mental health condition. *Noticing* when possible mental health difficulties may be affecting a student, but avoiding *labelling* is a key learning point offered. On this point, this section offers an empowering message: teachers, or indeed any professional, in contact with a student, are fully qualified to notice and quickly raise concerns with senior colleagues about a student's mental health (referred to by the term 'mental health concerns').

To aid practical action, the traveller is guided in this section through the three main current routes available to teachers in Australian schools for *referral* of students because of mental health concerns. Along this practical journey, there are stop points provided where the readers can dive into some of the deeper learning on this topic. Trauma and Adverse Childhood Experiences (ACEs) are discussed, along with trauma risk, and protective factors are detailed as a helpful framework for understanding why some students, such as those with disability, are more vulnerable to mental health conditions. Discrimination and disadvantage are highlighted as common root causes, and also accelerants, of a decline in a student's well-being.

This section ends with a tour of school-based programs to protect and nurture student mental health. Social-emotional learning (SEL) programs are introduced here as a broad family of programs used for this purpose.

For focus, a case study of nurture groups (Project X) is provided and as an example of an inclusive, multi-disciplinary, educational-therapeutic program delivered to students with a mental health condition who are at risk of exclusion from school because they present with challenging behaviour. We learn how students in Project X explicitly learn how to form and maintain relationships, engage in pro-social behaviours, and reduce their distress, plus advance their academic learning. The benefits of this dual therapeutic-educational approach are highlighted for students attending. Details are given on how the nurture group approach plays out in Project X in terms of how teachers interact with students, how teachers model appropriate behaviours in the project, the attitudes they hold about students, and, also, how they respond to a student in crisis. A case study, 'Jimmy', is given to illustrate how this approach works in practice.

Mental health in school: noticing, responding, and providing ongoing support to students ends by providing go-to resources for teachers in this topic, including helplines designed for children or young people's mental health. Helplines for teachers concerned about their own well-being are given, recognising that supporting students in distress can cause harm to the well-being of the teacher.

Up to this point in our journey, the 'how to' part of this book guides the reader through many of the key professional practices, professional knowledge, and often attitudes by professionals necessary for delivering inclusion in the classroom for students with a disability. How to plan for success in a student's learning and assessing educational progress for a student (are they learning effectively?) represent larger 'bookend' elements to professional practices already outlined in the 'how to' section of this book. We now come across **Planning and documenting inclusion: inclusive assessment and IEPs** in our journey, and quickly learn that the topics of assessment and of planning learning are important and, in the case of assessment, problematic for the inclusion of students with a disability.

This section is in two parts.

Part 1 Inclusive Assessment defines, evaluates, and explains inclusive assessment for students with a disability. This part evaluates whether assessment, as currently practised in Australia, is or can be inclusive. The involvement of students with a disability in senior school exams and in the National Assessment Program—Literacy and Numeracy (NAPLAN) is briefly discussed as prominent examples of assessment in the Australian education system. Our traveller will recall that national data on senior school exams and on NAPLAN indicate that neither cannot, as currently practised, be regarded as inclusive.

Inclusive alternative assessments are therefore explored, particularly, educational practices collectively called assessment for learning. We meet 'Carey', a case study student who has a disability, and observe how assessment for learning was used by the teaching assistant, Jay, and the class teacher, and how students can be supported across the curriculum (Roy et al., 2025).

Part 2 Individual Education Plans focuses on the why and how of planning and documenting learning. As we learn, the Individual Education Plan (IEP) is the key document where 'reasonable adjustments' are unpacked and detailed for a student with a disability.

Here, the authors draw on their considerable experience to guide the traveller through potential snakes (pitfalls) in the process of writing an IEP for a student and offer best-practice advice on how to avoid these problems. To illustrate best practices in action, Carey is referred to throughout Part 2 Individual Education Plans and as we move through the process of writing an IEP for a student with a disability. Carey's completed IEP is provided for the reader with annotations (notes) on this IEP explaining elements of good practice and other features in the completed document.

The final section of this book loops back to the start of our story and considers two essential conditions for the inclusion of students with a disability. These are, firstly, that the school is a physically and psychologically safe place for a student and, secondly, that a student is free from the harms caused by bullying. As with other educational issues discussed in this book, these conditions sound obvious, but, as we learn, too often the issue of school safety and the issue of bullying are major obstacles to inclusion in many Australian schools. The problems of occupational violence (OV) against teachers and of students with a disability being bullied are addressed (in that order) in this section: **Safety in schools and bullying prevention.**

The topic of school safety is explained, including incidents of aggressive, dangerous, or threatening behaviours against teachers known which make up OV. We make a connection with **Understanding inclusion**, given at the start of the journey, and with the fact that behaviour is given as grounds for the suspension or exclusion of a disproportionate number of students with a disability. The purpose of this highly practical part of our learning journey is to provide readers with the knowledge and tools to de-escalate incidents and, if that's not possible, offer advice that can protect health, safety and well-being in the classroom. To this purpose, the escalation cycle is explained, and stages in the cycle are unpacked for the reader. Opportunities for rapid *de-escalation* are identified and explained, and the reader is advised on how to create a plan for if the worst happens and a student enters the *crisis zone* stage. Advice is also given on the post-incident *recovery* stage in the escalation cycle and how to reduce the post-incident harms to a teacher, the student directly involved, and other students present during an incident.

Case study students Shona, Anj, and Darren are presented to explore some of the deeper issues, complexities, and dilemmas that can present in real examples of OV, including an example (Anj) which is really about student safety rather than OV. On the topic of safety in school, a critical incident plan is provided, with Shona, Anj, and Darren, referenced to help our traveller understand and navigate different elements in a critical incident plan.

The important issue of bullying is our final stop in **Safety in schools and bullying prevention.** As we highlighted, students with a disability are at elevated risk of being bullied, so addressing this topic is vital for schools in protecting their safety and well-being. Bullying itself is defined and unpacked. The associated category of victimisation is discussed. We hear from Quaden, a young man who spoke about his experience of bullying at school at the

Disability Royal Commission in 2020. This discussion about bullying ends with a focus on whole-school bullying prevention programs, which can benefit students with a disability, and connects with the suggested **Australian school-wide anti-bullying programs and resources** given at the end of the section. The final learning point is made about connections between OV and bullying when thinking about why too many students with a disability are suspended or excluded in Australia on account of their behaviour. Given that students with a disability are at known elevated risk of experiencing bullying or victimisation in school, it is entirely predictable, from a behavioural perspective, that some will respond with aggressive, dangerous, or violent behaviours. In such cases, we urge teachers to make proportional and compassionate responses.

Your return to **Key learnings from this book** brings you back to where you are reading right now. Remember, you can re-read this section as many times as you wish to help you recall, retain, and recognise your learning as a result of your travel through this book. Re-readings will bring new insights and strengthen your maintenance of learning (see **Disability: becoming a developmentally-informed teacher**).

The core finding from this book is to try to find ways to support all learners to succeed and achieve all they are capable of.

Your professional learning plan

You may have reached the end of your learning journey reading this book, but we encourage the reader to extend this learning into the future. If you are, or intend to be, a teacher, then this requirement is set out in AITSL Standards:

6.2 Engage in professional learning and improve practice.
6.3 Engage with colleagues and improve practice.
6.4 Apply professional learning and improve student learning.
7.4 Engage with professional teaching networks and broader communities.

The professional learning plan given below provides a framework to help you learn into the future, progressing your learning and capabilities as a result of this book.

Professional learning plan

Online Resource link here.

https://education.nsw.gov.au/teaching-and-learning/professional-learning/high-impact-professional-learning/resources/professional-learning-planning-guide

References

Adey, P., & Dillon, J. (2012). *Bad education: Debunking myths in education*. McGraw-Hill Education (UK).
Ainscow, M., Booth, T., & Dyson, A. (2006). *Improving schools, developing inclusion*. Routledge.
Alvares, G. A., Bebbington, K., Cleary, D., Evans, K., Glasson, E. J., Maybery, M. T., ... & Whitehouse, A. J. (2020). The misnomer of 'high functioning autism': Intelligence is an imprecise predictor of functional abilities at diagnosis. *Autism*, 24(1), 221–232.
American Psychiatric Association (2022). *Diagnostic and statistical manual of mental disorders* (5th ed., text rev. DSM-5-TR). American Psychiatric Publishing.
American Psychological Association (2021). *APA dictionary of psychology* (2nd ed.). American Psychological Association.
Anderson, S., & Bigby, C. (2017). Self-advocacy as a means to positive identities for people with intellectual disability: 'We just help them, be them really'. *Journal of Applied Research in Intellectual Disabilities*, 30(1), 109–120.
Anderson, J., & Boyle, C. (2019). Looking in the mirror: Reflecting on 25 years of inclusive education in Australia. *International Journal of Inclusive Education*, 23(7–8), 796–810.
Anastasiou, D., & Kauffman, J. M. (2011). A social constructionist approach to disability: Implications for special education. *Exceptional Children*, 77(3), 367–384.
Arden, S. V., Gandhi, A. G., Zumeta Edmonds, R., & Danielson, L. (2017). Toward more effective tiered systems: Lessons from national implementation efforts. *Exceptional Children*, 83(3), 269–280.
Armstrong, D. (2023). We don't need a hydrotherapy pool in every school, but we do need quality public education for all kids. The Conversation. Available at: https://theconversation.com/we-dont-need-a-hydrotherapy-pool-in-every-school-but-we-do-need-quality-public-education-for-all-kids-214716
Armstrong, D., & Armstrong, G. (2021). *Educational trends exposed: How to be a critical consumer*. Routledge.
Armstrong, D., Macleod, G., & Brough, C. (2019). Work done in the margins: A comparative study of mental health literacy in pre-service teacher education in Australia and in Scotland. *Journal of Research in Special Educational Needs*, 19(4), 334–343.
Armstrong, D. (2018). Addressing the wicked problem of behaviour in schools. *International Journal of Inclusive Education*, 22(9), 997–1013.
Armstrong, D. (2018). Am I Just Stupid? Key Issues for Teachers Involved in High-Stakes Testing with Children Who Have Dyslexia. In: Xerri, D., & Vella Briffa, P. (Eds.). *Teacher involvement in high-stakes language testing* (pp. 67–82). Cham: Springer.
Armstrong, D. (2017). Wicked problems in special and inclusive education. *Journal of Research in Special Educational Needs*, 17(4), 229–236.

Armstrong, D., Hallett, F., Elliott, J., & Hallett, G. (2015). *Understanding behaviour*. Cambridge University Press.

Armstrong, D., & Squires, G. (2014). *Key perspectives on dyslexia: An essential text for educators*. Routledge.

Armstrong, D., & Hallett, F. (2012). Private knowledge, public face: Conceptions of children with SEBD by teachers in the UK-a case study. *Educational & Child Psychology*, 29(4), 77–87.

Armstrong, D. (2012). The Ideal School? In Armstrong, D., & Squires, G. (Eds.). *Contemporary issues in special educational needs: Considering the whole child* (pp. 107–116). Open University Press.

Armstrong, D., & Humphrey, N. (2009). RESEARCH SECTION: Reactions to a diagnosis of dyslexia among students entering further education: Development of the 'resistance–accommodation' model. *British Journal of Special Education*, 36(2), 95–102.

Arnheim, R. (1997). *Visual thinking*. University of California Press.

Askell-Williams, H., Dix, K. L., Lawson, M. J., & Slee, P. T. (2012). Quality of implementation of a school mental health initiative and changes over time in students' social and emotional competencies. *School Effectiveness and School Improvement*, 24(3), 357–381. https://doi.org/10.1080/09243453.2012.692697

Aspland, T., Datta, P., & Talukdar, J. (2012). Curriculum policies for students with special needs in Australia. *International Journal of Special Education*, 27(3), 36–44.

Avery, J. C., Morris, H., Galvin, E., Misso, M., Savaglio, M., & Skouteris, H. (2021). Systematic review of school-wide trauma-informed approaches. *Journal of Child & Adolescent Trauma*, 14(3), 381–397.

Australian Alliance for Inclusive Education (2021). Driving change: A roadmap for achieving inclusive education in Australia. All Means All. Available at: https://allmeansall.org.au/driving-change-roadmap-achieving-inclusive-education-australia/

Australian Broadcasting Corporation (ABC) (2020). Meet the school principal who has never expelled or suspended a student. Available at: https://www.abc.net.au/news/2020-08-23/school-suspensions-expulsions-rise-student-engagement-education/12447104

Australian Curriculum and Assessment Reporting Authority (ACARA). (2024). Student Attendance. Available at: https://www.acara.edu.au/reporting/national-report-on-schooling-in-australia/student-attendance

Australian Curriculum, Assessment and Reporting Authority (n.d.). NAPLAN National Results. In National Report on Schooling in Australia. Retrieved August 27, 2025, from https://www.acara.edu.au/reporting/national-report-on-schooling-in-australia/naplan-national-results

Australian Education Research Organisation (AERO) (2024). Introduction Multi-Tiered System Support (MTSS). Available at: https://www.edresearch.edu.au/summaries-explainers/explainers/introduction-multi-tiered-system-supports

Australian Federation of Disability Organisations (AFDO) (2019). Disability Rights Now 2019: UN CRPD Review of Australia. CRPD Factsheet. Available at: https://www.afdo.org.au/uncrpd/

Australian Government (1992). Disability Discrimination Act 1992. https://www.legislation.gov.au/Details/C2004A04426

Australian Government (2005). Disability Standards for Education 2005. https://www.legislation.gov.au/Details/F2005L00767

Australian Government (2024). Australia's Disability Strategy 2021–2031. Department of Social Services. Available at: https://www.dss.gov.au/australias-disability-strategy

Australian Government Department of Education. (2024). Nationally Consistent Collection of Data on School Students with Disability: 2025 Guidelines. https://www.nccd.edu.au/sites/default/files/2024-09/2025%20NCCD%20Guidelines_02.pdf

Australian Government Department of Health; National Mental Health Commission. (2017, August 4). *The Fifth National Mental Health and Suicide Prevention Plan.* Council of Australian Governments Health Council. Retrieved [insert access date], from https://www.mentalhealthcommission.gov.au/monitoring-and-reporting/fifth-plan

Australian Human Rights Commission (2022, February 24). *Annual report 2020–2021.* https://humanrights.gov.au/our-work/commission-general/publications/annual-report-2020-2021

Australian Institute of Health and Welfare (AIHW) (2021). Autism in Australia. Available at: https://www.aihw.gov.au/reports/disability/autism-in-australia/contents/autism

Australian Institute for Teaching and School Leadership (2011). *Australian Professional Standards for Teachers* (ISBN 978-1-925192-64-3). AITSL. https://www.aitsl.edu.au/docs/default-source/national-policy-framework/australian-professional-standards-for-teachers.pdf

Axe, J. B., & Laprime, A. P. (2017). The effects of contingent pairing on establishing praise as a reinforcer with children with autism. *Journal of Developmental and Physical Disabilities, 29*(2), 325–340.

Axford, N., Berry, V., Lloyd, J., Moore, D., Rogers, M., Hurst, A., ... & Minton, J. (2019). *How can schools support parents' engagement in their children's learning? Evidence from research and practice.* Education Endowment Foundation.

Bailey, R., Meland, E. A., Brion-Meisels, G., & Jones, S. M. (2019). Getting developmental science back into schools: Can what we know about self-regulation help change how we think about "no excuses"? *Frontiers in Psychology, 10.* https://doi.org/10.3389/fpsyg.2019.01885

Barton, L. (ed.) (1996). *Disability and society: Emerging issues and insights.* Routledge.

Baron-Cohen, S. (2008). *Autism and Asperger syndrome.* Oxford University Press.

Bayat, M. (2011). Clarifying issues regarding the use of praise with young children. *Topics in Early Childhood Special Education, 31*(2), 121–128.

Bayer, J. K., Ukoumunne, O. C., Lucas, N., Wake, M., Scalzo, K., & Nicholson, J. M. (2011). Risk factors for childhood mental health symptoms: National longitudinal study of Australian children. *Pediatrics, 128*(4), e865–e873. https://doi.org/10.1542/peds.2011 0491

Bear, G. G. (2013). Teacher resistance to frequent rewards and praise: Lack of skill or a wise decision?. *Journal of Educational and Psychological Consultation, 23*(4), 318–340.

Bennett, H. (2015). Results of the systematic review on nurture groups' effectiveness. *The International Journal of Nurture in Education, 1*(1), 3–7.

Bertilsdotter Rosqvist, H., Chown, N., & Stenning, A. (Eds.). (2020). *Neurodiversity studies: A new critical paradigm.* Routledge. https://library.oapen.org/handle/20.500.12657/39438

Bigby, C., & O'Connor, M. (2019). Introduction to the Australasian Society for Intellectual Disability Position Statement on Intellectual Disability and Complex Support Needs. *Research and Practice in Intellectual and Developmental Disabilities, 6*(1), 1–4.

Billingsley, B., & Bettini, E. (2019). Special education teacher attrition and retention: A review of the literature. *Review of Educational Research, 89*(5), 697–744.

Bills, A., & Howard, N. (2023). School attendance rates are dropping. We need to ask students why. The Conversation. Available at: https://theconversation.com/school-attendance-rates-are-dropping-we-need-to-ask-students-why-200537

Bills, A., Armstrong, D., & Howard, N. (2020). Scaled-up 'safety-net' schooling and the 'wicked problem' of educational exclusion in South Australia: Problem or solution? *The Australian Educational Researcher, 47*(2), 239–261.

Bills, A., & Howard, N. (2017). Social inclusion education policy in South Australia: What can we learn?. *Australian Journal of Education*, *61*(1), 54–74.

Binagwaho, A., & Senga, J. (2021). Children and adolescent mental health in a time of COVID-19: A forgotten priority. *Annals of Global Health*, *87*(1), 57. https://doi.org/10.5334/aogh.3330

Binnie, L. M., & Allen, K. (2008). Whole school support for vulnerable children: The evaluation of a part-time nurture group. *Emotional and Behavioural Difficulties*, *13*(3), 201–216.

Bloom, B. S. (1968). Learning for Mastery. Instruction and Curriculum. Regional Education Laboratory for the Carolinas and Virginia, Topical Papers and Reprints, Number 1. *Evaluation Comment*, *1*(2), n2.

Booth, T., & Ainscow, M. (2002). *Index for inclusion: Developing learning and participation in schools* (English version) [PDF]. Centre for Studies on Inclusive Education. Retrieved from https://www.sipimpact.org/documents/Why-Inclusion/Index-English.pdf

Boxall, M., & Lucas, S. (2010). *Nurture groups in schools: Principles and practice* (2nd ed.). SAGE Publications.

Boyle, C., & Anderson, J. (2020). The justification for inclusive education in Australia. *Prospects*, *49*(3–4), 203–217. https://doi.org/10.1007/s11125-020-09494-x

Boyle, C., Topping, K., & Jindal-Snape, D. (2013). Teachers' attitudes towards inclusion in high schools. *Teachers and Teaching*, *19*(5), 527–542.

Bos, A. E., Pryor, J. B., Reeder, G. D., & Stutterheim, S. E. (2013). Stigma: Advances in theory and research. *Basic and Applied Social Psychology*, *35*(1), 1–9.

Brisenden, S. (1986). Independent living and the medical model of disability. *Disability, Handicap & Society*, *1*(2), 173–178.

Brown, P. M., & Byrnes, L. J. (2014). The development and use of individual learning plans for deaf and hard of hearing students in Victoria, Australia. *Deafness & Education International*, *16*(4), 204–217.

Buckman, M. M., Lane, K. L., Common, E. A., Royer, D. J., Oakes, W. P., Allen, G. E., Lane, K. S., & Brunsting, N. C. (2021). Treatment integrity of primary (Tier 1) prevention efforts in tiered systems: Mapping the literature. *Education and Treatment of Children*, *44*(1), 145–168. https://doi.org/10.1007/s43494-021-00044-4

Burnett, P. C., & Mandel, V. (2010). Praise and feedback in the primary classroom: Teachers' and Students' perspectives. *Australian Journal of Educational & Developmental Psychology*, *10*, 145–154.

Burns, C. O., Lemon, J., Granpeesheh, D., & Dixon, D. R. (2019). Interventions for daily living skills in individuals with intellectual disability: A 50-year systematic review. *Advances in Neurodevelopmental Disorders*, *3*, 235–245.

Carey, G. J. (2015). *Game to work: The social capital of employees with an intellectual disability in a supported workplace* (Doctoral dissertation, University of South Australia).

Cameron, A., Burns, P., Garner, A., Lau, S., Dixon, R., Pascoe, C., & Szafraniec, M. (2020). Making sense of multi-sensory environments: A scoping review. *International Journal of Disability, Development and Education*, *67*(6), 630–656.

Caldarella, P., Larsen, R. A., Williams, L., Downs, K. R., Wills, H. P., & Wehby, J. H. (2020). Effects of teachers' praise-to-reprimand ratios on elementary students' on-task behaviour. *Educational Psychology*, *40*(2), 1–17.

Campoy-Cubillo, M. C. (2019). Functional diversity and the multimodal listening construct. *European Journal of Special Needs Education*, *34*(2), 204–219.

Carruthers, S. E., Pickles, A., Slonims, V., Howlin, P. A., & Charman, T. (2020). Beyond intervention into daily life: A systematic review of generalisation following social communication interventions for young children with autism. *Autism Research*, *13*(4), 506–522. https://doi.org/10.1002/aur.2264

Caruana, E. J., Roman, M., Hernández-Sánchez, J., & Solli, P. (2015). Longitudinal studies. *Journal of Thoracic Disease*, 7(11), 1253–1257. https://doi.org/10.3978/j.issn.2072-1439.2015.10.63

Cefai, C., & Pizzuto, S. A. S. (2017). Listening to the voices of young children in a nurture class. *Emotional and Behavioural Difficulties*, 22(3), 248–260.

Chafouleas, S. M., Koriakin, T. A., Roundfield, K. D., & Overstreet, S. (2019). Addressing childhood trauma in school settings: A framework for evidence-based practice. *School Mental Health*, 11(1), 40–53. https://doi.org/10.1007/s12310-018-9256-5

Chambers, D., & Forlin, C. (2021). An historical review from exclusion to inclusion in Western Australia across the past five decades: What have we learnt?. *Education Sciences*, 11(3), 119.

Chan, R. C., Yi, H., & Siu, Q. K. (2020). Polymorbidity of developmental disabilities: Additive effects on child psychosocial functioning and parental distress. *Research in Developmental Disabilities*, 99, 103579.

Chen, H., Evans, D., & Luu, B. (2023). Moving towards inclusive education: Secondary school teacher attitudes towards universal design for learning in Australia. *Australasian Journal of Special and Inclusive Education*, 47(1), 1–13. https://doi.org/10.1017/jsi.2023.1

Cheney, D., Flower, A., & Templeton, T. (2008). Applying response to intervention metrics in the social domain for students at risk of developing emotional or behavioral disorders. *The Journal of Special Education*, 42(2), 108–126.

Child Trends (2013). Mental health disorders (Adolescent Health Highlight No. 2013-1). *Child Trends*. https://cms.childtrends.org/wp-content/uploads/2013/03/Child_Trends-2013_01_01_AHH_MentalDisordersl.pdf

Children and Young People with Disability Australia (2019). Time for change: The state of play for inclusion of students with disability. Available at https://cyda.org.au/time-for-change-the-state-of-play-for-inclusion-of-students-with-disability/

Chrysanthos, N. (2023). Royal commission split on future of special schools, group homes and workshops for the disabled. *Sydney Morning Herald*. Available at: https://www.smh.com.au/politics/federal/disability-royal-commission-calls-for-legal-overhaul-but-split-over-segregation-20230928-p5e8cp.html

Clare, J. (2023). Ministers Media Centre. 2023. 'Transcript of Interview with Sky News by Minister Clare.' January 20 2023. https://ministers.education.gov.au/clare/interview-sky-news-0

Clunies-Ross, P., Little, E., & Kienhuis, M. (2008). Self-reported and actual use of proactive and reactive classroom management strategies and their relationship with teacher stress and student behaviour. *Educational Psychology*, 28(6), 693–710. https://doi.org/10.1080/01443410802206700

Cocks, K., King, M. T., Velikova, G., Martyn St-James, M., Fayers, P. M., & Brown, J. M. (2011). Evidence-based guidelines for determination of sample size and interpretation of the European Organisation for the Research and Treatment of Cancer Quality of Life Questionnaire Core 30 (EORTC QLQ-C30). *Journal of Clinical Oncology*, 29(1), 89–96. https://doi.org/10.1200/JCO.2010.28.0107

Cohen, J. (1988). *Statistical power analysis for the behavioral sciences* (2nd ed.). Lawrence Erlbaum Associates.

Cohen, A., & Demchak, M. (2018). Use of visual supports to increase task independence in students with severe disabilities in inclusive educational settings. *Education and Training in Autism and Developmental Disabilities*, 53(1), 84–99.

Cohen, M. S., Rissman, J., Hovhannisyan, M., Castel, A. D., & Knowlton, B. J. (2017). Free recall test experience potentiates strategy-driven effects of value on memory. *Journal of Experimental Psychology: Learning, Memory, and Cognition*, 43(10), 1581.

Cole, S. F., Eisner, A., Gregory, M., & Ristuccia, J. (2013). *Creating and advocating for trauma sensitive schools*. Available at: https://traumasensitiveschools.org/

Coleman Brown, L. (2013). Stigma: An enigma demystified. *The Disability Studies Reader*, 147–162.

Collings, S., Dew, A., & Dowse, L. (2018). Unpacking the complexity of planning with persons with cognitive disability and complex support needs. *Journal of Applied Research in Intellectual Disabilities, 31*(1), 142–151.

Collings, S., & Llewellyn, G. (2012). Children of parents with intellectual disability: Facing poor outcomes or faring okay? *Journal of Intellectual & Developmental Disability, 37*(1), 65–82. https://doi.org/10.3109/13668250.2011.648610

Colvin, G., & Scott, T. M. (2014). *Managing the cycle of acting-out behavior in the classroom* (2nd ed.). Behavior Associates.

Cooke, C., Yeomans, J., & Parkes, J. (2008). The Oasis: Nurture group provision for Key Stage 3 pupils. *Emotional and Behavioural Difficulties, 13*(4), 291–303.

Cooper, P., Arnold, R., & Boyd, E. (2001). The effectiveness of nurture groups: Preliminary research findings. *British Journal of Special Education, 28*(4), 160–166.

Cooper, P. (2011). Teacher strategies for effective intervention with students presenting social, emotional and behavioural difficulties: An international review. *European Journal of Special Needs Education, 26*(1), 71–86.

Cooper, P. (2017). Evidence Based Approaches to Mental Health Issues in Schools. In: C. Cefai & P. Cooper (Eds.). *Mental health promotion in schools* (pp. 11–21). SensePublishers.

Cooper, P., Smith, C.J., & Upton, G. (1994). *Emotional and behavioural difficulties: Theory to practice* (1st ed.). Routledge. https://doi.org/10.4324/9780203416297

Cross, D., Monks, H., Hall, M., Shaw, T., Pintabona, Y., Erceg, E., Hamilton, G., Roberts, C., Waters, S., & Lester, L. (2011). Three-year results of the friendly schools whole-of-school intervention on children's bullying behaviour. *British Educational Research Journal, 37*(1), 105–129. https://doi.org/10.1080/01411920903420024

Cross, D., Shaw, T., Hearn, L., Epstein, M., Monks, H., Lester, L., & Thomas, L. (2009). *Australian Covert Bullying Prevalence Study (ACBPS)*. Child Health Promotion Research Centre, Edith Cowan University.

Cruz-Torres, E., Duffy, M. L., Brady, M. P., Bennett, K. D., & Goldstein, P. (2020). Promoting daily living skills for adolescents with autism spectrum disorder via parent delivery of video prompting. *Journal of Autism and Developmental Disorders, 50*, 212–223.

Cubeddu, D., & MacKay, T. (2017). The attunement principles: A comparison of nurture group and mainstream settings. *Emotional and Behavioural Difficulties, 22*(3), 261–274.

Cumming, J. J., & Dickson, E. (2013). Educational accountability tests, social and legal inclusion approaches to discrimination for students with disability: A national case study from Australia. *Assessment in Education: Principles, Policy & Practice, 20*(2), 221–239.

Davies, M. (2012). Accessibility to NAPLAN assessments for students with disabilities: A 'fair go'. *Australasian Journal of Special Education, 36*, 62–78.

Daley, S. G., & McCarthy, M. F. (2020). Students with disabilities in social and emotional learning interventions: A systematic review. *Remedial and Special Education, 42*(6), 384–397. https://doi.org/10.1177/0741932520964917.

Danese, A. (2020). Annual research review: Rethinking childhood trauma—new research directions for measurement, study design and analytical strategies. *Journal of Child Psychology and Psychiatry, 61*(3), 236–250. https://doi.org/10.1111/jcpp.13195

Davidson, M. (2013). Universal Design: The Work of Disability in an Age of Globalization. In L. Davis (Ed.), *The disability studies reader* (2nd ed., pp. 117–128). Routledge.

Davis, J. (2013). *A sensory approach to the curriculum: For pupils with profound and multiple learning difficulties.* Routledge.

Davis, H. A. (1998). *Variables influencing the development of the student-teacher relationship* (Doctoral dissertation, University of Georgia).

de Giambattista, C., Ventura, P., Trerotoli, P., Margari, M., Palumbi, R., & Margari, L. (2019). Subtyping the autism spectrum disorder: Comparison of children with high functioning autism and Asperger syndrome. *Journal of Autism and Developmental Disorders, 49*(1), 138–150.

Dean, J., Roberts, P., & Perry, L. B. (2021). School equity, marketisation and access to the Australian senior secondary curriculum. *Educational Review, 75*(2), 243–263.

den Houting, J. (2019). Neurodiversity: An insider's perspective. *Autism, 23*(2), 271–273. https://doi.org/10.1177/1362361318820762.

Department of Education and Training (n.d.). *Policies.* ACT Government. Retrieved August 27, 2025, from https://www.education.act.gov.au/publications_and_policies/policies

Department of Education and Training (DET) (2019). High Impact Teaching Strategies (HITS). Available at: https://www.education.vic.gov.au/school/teachers/teachingresources/practice/improve/Pages/hits.aspx

Department of Education and Training (DET) (2021). Behaviour Support Plan. (BSP). Available at: https://www2.education.vic.gov.au/pal/behaviour-students/guidance/behaviour-support-plans

Department of Education and Training (DET) (2021). Selective Schools. Available at: https://www.vic.gov.au/selective-entry-high-schools

Department of Education and Training (DET) (2021). Individual education Plans (IEPs). Available at: https://www2.education.vic.gov.au/pal/individual-education-plans-ieps/resources

Department of Education and Training (DET) (2025). Vocational education and training delivered to school students: Policy. Victorian government. Retrieved August 27, 2025, from https://www2.education.vic.gov.au/pal/vet-delivered-school-students/policy

Disability Royal Commission (DRC) (2020a). Public hearing 7: Barriers to accessing a safe, quality and inclusive school education and life course impacts. EXHIBIT 7-11 - STAT.0170.0001.0001 - Statement of David Armstrong. Available at: https://disability.royalcommission.gov.au/publications/exhibit-7-11-stat017000010001-statement-david-armstrong

Disability Royal Commission (DRC) (2020b). Royal Commission into Violence, Abuse, Neglect and Exploitation of People with Disability. *Public hearing 7: Barriers to accessing a safe, quality and inclusive school education and life course impacts.* Closing Address. Available at: https://disability.royalcommission.gov.au/public-hearings/public-hearing-7

Disability Royal Commission (DRC) (2023). Royal Commission into Violence, Abuse, Neglect and Exploitation of People with Disability. Final Report. *Volume 7, Inclusive education, employment and housing.* Available at: https://disability.royalcommission.gov.au/publications/final-report-volume-7-inclusive-education-employment-and-housing

Doronkin, J. L., Martin, J. E., Greene, B. A., Choiseul-Praslin, B., & Autry-Schreffler, F. (2020). Opening Oz's curtain: who's really running the annual IEP meeting to discuss secondary transition issues?. *Journal of Research in Special Educational Needs, 20*(3), 206–216.

Dray, J., Bowman, J., Campbell, E., Freund, M., Wolfenden, L., Hodder, R. K., McElwaine, K., Tremain, D., Bartlem, K., Bailey, J., Small, T., Palazzi, K., Oldmeadow, C., & Wiggers, J. (2017). Systematic review of universal resilience-focused interventions targeting child and adolescent mental health in the school setting. *Journal of the American Academy of Child & Adolescent Psychiatry, 56*(10), 813–824. https://doi.org/10.1016/j.jaac.2017.07.780

Duncan, J., Punch, R., Gauntlett, M., & Talbot-Stokes, R. (2020). Missing the mark or scoring a goal? Achieving non-discrimination for students with disability in primary and secondary education in Australia: A scoping review. *Australian Journal of Education*, *64*(1), 54–72.

Duong, J., & Bradshaw, C. P. (2013). Using the extended parallel process model to examine teachers' likelihood of intervening in bullying. *The Journal of School Health*, *83*(6), 422–429.

Durlak, J. A., & DuPre, E. P. (2008). Implementation matters: A review of research on the influence of implementation on program outcomes and the factors affecting implementation. *American Journal of Community Psychology*, *41*(3–4), 327–350.

Durlak, J. A., Weissberg, R. P., Dymnicki, A. B., Taylor, R. D., & Schellinger, K. B. (2011). The impact of enhancing students' social and emotional learning: A meta-analysis of school-based universal interventions. *Child Development*, *82*(1), 405–432.

Dweck, C. S. (1999). *Self-theories: Their role in motivation, personality, and development*. Psychology Press.

Eisenberg, N., VanSchyndel, S. K., & Hofer, C. (2015). The association of maternal socialization in childhood and adolescence with adult offsprings' sympathy/caring. *Developmental Psychology*, *51*(1), 7–16. https://doi.org/10.1037/a0038137

Elder, B. C., Rood, C. E., & Damiani, M. L. (2018). Writing strength-based IEPs for students with disabilities in inclusive classrooms. *International Journal of Whole Schooling*, *14*(1), 116–155.

Elliott, J. (2015). Teacher Expertise. In Armstrong, D., Hallett, F., Elliott, J., & Hallett, G. (Eds.). *Understanding child and adolescent behaviour in the classroom* (pp. 87–98). Cambridge University Press.

Elliott, J., & Place, M. (2012). *Children in difficulty: A guide to understanding and helping*. Routledge.

Eilts, J., & Koglin, U. (2022). Bullying and victimization in students with emotional and behavioural disabilities: A systematic review and meta-analysis of prevalence rates, risk and protective factors. *Emotional and Behavioural Difficulties*, *27*(2), 133–151.

Elliott, J. G., Stemler, S. E., Sternberg, R. J., Grigorenko, E. L., & Hoffman, N. (2011). The socially skilled teacher and the development of tacit knowledge. *British Educational Research Journal*, *37*(1), 83–103.

Fazel, M., Reed, R. V., Panter-Brick, C., & Stein, A. (2012). Mental health of displaced and refugee children resettled in high-income countries: Risk and protective factors. *The Lancet*, *379*(9812), 266–282. https://doi.org/10.1016/S0140-6736(11)60051-2

Ferri, B. A. (2012). Undermining inclusion? A critical reading of response to intervention (RTI). *International Journal of Inclusive Education*, *16*(8), 863–880.

Floress, M. T., & Jenkins, L. N. (2015). A preliminary investigation of kindergarten teachers' use of praise in general education classrooms. *Preventing School Failure: Alternative Education for Children and Youth*, *59*(4), 253–262. https://doi.org/10.1080/1045988X.2014.942834

Floress, M. T., Jenkins, L. N., Reinke, W. M., & McKown, L. (2018). General education teachers' natural rates of praise: A preliminary investigation. *Behavioral Disorders*, *43*(4), 411–422.

Florian, L. (2019). On the necessary co-existence of special and inclusive education. *International Journal of Inclusive Education*, *23*(7-8), 691–704.

Forlin, C. (2006). Inclusive education in Australia ten years after Salamanca. *European Journal of Psychology of Education*, *21*(3), 265–277.

Frisén, A., Holmqvist, K., & Oscarsson, D. (2008). 13-year-olds' perception of bullying: Definitions, reasons for victimisation and experience of adults' response. *Educational Studies*, *34*(2), 105–117.

Fuchs, D., Fuchs, L. S., & Compton, D. L. (2012). Smart RTI: A next-generation approach to multilevel prevention. *Exceptional Children*, *78*(3), 263–279.

Gable, R. A., Hester, P. H., Rock, M. L., & Hughes, K. G. (2009). Back to basics: Rules, praise, ignoring, and reprimands revisited. *Intervention in School and Clinic*, 44(4), 195–205.

Gallagher, E. K., Dever, B. V., Hochbein, C. et al. (2019). Teacher caring as a protective factor: The effects of behavioral/emotional risk and teacher caring on office disciplinary referrals in middle school. *School Mental Health*, 11, 754–765. https://doi.org/10.1007/s12310-019-09318-0

Gatwiri, K., McPherson, L., Parmenter, N., Cameron, N., & Rotumah, D. (2019). Indigenous children and young people in residential care: A systematic scoping review. *Trauma, Violence, & Abuse*, 22(4), 829–842. https://doi.org/10.1177/1524838019881707

Ghirlanda, S., & Enquist, M. (2003). A century of generalization. *Animal Behaviour*, 66(1), 15–36.

Giangreco, M. F. (2010). Utilization of teacher assistants in inclusive schools: Is it the kind of help that helping is all about? *European Journal of Special Needs Education*, 25(4), 341–345.

Gibby-Leversuch, R., Hartwell, B. K., & Wright, S. (2021). Dyslexia, literacy difficulties and the self-perceptions of children and young people: A systematic review. *Current Psychology*, 40(11), 5595–5612.

Gleeson, J., Klenowski, V., & Looney, A. (2020). Curriculum change in Australia and Ireland: A comparative study of recent reforms. *Journal of Curriculum Studies*, 52(4), 478–497.

Goffman, I. (1963). *Stigma: Notes on the management of spoiled identity*. Prentice-Hall.

Gonski, D., Arcus, T., Boston, K., Gould, V., Johnson, W., O'Brien, L., Perry, L., & Roberts, M. (2018). Through Growth to Achievement: Report of the Review to Achieve Educational Excellence in Australian Schools. Canberra: Commonwealth of Australia. https://www.education.gov.au/recurrent-funding-schools/resources/through-growth-achievement-report-review-achieve-educational-excellence-australian-schools

Graham, L. J. (2020). Questioning the impacts of legislative change on the use of exclusionary discipline in the context of broader system reforms: A Queensland case-study. *International Journal of Inclusive Education*, 24(14), 1473–1493.

Grantham, R., & Primrose, F. (2017). Investigating the fidelity and effectiveness of Nurture Groups in the secondary school context. *Emotional and Behavioural Difficulties*, 22(3), 219–236.

Grattan, M. (6/10/2023). Podcasts/Politics with Michelle Grattan. The Conversation. Available at: https://theconversation.com/politics-with-michelle-grattan-greens-jordon-steele-john-on-the-disability-royal-commission-and-bill-shortens-ndis-reforms-215072

Griffiths, R., Stenner, R., & Hicks, U. (2014). Hearing the unheard: Children's constructions of their Nurture Group experiences. *Educational & Child Psychology*, 31(1), 124–136.

Groch, S. (29/09/2023). Lili thrived at special schools. The royal commission is split on a plan to phase them out. *Sydney Morning Herald*. Available at: https://www.smh.com.au/politics/federal/julius-loves-his-mainstream-school-does-australia-still-need-special-schools-20230928-p5e8cq.html

Grosche, M., & Volpe, R. J. (2013). Response-to-intervention (RTI) as a model to facilitate inclusion for students with learning and behaviour problems. *European Journal of Special Needs Education*, 28(3), 254–269.

Guercio, J. M. (2020). The importance of a deeper knowledge of the history and theoretical foundations of behaviorism and behavior therapy: Part 2—1960–1985. *Behavior Analysis: Research and Practice*, 20(3), 174–195. https://doi.org/10.3402/snp.v5.28004

Hanbury, M. (2011). *Educating students on the autistic spectrum: A practical guide.* Sage.

Harris, C. (2019). In praise of praise...for pupils and teachers. *Times Educational Supplement.* Available at: https://www.tes.com/news/praise-praisefor-pupils-and-teachers

Harris, J. C., & Greenspan, S. (2016). Definition and nature of intellectual disability. In N. N. Singh (Ed.), *Handbook of evidence-based practices in intellectual and developmental disabilities* (pp. 11–39). Springer. https://doi.org/10.1007/978-3-319-26583-4_2

Hart, J. E., & Brehm, J. (2013). Promoting self-determination: A model for training elementary students to self-advocate for IEP accommodations. *Teaching Exceptional Children, 45*(5), 40–48.

Hart, L. M., Morgan, A. J., Rossetto, A., Kelly, C. M., Mackinnon, A., & Jorm, A. F. (2018). Helping adolescents to better support their peers with a mental health problem: A cluster-randomised crossover trial of teen mental health first aid. *Australian & New Zealand Journal of Psychiatry, 52*(7), 638–651. https://doi.org/10.1177/0004867417753552

Hart, R. (2010). Classroom behaviour management: Educational psychologists' views on effective practice. *Emotional and Behavioural Difficulties, 15*(4), 353–371.

Hawkins, S. M., & Heflin, L. J. (2011). Increasing secondary teachers' behavior-specific praise using a video self-modeling and visual performance feedback intervention. *Journal of Positive Behavior Interventions, 13*(2), 97–108.

Healthdirect Australia (n.d.). *Autism spectrum disorder (ASD).* https://www.healthdirect.gov.au/autism

Heffernan, A., Bright, D., Kim, M., Longmuir, F., & Magyar, B. (2022). 'I cannot sustain the workload and the emotional toll': Reasons behind Australian teachers' intentions to leave the profession. *Australian Journal of Education, 66*(2), 196–209.

Hehir, T., Grindal, T., Freeman, B., Lamoreau, R., Borquaye, Y., & Burke, S. (2016). A Summary of the Evidence on Inclusive Education. *Abt Associates.* Available at: https://files.eric.ed.gov/fulltext/ED596134.pdf

Hepburn, L., & Beamish, W. (2019). Towards implementation of evidence-based practices for classroom management in Australia: A review of research. *Australian Journal of Teacher Education, 44*(2), 82–98.

Hoare, E., Thorp, A., Bartholomeusz-Raymond, N., McCoy, A., Butler, H., & Berk, M. (2020). Be you: A national education initiative to support the mental health of Australian children and young people. *Australian & New Zealand Journal of Psychiatry, 54*(11), 1061–1066. https://doi.org/10.1177/0004867420946840

Holloway, J., & Brass, J. (2018). Making accountable teachers: The terrors and pleasures of performativity. *Journal of Education Policy, 33*(3), 361–382.

Houchins, D., Oakes, W. P., & Johnson, Z. (2016). Bullying and students with disabilities: A systematic literature review of intervention studies. *Remedial and Special Education, 37*(5), 259–273.

Howarth, C., McCartney, C., Mansfield, M., & Main, G. (2021). A different take: Reflections on an intergenerational participatory research project on child poverty. *Social Work & Society, 18*(3), 673. https://ejournals.bib.uni-wuppertal.de/index.php/sws/article/view/673

Hughes, C. A., Morris, J. R., Therrien, W. J., & Benson, S. K. (2017). Explicit instruction: Historical and contemporary contexts. *Learning Disabilities Research & Practice, 32*(3), 140–148.

Humphrey, N., Barlow, A., & Lendrum, A. (2018). Quality matters: Implementation moderates student outcomes in the PATHS curriculum. *Prevention Science, 19*(2), 197–208. https://doi.org/10.1007/s11121-017-0802-4

Humphrey, N., & Hebron, J. (2014). Bullying of children and adolescents with autism spectrum conditions: A 'state of the field' review. *International Journal of Inclusive Education, 19*(8), 845–862. https://doi.org/10.1080/13603116.2014.981602

Humphrey, N., Lendrum, A., Wigelsworth, M., & Greenberg, M. T. (Eds.). (2020). *Social and emotional learning*. Routledge.

Humphrey, N., & Lewis, S. (2008). 'Make me normal': The views and experiences of pupils on the autistic spectrum in mainstream secondary schools. *Autism*, 12(1), 23–46.

Iacono, T., Keeffe, M., Kenny, A., & McKinstry, C. (2019). A document review of exclusionary practices in the context of Australian school education policy. *Journal of Policy and Practice in Intellectual Disabilities*, 16(4), 264–272.

Jacob, R., & Parkinson, J. (2015). The potential for school-based interventions that target executive function to improve academic achievement: A review. *Review of Educational Research*, 85(4), 512–552.

Jalali, R., & Morgan, G. (2018). 'They won't let me back.' Comparing student perceptions across primary and secondary Pupil Referral Units (PRUs). *Emotional and Behavioural Difficulties*, 23(1), 55–68.

Jamil, F. M., Downer, J. T., & Pianta, R. C. (2012). Association of pre-service teachers' performance, personality, and beliefs with teacher self-efficacy at program completion. *Teacher Education Quarterly*, 39(4), 119–138.

Jarvis, J. M., Jolly, J. L., & Moltzen, R. (2018). Gifted Education in Australia and New Zealand: Reflections and Future Directions. In *Exploring gifted education* (pp. 206–211). Routledge.

Jenkins, L. N., Floress, M. T., & Reinke, W. (2015). Rates and types of teacher praise: A review and future directions. *Psychology in the Schools*, 52(5), 463–476.

Jones-Smith, E. (2011). *Spotlighting the strengths of every single student: Why U.S. schools need a new, strengths-based approach*. Praeger.

Joseph, L. M., Alber-Morgan, S., & Neef, N. (2016). Applying behavior analytic procedures to effectively teach literacy skills in the classroom. *Psychology in the Schools*, 53(1), 73–88.

Joyner, R. E., & Wagner, R. K. (2020). Co-occurrence of reading disabilities and math disabilities: A meta-analysis. *Scientific Studies of Reading*, 24(1), 14–22.

Johnson, A. H., Goldberg, T. S., Hinant, R. L., & Couch, L. K. (2019). Trends and practices in functional behavior assessments completed by school psychologists. *Psychology in the Schools*, 56(3), 360–377.

Kauffman, J. M., Anastasiou, D., & Maag, J. W. (2017). Special education at the crossroad: An identity crisis and the need for a scientific reconstruction. *Exceptionality*, 25(2), 139–155.

Kavanagh, A. M., Aitken, Z., Baker, E., LaMontagne, A. D., Milner, A., & Bentley, R. (2016). Housing tenure and affordability and mental health following disability acquisition in adulthood. *Social Science & Medicine*, 151, 225–232. https://doi.org/10.1016/j.socscimed.2016.01.010

Kenny, L., Hattersley, C., Molins, B., Buckley, C., Povey, C., & Pellicano, E. (2016). Which terms should be used to describe autism? Perspectives from the UK autism community. *Autism*, 20(4), 442–462.

Kellam, S. G., Mackenzie, A. C., Brown, C. H., Poduska, J. M., Wang, W., Petras, H., & Wilcox, H. C. (2011). The good behavior game and the future of prevention and treatment. *Addiction Science & Clinical Practice*, 6(1), 73.

Kelly, C. (02/10/2023). Disability advocates urge faster phase-out of segregated education following royal commission report. *The Guardian*. Available at: https://www.theguardian.com/australia-news/2023/oct/02/neurodiverse-kids-dumped-from-mainstream-education-amid-debate-over-special-schools

Knowlton, B. J., & Castel, A. D. (2022). Memory and reward-based learning: A value-directed remembering perspective. *Annual Review of Psychology*, 73, 25–52. https://doi.org/10.1146/annurev-psych-032921-050951

Kor, K., Simpson, H., & Fabrianesi, B. (2023). Strengthening schools' responses to Students' harmful sexual behaviors: A scoping review. *Trauma, Violence, & Abuse*, 24(4), 2726–2742.

Kounin, J. S. (1970). *Discipline and group management in classrooms*. Holt, Rinehart & Winston.

Korkodilos, M. (2016). The mental health of children and young people in England. *Public Health England, London*.

King-Sears, M. E., Swanson, C., & Mainzer, L. (2011). TECHnology and literacy for adolescents with disabilities. *Journal of Adolescent & Adult Literacy*, 54(8), 569–578.

Kubina, R. M., Jr, Kostewicz, D. E., & Lin, F. Y. (2009). The taxonomy of learning and behavioral fluency. *Journal of Precision Teaching and Celebration*, 25, 17.

Kulinski, A. R. (2023). Finding my way: Using journals to forge a path of resilience and resistance. *International Journal of Education & the Arts*, 24(12), 12. https://doi.org/10.26209/ijea24n12

Landes, S., Stevens, D., & Turk, J. D. (2020). Cause of death in adults with Down syndrome in the United States. *Disability and Health Journal*, 13(4), 100947.

Lassig, C., Poed, S., Mann, G., Saggers, B., Carrington, S., & Mavropoulou, S. (2024). The future of special schools in Australia: Complying with the convention on the rights of persons with disabilities. *International Journal of Inclusive Education*, 28(9), 1701–1719.

Larcombe, T. J., Joosten, A. V., Cordier, R., & Vaz, S. (2019). Preparing children with autism for transition to mainstream school and perspectives on supporting positive school experiences. *Journal of Autism and Developmental Disorders*, 49(8), 3073–3088.

Lau, W., Silove, D., Edwards, B., Forbes, D., Bryant, R., McFarlane, A., Hadzi-Pavlovic, D., Steel, Z., Nickerson, A., Van Hooff, M., Felmingham, K., Cowlishaw, S., Alkemade, N., Kartal, D., & O'Donnell, M. (2018). Adjustment of refugee children and adolescents in Australia: Outcomes from wave three of the building a new life in Australia study. *BMC Medicine*, 16, 157. https://doi.org/10.1186/s12916-018-1124-5

Lawrence, D., Dawson, V., Houghton, S., Goodsell, B., & Sawyer, M. G. (2019). Impact of mental disorders on attendance at school. *Australian Journal of Education*, 63(1), 5–21. https://doi.org/10.1177/0004944118823576

Le, L. K. D., Engel, L., Lee, Y. Y., Lal, A., & Mihalopoulos, C. (2021). The cost-effectiveness of a school-based intervention for bullying prevention: An Australian case study. *Mental Health & Prevention*, 24, 200224.

Leadbitter, K., Buckle, K. L., Ellis, C., & Dekker, M. (2021). Autistic self-advocacy and the neurodiversity movement: Implications for autism early intervention research and practice. *Frontiers in Psychology*, 12, 782.

Learning difficulties Australia Inc (n.d.). *Learning Difficulties*. Retrieved August 25, 2025, from https://ldaustralia.org/information-resources/learning-difficulties/

Lengetti, E., Kronk, R., & Cantrell, M. A. (2020, November 3). A theory analysis of mastery learning and self-regulation. *Nurse Education in Practice*. https://doi.org/10.1016/j.nepr.2020.102911

Leuschner, V., Fiedler, N., Schultze, M., Ahlig, N., Göbel, K., Sommer, F., Scholl, J., Cornell, D., & Scheithauer, H. (2017). Prevention of targeted school violence by responding to students' psychosocial crises: The NETWASS program. *Child Development*, 88(1), 68–82. https://doi.org/10.1111/cdev.12690

Liasidou, A. (2024). (Internalising) challenging behaviours and trauma-informed Positive Behavioural Interventions and Supports (PBIS). *Emotional and Behavioural Difficulties*, 29(3–4), 138–151. https://doi.org/10.1080/13632752.2024.2426433

Lory, C., Mason, R. A., Davis, J. L., Wang, D., Kim, S. Y., Gregori, E., & David, M. (2020). A meta-analysis of challenging behavior interventions for students with developmental disabilities in inclusive school settings. *Journal of Autism and Developmental Disorders*, 50(4), 1221–1237.

Lifton, R. J. (1989) [1961]. Chapter 22, Ideological Totalism. In *Thought reform and the psychology of totalism: A study of brainwashing in China* (reprint ed.). UNC Press.

Lingard, B. (2013). *Politics, policies and pedagogies in education: The selected works of Bob Lingard*. Routledge.

Lingard, B. (2010). Policy borrowing, policy learning: Testing times in Australian schooling. *Critical Studies in Education, 51*(2), 129–147.

Lu, L., Williams, L., Groves, O., Wan, W., & Lee, E. (2023). *NAPLAN participation: Who is missing the tests and why it matters*. Australian Education Research Organisation (AERO). Available at: https://www.edresearch.edu.au/

Lyons, G. S., & Cassebohm, M. (2012). Student wellbeing for those with profound intellectual and multiple disabilities: Same, same but different?. *The Journal of Student Wellbeing, 5*(2), 18–33.

MacFarlane, K., & Woolfson, L. M. (2013). Teacher attitudes and behavior toward the inclusion of children with social, emotional and behavioral difficulties in mainstream schools: An application of the theory of planned behavior. *Teaching and Teacher Education, 29*, 46–52.

Macdonald, S. J. (2009). Windows of reflection: Conceptualizing dyslexia using the social model of disability. *Dyslexia, 15*(4), 347–362.

Madigan, D. J., & Kim, L. E. (2021). Towards an understanding of teacher attrition: A meta-analysis of burnout, job satisfaction, and teachers' intentions to quit. *Teaching and Teacher Education, 105*, 103425.

March, S., & Kearney, M. (2017). A psychological service contribution to nurture: Glasgow's nurturing city. *Emotional and Behavioural Difficulties, 22*(3), 237–247. https://doi.org/10.1080/13632752.2017.1331972

Mavropoulou, S., Mann, G., & Carrington, S. (2021). The divide between inclusive education policy and practice in Australia and the way forward. *Journal of Policy and Practice in Intellectual Disabilities, 18*(1), 44–52.

McClelland, M. M., Tominey, S. L., Schmitt, S. A., & Duncan, R. (2017). SEL interventions in early childhood. *The Future of Children, 27*(1), 33–47. https://www.jstor.org/stable/44219020

McDowell, M. (2018). Specific learning disability. *Journal of Paediatrics and Child Health, 54*(10), 1077–1083.

McGaghie, W. C., Issenberg, S. B., Barsuk, J. H., & Wayne, D. B. (2014). A critical review of simulation-based mastery learning with translational outcomes. *Medical Education, 48*(4), 375–385. https://doi.org/10.1111/medu.12391

McKenzie, R. G. (2009). Obscuring vital distinctions: The oversimplification of learning disabilities within RTI. *Learning Disability Quarterly, 32*(4), 203–215.

Mellard, D., McKnight, M., & Jordan, J. (2010). RTI tier structures and instructional intensity. *Learning Disabilities Research & Practice, 25*(4), 217–225. https://doi.org/10.1111/j.1540-5826.2010.00319.x

Meltzer, A., & Saunders, I. (2020). Cultivating supportive communities for young people – Mentor pathways into and following a youth mentoring program. *Children and Youth Services Review, 110*, 104815. https://doi.org/10.1016/j.childyouth.2020.104815

Mitchell, D. (2014). *What really works in special and inclusive education: Using evidence-based teaching strategies* (2nd ed.). Routledge. https://doi.org/10.4324/9780203105313

Moffat, A. K., Redmond, G., & Raghavendra, P. (2019). The impact of social network characteristics and gender on covert bullying in Australian students with disability in the middle years. *Journal of School Violence, 18*(4), 613–629.

Nakar, S., & Bagnall, R. G. (2024). Reasonable adjustment for inclusive development: A cautionary case study of Australian VET teachers' experience. *International Journal of Comparative Education and Development, 26*(3), 171–188. https://doi.org/10.1108/IJCED-05-2023-0042

National Collaborating Centre for Mental Health (UK). (2015). 5 Pre- and Immediately Pre-event. In *Violence and aggression: Short-term management in mental health, health and community settings: Updated edition*. British Psychological Society (UK); (NICE Guideline, No. 10.). Available from: https://www.ncbi.nlm.nih.gov/books/NBK356330/

Nationally Consistent Collection of Data on School Students with Disability (NCCD) (2021). 4-step model. Available at: https://www.nccd.edu.au/wider-support-materials/what-nccd-model-1?parent=%2Funderstanding-nccd&activity=%2Fwider-support-materials%2Fwhat-nccd-model-1&step=-1

Nationally Consistent Collection of Data on School Students with Disability (NCCD) (2021). What is the NCCD? Available at: https://www.nccd.edu.au/wider-support-materials/what-nccd?parent=%2Funderstanding-nccd&activity=%2Fwider-support-materials%2Fwhat-nccd&step=-1

National Institute for Health and Care Excellence (2015). Violence and aggression: Short-term management in mental health, health and community settings (NICE guideline NG10). https://www.nice.org.uk/guidance/ng10

Ní Bhroin, Ó., & King, F. (2020). Teacher education for inclusive education: A framework for developing collaboration for the inclusion of students with support plans. *European Journal of Teacher Education*, 43(1), 38–63.

Nicholson, T. (2014). Academic Achievement and Behavior. In Garner, P., James, K., & Julian, E. (Eds.). *The Sage handbook of emotional and behavioral difficulties* (Vol. 2, pp. 177–188). SAGE Publications.

Norwich, B. (2013). *Addressing tensions and dilemmas in inclusive education: Living with uncertainty*. Routledge.

NSW Department of Education (2020, January 28). *Trauma-informed practice in schools: An explainer*. Centre for Education Statistics and Evaluation. https://education.nsw.gov.au/about-us/education-data-and-research/cese/publications/research-reports/trauma-informed-practice-in-schools.html

NSW Standards Authority (2024). Assessment for, as and of Learning. Available at: https://educationstandards.nsw.edu.au/wps/portal/nesa/k-10/understanding-the-curriculum/assessment/approaches

O'Neill, S. C., & Stephenson, J. (2014). Evidence-based classroom and behaviour management content in Australian pre-service primary teachers' coursework: Wherefore art thou? *Australian Journal of Teacher Education*, 39(4), n4.

Odom, S. L., Hall, L. J., & Suhrheinrich, J. (2019). Implementation science, behavior analysis, and supporting evidence-based practices for individuals with autism. *European Journal of Behavior Analysis*, 21(1), 55–73.

Oldfield, J., Hebron, J., & Humphrey, N. (2016). The role of school level protective factors in overcoming cumulative risk for behaviour difficulties in children with special educational needs and disabilities. *Psychology in the Schools*, 53(8), 831–847. https://doi.org/10.1002/pits.21950

Olweus, D. (2013). School bullying: Development and some important challenges. *Annual Review of Clinical Psychology*, 9(1), 751–780.

Overstreet, S., & Chafouleas, S. M. (2016). Trauma-informed schools: Introduction to the special issue. *School Mental Health*, 8(1), 1–6. https://doi.org/10.1007/s12310-016-9184-1

Page, A., Barr, M., Rendoth, T., Roche, L., Foggett, J. L., Leonard, C., & Duncan, J. (2024). Making reasonable adjustments for students with disability in Australian mainstream classrooms: A scoping review. *Australasian Journal of Special and Inclusive Education*, 48(1), 46–63. https://doi.org/10.1017/jsi.2024.1

Panagiotidi, M., Overton, P. G., & Stafford, T. (2019). Co-occurrence of ASD and ADHD traits in an adult population. *Journal of Attention Disorders*, 23(12), 1407–1415.

Parents Victoria (PV) (2023). Special provision for VCE exams Available at: https://www.parentsvictoria.asn.au/special-provision-for-vce-exams/

Parker, R., Rose, J., & Gilbert, L. (2016). Attachment Aware Schools: An Alternative to Behaviourism in Supporting Children's Behaviour?. In: Lees, H., & Noddings, N. (Eds). *The Palgrave international handbook of alternative education* (pp. 463–483). Palgrave Macmillan.
Pawliczek, C. M., Derntl, B., Kellermann, T., Gur, R. C., Schneider, F., & Habel, U. (2013). Anger under control: Neural correlates of frustration as a function of trait aggression. *PLOS ONE, 8*(10), e78503. https://doi.org/10.1371/journal.pone.0078503
Payton, J., Weissberg, R. P., Durlak, J. A., Dymnicki, A. B., Taylor, R. D., Schellinger, K. B., & Pachan, M. (2008). *The positive impact of social and emotional learning for kindergarten to eighth-grade students: Findings from three scientific reviews.* Collaborative for Academic, Social, and Emotional Learning. https://files.eric.ed.gov/fulltext/ED505370.pdf
Peterson, R. L., & Pennington, B. F. (2015). Developmental dyslexia. *Annual Review of Clinical Psychology, 11,* 283–307.
Pfitzner-Eden, F. (2016). Why do I feel more confident? Bandura's sources predict preservice teachers' latent changes in teacher self-efficacy. *Frontiers in Psychology, 7,* 1486.
Phillips, L., Wilson, L., & Wilson, E. (2010). Assessing behaviour support plans for people with intellectual disability before and after the Victorian Disability Act 2006. *Journal of Intellectual and Developmental Disability, 35*(1), 9–13.
Poed, S., Cologon, K., & Jackson, R. (2020). Gatekeeping and restrictive practices by Australian mainstream schools: Results of a national survey. *International Journal of Inclusive Education, 26*(8), 766–779.
Polanyi, M., & Sen, A. (2009). *The tacit dimension.* University of Chicago press.
Price, D., & Slee, R. (2021). An Australian curriculum that includes diverse learners: The case of students with disability. *Curriculum Perspectives, 41*(1), 71–81.
Puiu, A. A., Wudarczyk, O., Goerlich, K. S., Votinov, M., Herpertz-Dahlmann, B., Turetsky, B., & Konrad, K. (2018). Impulsive aggression and response inhibition in attention-deficit/hyperactivity disorder and disruptive behavioral disorders: Findings from a systematic review. *Neuroscience & Biobehavioral Reviews, 90,* 231–246. https://doi.org/10.1016/j.neubiorev.2018.03.014
Queensland Government (2021). *Inclusive Education.* Available at: https://education.qld.gov.au/students/inclusive-education
Queensland Government (2021). *Special school eligibility ("person with a disability" criteria) policy.* Available at: https://education.qld.gov.au/students/students-with-disability/supports-for-students-with-disability/intellectual-disability/supports-at-school-for-students-with-intellectual-disability
Raaijmakers, M. A. J., Smidts, D. P., Sergeant, J. A., Maassen, G. H., Posthumus, J. A., van Engeland, H., & Matthys, W. (2008). Executive functions in preschool children with aggressive behavior: Impairments in inhibitory control. *Journal of Abnormal Child Psychology, 36*(7), 1097–1107. https://doi.org/10.1007/s10802-008-9235-7
Radford, J., Bosanquet, P., Webster, R., & Blatchford, P. (2015). Scaffolding learning for independence: Clarifying teacher and teaching assistant roles for children with special educational needs. *Learning and Instruction, 36,* 1–10.
Rasooli, A., Razmjoee, M., Cumming, J., Dickson, E., & Webster, A. (2021). Conceptualising a fairness framework for assessment adjusted practices for students with disability: An empirical study. *Assessment in Education: Principles, Policy & Practice, 28*(3), 301–321.
Reber, R., & Greifeneder, R. (2017). Processing fluency in education: How metacognitive feelings shape learning, belief formation, and affect. *Educational Psychologist, 52*(2), 84–103.

Reddy, L. A., Fabiano, G. A., Dudek, C. M., & Hsu, L. (2013). Instructional and behavior management practices implemented by elementary general education teachers. *Journal of School Psychology, 51*(6), 683–700.

Reynolds, J. L., Cochrane, W. S., Furey, W. M., & Matvichuk, T. A. (2020). Working together: A process to support teachers in increasing specific praise statements. *Intervention in School and Clinic, 55*(3), 162–168.

Richaud de Minzi, M. C. R., Lemos, V. N., & Oros, L. B. (2016). Empathy in children: Theory and assessment. In D. F. Watt & J. Panksepp (Eds.), *Psychology and neurobiology of empathy* (pp. 149–170). Nova Biomedical Books.

Rickwood, D. J., Telford, N. R., Mazzer, K. R., Parker, A. G., Tanti, C. J., & McGorry, P. D. (2015). The services provided to young people through the headspace centres across Australia. *The Medical Journal of Australia, 202*(10), 533–536. https://doi.org/10.5694/mja14.01695

Riddick, B. (2012). *Living with dyslexia: The social and emotional consequences of specific learning difficulties/disabilities*. Routledge.

Ritchhart, R., Church, M., & Morrison, K. (2011). *Making thinking visible*. Jossey-Bass.

Robson, D. A., Allen, M. S., & Howard, S. J. (2020). Self-regulation in childhood as a predictor of future outcomes: A meta-analytic review. *Psychological Bulletin, 146*(4), 324–354. https://doi.org/10.1037/bul0000227

Rose, J. (2009). *Identifying and teaching children and young people with dyslexia and literacy difficulties: An independent report*. DfES Publications.

Rose, J., Low-Choy, S., Singh, P., & Vasco, D. (2020). NAPLAN discourses: A systematic review after the first decade. *Discourse: Studies in the Cultural Politics of Education, 41*(6), 871–886.

Rouf, K., Fennell, M., Westbrook, D., Cooper, M., & Bennett-Levy, J. (2004). Devising effective behavioural experiments. In J. Bennett-Levy, G. Butler, M. Fennell, A. Hackman, M. Mueller, & D. Westbrook (Eds.), *Oxford guide to behavioural experiments in cognitive therapy* (pp. 21–58). Oxford University Press. https://doi.org/10.1093/med:psych/9780198529163.003.0002

Roy, D. (2016, August 25). Children with disability are being excluded from education. *The Conversation*. https://theconversation.com/children-with-disability-are-being-excluded-from-education-59825

Roy, D. (2020, April 20). *The NSW DoE are failing students with a disability, shocking new data shows*. EducationHQ. https://educationhq.com/news/the-nsw-doe-are-failing-students-with-a-disability-shocking-new-data-shows-76175/

Roy, D., Baker, W., & Hamilton, A. (2025). *Teaching the Arts: Early Childhood and Primary Education* (4th ed.). Cambridge University Press.

Roy, D., & Dock, C. (2014). Dyspraxia, drama and masks: Applying the school curriculum as therapy. *Journal of Applied Arts & Health, 5*(3), 369–375. https://doi.org/10.1386/jaah.5.3.369_1

Rzepecka, H., McKenzie, K., McClure, I., & Murphy, S. (2011). Sleep, anxiety and challenging behaviour in children with intellectual disability and/or autism spectrum disorder. *Research in Developmental Disabilities, 32*(6), 2758–2766.

Saggers, B., Klug, D., Harper-Hill, K., Ashburner, J., Costley, D., Clark, T., & Carrington, S. (2018). *Australian autism educational needs analysis–What are the needs of schools, parents and students on the autism spectrum*. Cooperative Research Centre for Living with Autism.

Saltmarsh, S., Barr, J., & Chapman, A. (2014). Preparing for parents: How Australian teacher education is addressing the question of parent-school engagement. *Asia Pacific Journal of Education, 35*(1), 69–84. https://doi.org/10.1080/02188791.2014.906385

Sancassiani, F., Pintus, E., Holte, A., Paulus, P., Moro, M. F., Cossu, G., Angermeyer, M. C., Carta, M. G., & Lindert, J. (2015). Enhancing the emotional and social skills of the youth to promote their wellbeing and positive development: A systematic review of universal school-based randomized controlled trials. *Clinical Practice & Epidemiology in Mental Health*, *11*(Suppl 1 M2), 21–40. https://doi.org/10.2174/1745017901511010021

Schalock, R. L., Luckasson, R., & Tassé, M. J. (2019). The contemporary view of intellectual and developmental disabilities: Implications for psychologists. *Psicothema*, *31*(3), 223–228.

Schulte-Körne, G. (2016). Mental health problems in a school setting in children and adolescents. *Deutsches Ärzteblatt International*, *113*(11), 183–190. https://doi.org/10.3238/arztebl.2016.0183

Schunk, D. H., & Zimmerman, B. J. (2012). Self-regulation and Learning. In Weiner, I., Reynolds, W.M., & Miller, G.E. (Eds.). *Handbook of psychology* (2nd ed., Vol. 7, pp. 59–78). Wiley.

Sentenac, M., Gavin, A., Nic Gabhainn, S., Molcho, M., Due, P., Ravens-Sieberer, U., Matos, M. G. de, Malkowska-Szkutnik, A., Gobina, I., Vollebergh, W., Arnaud, C., & Godeau, E. (2013). Peer victimization and subjective health among students reporting disability or chronic illness in 11 Western countries. *European Journal of Public Health*, *23*(3), 421–426. https://doi.org/10.1093/eurpub/cks073

Shaddock, A., MacDonald, N., Hook, J., Giorcelli, L., & Arthur-Kelly, M. (2009). *Disability, diversity and tides that lift all boats: Review of special education in the ACT*. Services Initiates.

Sharma, U., Furlonger, B., & Forlin, C. (2019). The impact of funding models on the education of students with autism spectrum disorder. *Australasian Journal of Special and Inclusive Education*, *43*(1), 1–11.

Sharma, U., & Salend, S. J. (2016). Teaching assistants in inclusive classrooms: A systematic analysis of the international research. *Australian Journal of Teacher Education*, *41*(8), 118–134.

Sheridan, M. (2008). Revised and updated by Sharma, A., & Frost, M. *From birth to five years: Children's developmental progress* (3rd ed.). Routledge.

Shelemy, L., Harvey, K., & Waite, P. (2019). Supporting students' mental health in schools: What do teachers want and need? *Emotional and Behavioural Difficulties*, *24*(1), 100–116. https://doi.org/10.1080/13632752.2019.1582742

Shute, R. H., & Slee, P. T. (Eds.). (2016). *Mental health and wellbeing through schools: The way forward*. Routledge. https://doi.org/10.4324/9781315764696

Silberman, S. (2015). *NeuroTribes: The legacy of autism and the future of neurodiversity*. Penguin.

Singh, V., Kumar, A., & Gupta, S. (2020). Mental health prevention and promotion—a narrative review. *Journal of Family Medicine and Primary Care*, *9*(6), 2648–2654. https://doi.org/10.4103/jfmpc.jfmpc_124_20

Skiba, R. J. (2014). The failure of zero tolerance. *Reclaiming Children and Youth*, *22*(4), 27–33.

Slee, R. (2018). *Inclusive education isn't dead, it just smells funny*. Routledge.

Slee, R. (2011). *The irregular school: Exclusion, schooling and inclusive education*. Routledge.

Sloan, S., Winter, K., Connolly, P., & Gildea, A. (2020). The effectiveness of Nurture Groups in improving outcomes for young children with social, emotional and behavioural difficulties in primary schools: An evaluation of Nurture Group provision in Northern Ireland. *Children and Youth Services Review*, *108*, 104619. https://doi.org/10.1016/j.childyouth.2019.104619

Smith, P. L., & Ragan, T. J. (2005). *Instructional design* (3rd ed.). Wiley

Solomon, T., Plamondon, A., O'Hara, A., Finch, H., Goco, G., Chaban, P., Huggins, L., Ferguson, B., & Tannock, R. (2018). A cluster randomized-controlled trial of the impact of the tools of the mind curriculum on self-regulation in Canadian preschoolers. *Frontiers in Psychology*, *8*, 2366. https://doi.org/10.3389/fpsyg.2017.02366

Sousa, D. A., & Tomlinson, C. A. (2011). *Differentiation and the brain: How neuroscience supports the learner-friendly classroom*. Solution Tree Press.

South Australian Government (SA Gov.) (2017). Report of the select committee on access to the South Australian Education system for students with disabilities. Parliament of South Australia. Available at: https://www.parliament.sa.gov.au/Committees/Pages/Committees.aspx?CTId=3&PId=53&CId=320

South Australian Department for Education (2021). Flexible Learning Options (FLO) and Enrolment. Available at: https://www.education.sa.gov.au/parents-and-families/enrol-school-or-preschool/school-enrolment/flexible-learning-options-flo-and-enrolment

SPELD Victoria (2021). *Our History*. Available at: https://www.speldvic.org.au/history/

Sprague, J. R., & Walker, H. M. (2021). *Safe and healthy schools: Practical prevention strategies* (2nd ed.). Guilford Press.

Sugai, G., Armstrong, D., & McMillan, J. (2016). School-based Positive Behavior Support. Presentation. Flinders University, School of Education. Courtesy George Sugai.

Staddon, J. E., & Cerutti, D. T. (2003). Operant conditioning. *Annual Review of Psychology, 54*(1), 115–144.

Stefanidi, A., Ellis, D. M., & Brewer, G. A. (2018). Free recall dynamics in value-directed remembering. *Journal of Memory and Language, 100*, 18–31.

Stevenson, D. J., Neill, J. T., Ball, K., Smith, R., & Shores, M. C. (2022). How do preschool to year 6 educators prevent and cope with occupational violence from students? *Australian Journal of Education, 66*(2), 154–170.

Strickland-Cohen, M. K., & Horner, R. H. (2015). Typical school personnel developing and implementing basic behavior support plans. *Journal of Positive Behavior Interventions, 17*(2), 83–94.

Squires, G. (2020). A European consideration of early school leaving as a process running through childhood: A model for inclusive action. *Education 3-13, 48*(3), 332–343.

Sullivan, A. M., Johnson, B., Owens, L., & Conway, R. (2014). Punish them or engage them? Teachers' views of unproductive student behaviours in the classroom. *Australian Journal of Teacher Education, 39*(6), 43–56.

Sutherland, K. S., Wehby, J. H., & Yoder, P. J. (2002). Examination of the relationship between teacher praise and opportunities for students with EBD to respond to academic requests. *Journal of Emotional and Behavioral Disorders, 10*(1), 5–13. https://doi.org/10.1177/106342660201000102

Symes, W., & Humphrey, N. (2012). Including pupils with autistic spectrum disorders in the classroom: The role of teaching assistants. *European Journal of Special Needs Education, 27*(4), 517–532.

Tallet, J., Albaret, J.-M., & Rivière, J. (2014). The role of motor memory in action selection and procedural learning: Insights from children with typical and atypical development. *Socioaffective Neuroscience & Psychology, 5*, 28004. https://doi.org/10.3402/snp.v5.28004

Tan, B. S., Wilson, E., Campain, R., Murfitt, K., & Hagiliassis, N. (2019). Understanding Negative Attitudes toward Disability to Foster Social Inclusion: An Australian Case Study. In Halder, S., & Argyropoulos, V. (Eds.). *Inclusion, equity and access for individuals with disabilities* (pp. 41–65). Palgrave Macmillan.

Temple, J. B., Kelaher, M., & Williams, R. (2018). Discrimination and avoidance due to disability in Australia: Evidence from a national cross-sectional survey. *BMC Public Health, 18*(1), 1–13.

The British Dyslexia Association (BDA) (2019). Definition of Dyslexia. Available at: https://www.bdadyslexia.org.uk/dyslexia/about-dyslexia

The Lancet. (2009). Disability: Beyond the medical model. *The Lancet, 374*(9704), 1793. https://doi.org/10.1016/S0140-6736(09)62043-2

Thompson, I. (2017). Tackling Social Disadvantage Through Teacher Education. In I. Menter (Ed.), Tackling Social Disadvantage Through Teacher Education (p. 84). Critical Publishing.

Tong, L., Shinohara, R., Sugisawa, Y., Tanaka, E., Yato, Y., Yamakawa, N., & Anme, T. (2012). Early development of empathy in toddlers: Effects of daily parent–child interaction and home-rearing environment. *Journal of Applied Social Psychology, 42*(10), 2464–2483. https://doi.org/10.1111/j.1559-1816.2012.00949.x

Tran, L., Sanchez, T., Arellano, B., & Lee Swanson, H. (2011). A meta-analysis of the RTI literature for children at risk for reading disabilities. *Journal of Learning Disabilities, 44*(3), 283–295.

Tsouloupas, C. N., Carson, R. L., Matthews, R., Grawitch, M. J., & Barber, L. K. (2010). Exploring the association between teachers' perceived student misbehaviour and emotional exhaustion: The importance of teacher efficacy beliefs and emotion regulation. *Educational Psychology, 30*(2), 173–189.

UNICEF (2017). Inclusive education: Including children with disabilities in quality learning: What needs to be done?. United Nations Children's Fund. Geneva. Available at: https://www.unicef.org/eca/sites/unicef.org.eca/files/IE_summary_accessible_220917_brief.pdf

United Nations (1990). Convention on the rights of the child. https://www.ohchr.org/en/instruments-mechanisms/instruments/convention-rights-child

United Nations (2008). Convention on the rights of persons with disabilities. https://www.un.org/disabilities/documents/convention/convoptprot-e.pdf

Vaughn, S., Cirino, P. T., Wanzek, J., Wexler, J., Fletcher, J. M., Denton, C. D., & Francis, D. J. (2010). Response to intervention for middle school students with reading difficulties: Effects of a primary and secondary intervention. *School Psychology Review, 39*(1), 3–21.

Venet, A. S. (2021). *Equity-cantered trauma-informed education (Equity and social justice in education)*. WW Norton & Company.

Victorian Curriculum and Assessment Authority (VCAA) (2023a). Overview Available at: https://victoriancurriculum.vcaa.vic.edu.au/overview/about

Victorian Curriculum and Assessment Authority (VCAA) (2023b). Special Examination Arrangements. Available at: https://www.vcaa.vic.edu.au/administration/special-provision/special-examination-arrangements-vce-external-assessments

Walker, P. M., Carson, K. L., Jarvis, J. M., McMillan, J. M., Noble, A. G., Armstrong, D., & Palmer, C. D. (2018). How do educators of students with disabilities in specialist settings understand and apply the Australian Curriculum framework?. *Australasian Journal of Special and Inclusive Education, 42*(2), 111–126.

Walsh, T. (2012). Adjustments, accommodation and inclusion: Children with disabilities in Australian primary schools. *International Journal of Law and Education, 17*(2), 33–48.

Wardale, S., Davis, F., Vassos, M., & Nankervis, K. (2018). The outcome of a statewide audit of the quality of positive behaviour support plans. *Journal of Intellectual & Developmental Disability, 43*(2), 202–212.

Warrier, V., Toro, R., Won, H., Leblond, C. S., Cliquet, F., Delorme, R., De Witte, W., Bralten, J., Chakrabarti, B., Børglum, A. D., Grove, J., Poelmans, G., Hinds, D. A., Bourgeron, T., & Baron-Cohen, S. (2019). Social and non-social autism symptoms and trait domains are genetically dissociable. *Communications Biology, 2*(1), 328. https://doi.org/10.1038/s42003-019-0558-4

Westling, D. L. (2010). Teachers and challenging behavior: Knowledge, views, and practices. *Remedial and Special Education, 31*(1), 48–63. https://doi.org/10.1177/0741932508327466

Whitley, J., Smith, J. D., Vaillancourt, T., & Neufeld, J. (2018). Promoting mental health literacy among educators: A critical aspect of school-based prevention and intervention. In A. Leschied, D. Saklofske, & G. Flett (Eds.), *Handbook of school-based mental health promotion: An evidence-informed framework for implementation* (pp. 143–165). Springer. https://doi.org/10.1007/978-3-319-89842-1_9

WHO (2013). *International statistical classification of diseases and related health problems-*9th revision. 2nd edn. World Health Organization

WHO (2023). Disability: Fact Sheet. World Health Organisation, Geneva. https://www.who.int/news-room/fact-sheets/detail/disability-and-health

Williams, J. J., & Lombrozo, T. (2010). The role of explanation in discovery and generalization: Evidence from category learning. *Cognitive Science, 34*(5), 776–806.

Wilson, R., & Sahlberg, P. (2021). Putting NAPLAN to the test: Towards a new national assessment system. *Professional Voice — Assessment, Technology and the Impact of Social Concerns, 14*(1) 9–20. Available at: https://www.aeuvic.asn.au/sites/default/files/Professional%20Voice/PV_14.1/PV_2021_14.1_Complete.pdf#page=9

Wilson, C., Woolfson, L. M., Durkin, K., & Elliott, M. A. (2016). The impact of social cognitive and personality factors on teachers' reported inclusive behaviour. *British Journal of Educational Psychology, 86*(3), 461–480.

Winget, M., & Persky, A. M. (2022). A practical review of mastery learning. *American Journal of Pharmaceutical Education, 86*(10), 8906. https://doi.org/10.5688/ajpe8906

Winter, S., & Bunn, H. (2019). Work to be done? A survey of educational psychologists' contribution to special schools for profound and multiple learning difficulties. *British Journal of Special Education, 46*(1), 53–74.

Wood, D., Bruner, J. S., & Ross, G. (1976). The role of tutoring in problem solving. *Journal of Child Psychology and Psychiatry, 17*(2), 89–100.

Woodcock, S., & Faith, E. (2021). Am I to blame? Teacher self-efficacy and attributional beliefs towards students with specific learning disabilities. *Teacher Development, 25*(2), 215–238.

Young, E., Edmonds, C., & Campagnella, N. (29/09/2023). Disability royal commission hands down final report with 222 recommendations for change. *Australian Broadcasting Corporation* (ABC). Available at: https://www.abc.net.au/news/2023-09-29/disability-royal-commission-final-report-recommendations/102913028

Zeng, S., Corr, C. P., O'Grady, C., & Guan, Y. (2019). Adverse childhood experiences and preschool suspension expulsion: A population study. *Child Abuse & Neglect, 97*, 104149. https://doi.org/10.1016/j.chiabu.2019.104149

Zhang, J., Martella, R. C., Kang, S., & Yenioglu, B. Y. (2023). Response to intervention (RTI)/multi-tiered systems of support (MTSS): A nationwide analysis. *Journal of Educational Leadership and Policy Studies, 7*(1), 1–26. https://eric.ed.gov/?id=EJ1396417

Zwosta, K., Ruge, H., & Wolfensteller, U. (2015). Neural mechanisms of goal-directed behavior: Outcome-based response selection is associated with increased functional coupling of the angular gyrus. *Frontiers in Human Neuroscience, 9*, 180. https://doi.org/10.3389/fnhum.2015.00180

Index

Note: **Bold** indicates tables in the text.

Abilities Based Learning and Educational Support (ABLES) 148–149
Additional Support Class (ASC) 19
adverse childhood experiences (ACEs) 123, 125, 187
allied professionals xiv, 20, 53
alternative settings 13
Antecedent Behaviour Consequences (ABC) observation 104–105, 107
Applied Behaviour Analysis (ABA) 92, **101**
Armstrong, D. 9, 18–19, 23, 37, 90–91, 96, 100, 110, 118, 123
Armstrong, G. 9, 23, 37, 123
Asperger Syndrome 32
assessment of learning 148–149
attendance, declining 4–5, 184, 186
attention-deficit/hyperactivity disorder (ADHD) 29, 37, 41, 59, 168–169
Australian Bureau of Statistics (ABS) 35–36
Australian Child Wellbeing Project (ACWP) 176
Australian Educational Research Organisation (AERO) 22, 74–75, 113, 147
Australian education system 3, 13–14, 36, 188
Australian Institute for Teaching and School Leadership (AITSL) xv, 11, 115
Australian Institute of Welfare and Health (AIWH) 146
Australian schoolwide anti-bullying programs and resources 178, 190
Autism spectrum disorder (ASD) 41, 77, 91, 120, 129, 169

avoidance behaviours 35
Axe, J. B. 70
Axford, N. 84–85

Bayer, J. K. 120
Bear, G. G. 108
behaviourism theory 92–93
behaviour of concern (BoC) 94; challenges faced by children 94–95; evidence-based strategies and 100–102, **101**
behaviours, students 6, 101, 187; approaches and practices 95; challenging 90–91, 113; desired 68, 70; disruptive 89–90; evidence-based strategies to positive 110, **111**, **170**; individual and class level 96–98; in learning process 46–50; scale and 95–96; teacher self-efficacy and 98–99; teaching replacement/coping 106–108
Behaviour Support Plan (BSP) 43, 110
Bills, A. 5
The Blob Tree 113
Boxhall, M. 134
Boyle, C 36

Caldarella, P. 71
Campagnella, N. 18
Castel, A. D. 47
casual relief teacher (CRT) 59, 69
Cerutti, D. T. 79
challenging behaviour 90–92, 94–95, 113, 136
Chambers, D. 14
Chen, H. 63–64
Chief Operation Officer (CEO) 84

Child and Adolescent Mental Health Services (CAMHS) 20, 118, 121, 126–128, **126**, 136
Clare, J. 4–**5**
classroom-based issues xiii
cognitive-behavioural theory/interventions 98, 100–102, **101**
Cohen, J. 140
Coleman, B. L. 36
Collaborative for Academic, Social, and Emotional Learning (CASEL) 131
Collings, S. 42
complex support needs 41–42
co-occurrence 41–43
Cooper, P. 135
covert bullying 174, 176–177
Cubeddu, D. 136
Cumming, J. J. 145

Davies M. 147
Davis, H. A. 98
de-escalation 166–168, 189
demotivation cycle 71
Developmental Coordination Disorder (CDC) 79
developmental delay 38–40
diagnostic overshadowing 129
Dickson, E. 145
differentiation 6, 57–59, 61; learning resources to enable 62–63; UDL and 63–66, 185–186
disability: assessment via senior school examinations 146; categories of **38**; definition 28, 31; developmental. co-occurrence and complex support needs 41–43; developmental delay 38–39; evidence based strategies for students 50–55; hidden and learning 43–44; inclusion and 35; and intelligence 40; medical model of 33–34; neurodiversity 37; praise the students 70; role of academic assessment 147–148; social model of 34; special examination arrangement for 158–160; stigma and attitudes in education 35–37; teaching approaches and strategies 45; *see also* Educational inclusion for disability students
Disability Discrimination Act (DDA) 11, 21, 31, 34, 64, 125, 159
Disability Royal Commission (DRC) Final Report 16–17, 23, **23**, 63, 164, 184; publication of 18; response to 17–18

Disability Standards for Education (DSE) 11, 82
disciplinary sanctions 97, 108
disruptive behaviour 68, 89–90, 94, 97
Down Syndrome 34, 41, 76, 91, 120
dropout 38–39

Edmonds, C. 18
educational inclusion for disability students xiv, 7, 12–13; in Australia laws and regulations 10–12; Australian school systems and lack of 15; declining attendance 4–5, 184; implications for quality teaching and 4; school suspensions 5; setting classroom environment 11–13, **12**; special examination arrangement for 158; vignettes/case studies 28–35, 42–46, 48–50, 64–65, 85–87, 104–105, 116–117, 150–155, 170–173, 185; *see also* Disability; Inclusive/educational assessment; Learning
Education Endowment Foundation (EEF) 84
effective academic instruction 109–110
Eilts, J. 174
Elder, B. C. 38
Elliott, J. 45, 99
Emotional Behavioural Difficulty (EBD) 71
encoding 47
escalation 166–168, 170–171, 174
existing/qualified teachers xiv, 3
experimental manipulation 105–106

First Nations xiv, 16, 59–60, 120
Flexible Learning Options (FLO) 13, 21, 55, 108, 177
Forlin, C. 14
formative assessment 149–150, 153
Friendly Schools program 179
Functional Behaviour Assessment (FBA) 53, 89, 102–104, 110
funding issues in school 8–9

Gable, R. A. 72
gatekeeping practices 17
Gaussian (bell) curve 39
Generalised Anxiety Disorder (GAD) 119, 125
goal-orientated behaviour 46
Goffman, E. 36
Gonski, D. 13–14

Graham, L. J. 61
group alerting 99–100
Guercio, J. M. 92

Hallett, F. 96
Hattie, J. 72–73
Hehir, T. 15
high-functioning autism (HFA) 29, 32, 41
High Impact Teaching Strategies (HITS) 50
Howard, N. 5
Humphrey, N. 131

impulse aggression 168–169
Inclusion Centre 19–20
inclusive/educational assessment 145, 188; alternative sources for 148; barriers to 158–161, **159**; for learning 149–150; purchasing 149; purpose of 145–146; role of 147–148; unexpected learning and 153–154
inclusive education system 13, 108
Individual Education Plan (IEP) 19, 38, 82, 110, 188–189
individualised learning plan (ILP) 52–53, 106, 128
inhibitory response 168–169
initial teacher education (ITE) xiv
intellectual disability (ID) 29, 40–41, 70, 150, 171
Intelligence Quotient (IQ) Test 40, 185

Jarvis, J. M. 58–60, 64
Jenkins, L. N. 69

Kim, L. E. 98
Knowlton, B. J. 47
Koglin, U. 174
Korkodilos, M. 120
Kounin, J. S. 99

The Lancet (journal) 32
Laprime, A. P. 70
Lassig, C. 15
Lau, W. 123
Lawrence, D. 96
law *vs.* regulations 11
learning: assessment and 149–150, 153–154; and differentiation 62–63; disabilities 43–44; stages and behaviours in 46–50; support and interventions 53–54; teaching and 7

Learning Difficulties Australia 44
Lee, V. 132

MacKay, T. 136
Madigan, D. J. 98
mainstream schools 13–14, 16, 41, 55
maladaptive behaviour 121
Maslach, S. 96
mastery learning 47–48
McClelland, M. M. 133
mental health 187–188; challenges 121–124; difficulties 119–120; jurisdiction 127; referral 127–128, 187
Mental Health Care Plans (MHCPs) 128
mental health first aid (MHFA) 122
mental health literacy programs 129–130
Moffat, A. K. 176–177
motor memory 79
Mount Donna Buang 150–155, 157, 161
Multi-Tiered Systems Supports (MTSS) 22

National Assessment Program – Literacy and Numeracy (NAPLAN) 144–147, 188
National Disability Strategy (NDS) 10
National Safe Schools Framework (NSSF) 179
Nationally Consistent Collection of Data (NCCD) 12
New South Wales (NSW) xv, 4, 46, 124, 146, 158
New South Wales Education Standards Authority (NESA) 149
notice, plan, document, implement and review (NPDIR) 51–52
nurture groups 134–138, 187–188

occupational violence (OV) 90, 165–166, 178, 189
O'Neill, S. C. 93
operant behaviour 79
overlapping, teacher ability 99–100

parent-school partnerships 7, 186; barriers and obstacles 83; benefit of 84; 'hard-to-reach' phrase 85; Parents Victoria (PV) advice 83–84; teacher and parents 82–83
Parents Victoria (PV) 83–84, 158
Pfitzner-Eden, F. 98
Positive Behavioural Interventions and Support (PBIS) 89, 107–110

positive mental health 119–121, 133, 140
pragmatic guidance xiii
praise 67–68; Autism/ID students 70; effective 69; feedback and 72–73, **73**; to raise student concentration 70–71; recommendations for 71–72; students with disability 70
pre-service teachers/students of ITE xiv, 84, 117–119
Professional Standards xv, 11, 23
Project X 136, 187–188; aims 136–137; classroom-level practice in 137–138; delivery 137; outcomes of 139
public service professionals xv

Queensland (QLD) 46, 146

Rasooli, A. 145
reasonable adjustment in classroom 11–12, **12**, 17, 28, 157, 185
rehearsal 47
reprimands 70–71, 171–172
Response to Intervention (RtI) 22, 50–51
routines 74–75, 186; connections and 79–80; myths around 75–77, **75**; recommendations 77–79, **78**; task analysis and 80–81; teaching 77

safety-disability connection 164
Sancassiani, F. 130
scales of intervention 95–96
school leaders xiv, **12**, 17, 140–141, 160, 173, 186
school safety and bullying 8, 189–190; and critical incident response plan 174, **175**; definition 174; prevention of 176–177
schools for specific purposes (SSPs) 8
school support staff xiv
Sharma, U. 45
Sheridan, M. 39
Slee, R. xiv, 14–15
Sloan, S. 136
social and emotional learning (SEL) 53–54, 110, 130–131, 169, 187; empathy and 132; evidence base for 133–134; strategies to encourage 132–133; types of 131
Sousa, D. A. 57, 60
South Australia (SA) 46, 94, 146–147, 179
special schools 7–8, 13, 15, 18–19, 35, 61

SPELD (Specific Educational Learning Disorders) Victoria 45–46
Sprague, J. R. 174
Squires, G. 38
Staddon, J. E. 79
state secondary exam (SSE) 21
Stephenson, J. 93
Stevenson, D. J. 173
story sequence 155–156
Stringer, J. 37
Sullivan, A. M. 94
suspensions and exclusions xiv, 5, 20, 103, 108, 113, 164, 174
The Sydney Morning Herald 18

tacit knowledge 45, 53, 99
target behaviour 103–104, 106–107
teacher attrition 4
teacher self-efficacy (TSE) 98, 112
teaching: approaches and strategies 45, 95; and learning 7; in Project X 137; quality and inclusion 4; replacement/coping behaviours 106–107; routines 77
Temple, J. B. 35–36
'thought termination cliché' 6
Titchener, E. B. 132
Tomlinson, C. A. 57, 60
Tong, L. 132
transtheoretical model (TTM) theory **101**, 110, 169
trauma 122–123
trauma-informed educational practice 123–124

United Nations Convention on the Rights of Persons with Disabilities (UNCRPD) 8
United Nations Human Rights Commission (UNHRC) 15
Universal Design for Learning (UDL) xiii, 7, 63–66, 185–186

Venet, A. S. 124
vicious circle 4
victimisation 174, 176, 178
Victorian Certificate of Education (VCE) 146, 160
Victorian Curriculum and Assessment Authority (VCAA) 158–160
visual journal 144, 155–157, 161
vocabulary 155–157
Vocational Education and Training (VET) 148

Walker, H. M. 174
Western Australia (WA) 14, 46, 146
Western Thornbury Primary School (WTPS) 64
Whitley, J. 129
whole-school bullying prevention program 177, 190
Wide-Ranging Achievement Test (WRAT) 52
withiness 99
Work Health Safety (WHS) 163
World Health Organisation (WHO) 28, 41

Young, E. 18

Zeng, S. 125
Zero Tolerance 107–108

For Product Safety Concerns and Information please contact our EU representative GPSR@taylorandfrancis.com
Taylor & Francis Verlag GmbH, Kaufingerstraße 24, 80331 München, Germany

www.ingramcontent.com/pod-product-compliance
Lightning Source LLC
Chambersburg PA
CBHW061712300426
44115CB00014B/2659